The Ultimate
Guide to
Umrah

© **Maktaba Dar-us-Salam, 2005**

King Fahd National Library Cataloging-in-Publication Data

Davids Ismail

The Ultimate guide to Umrah bassed on the famous book
getting the best out of Hajj. / Ismail Davids. -
Riyadh, 2005

300 p; 21cm

ISBN: 9960-9690-4-5

1-Al-Umrah   1-Title

252.6 dc   1426/5946

L.D. no. 1426/5946

ISBN: 9960-9690-4-5

The Ultimate Guide to

UMRAH

based on the famous book
Getting the Best out of Hajj

with special chapters on
Umrah in Ramadaan
and Visiting Madinah

Abu Muneer Ismail Davids

DARUSSALAM
GLOBAL LEADER IN ISLAMIC BOOKS
Riyadh, Jeddah, Sharjah, Lahore
London, Houston, New York

1st Edition: January 2006

HEAD OFFICE

P.O. Box: 22743, Riyadh 11416 K.S.A.Tel: 0096 -1-4033962/4043432 Fax: 4021659

E-mail: riyadh@dar-us-salam.com, darussalam@awalnet.net.sa Website: www.dar-us-salam.com

K.S.A. Darussalam Showrooms:
Riyadh
Olaya branch: Tel 00966-1-4614483 Fax: 4644945
Malaz branch: Tel 00966-1-4735220 Fax: 4735221
- **Jeddah**
  Tel: 00966-2-6879254 Fax: 6336270
- **Madinah**
  Tel: 00966-503417155 Fax: 04-8151121
- **Al-Khobar**
  Tel: 00966-3-8692900 Fax: 8691551
- **Khamis Mushayt**
  Tel & Fax: 00966-072207055

U.A.E
- **Darussalam, Sharjah U.A.E**
  Tel: 00971-6-5632623 Fax: 5632624
  Sharjah@dar-us-salam.com.

PAKISTAN
- **Darussalam, 36 B Lower Mall, Lahore**
  Tel: 0092-42-724 0024 Fax: 7354072
- **Rahman Market, Ghazni Street,**Urdu Bazar Lahore
  Tel: 0092-42-7120054 Fax: 7320703
- **Karachi,** Tel: 0092-21-4393936 Fax: 4393937
- **Islamabad,** Tel: 0092-51-2500237

U.S.A
- **Darussalam, Houston**
  P.O Box: 79194 Tx 77279
  Tel: 001-713-722 0419 Fax: 001-713-722 0431
  E-mail: sales@dar-us-salam.com
- **Darussalam, New York** 481 Atlantic Ave, Brooklyn
  New York-11217, Tel: 001-718-625 5925
  Fax: 718-625 1511
  E-mail: newyork@dar-us-salam.com.

U.K
- **Darussalam International Publications Ltd.**
  Leyton Business Centre
  Unit-17, Etloe Road, Leyton, London, E10 7BT
  Tel: 0044 20 8539 4885 Fax:0044 20 8539 4889
  Website: www.darussalam.com
  Email: info@darussalam.com
- **Darussalam International Publications Limited**
  Regents Park Mosque, 146 Park Road
  London NW8 7RG Tel: 0044- 207 725 2246

AUSTRALIA
- **Darussalam:** 153, Haldon St, Lakemba (Sydney)
  NSW 2195, Australia
  Tel: 0061-2-97407188 Fax: 0061-2-97407199
  Mobile: 0061-414580813 Res: 0061-2-97580190
  Email: abumuaaz@hotamail.com

CANADA
- **Islmic Books Service**
  2200 South Sheridan way Mississauga,
  Ontario Canada L5K 2C8
  Tel: 001-905-403-8406 Ext. 218 Fax: 905-8409

HONG KONG
- **Peacetech**
  A2, 4/F Tsim Sha Mansion
  83-87 Nathan Road Tsimbatsui
  Kowloon, Hong Kong
  Tel: 00852 2369 2722 Fax: 00852-23692944
  Mobile: 00852 97123624

MALAYSIA
- **Darussalam International Publication Ltd.**
  No.109A, Jalan SS 21/1A, Damansara Utama,
  47400, Petaling Jaya, Selangor, Darul Ehsan, Malaysia
  Tel: 00603 7710 9750 Fax: 7710 0749
  E-mail: darussalm@streamyx.com

FRANCE
- **Editions & Librairie Essalam**
  135, Bd de Ménilmontant- 75011 Paris
  Tél: 0033-01- 43 38 19 56/ 44 83
  Fax: 0033-01- 43 57 44 31 E-mail: essalam@essalam com-

SINGAPORE
- **Muslim Converts Association of Singapore**
  32 Onan Road The Galaxy
  Singapore- 424484
  Tel: 0065-440 6924, 348 8344 Fax: 440 6724

SRI LANKA
- **Darul Kitab 6, Nimal Road, Colombo-4**
  Tel: 0094 115 358712 Fax: 115-358713

INDIA
- **Islamic Dimensions**
  56/58 Tandel Street (North)
  Dongri, Mumbai 4000 009,India
  Tel: 0091-22-3736875, Fax: 3730689
  E-mail:sales@irf.net

SOUTH AFRICA
- **Islamic Da`wah Movement (IDM)**
  48009 Qualbert 4078 Durban,South Africa
  Tel: 0027-31-304-6883 Fax: 0027-31-305-1292
  E-mail: idm@ion.co.za

CONTENTS

Acknowledgments

First and foremost I thank Almighty Allah for having granted me the health, strength, and time to complete this second major project. Without the Mercy and Blessings of our Sustainer we can achieve nothing.

As with the *Hajj* book, a very special thanks to Imam Ahmad Al-Jehani; Imam Said Al-Mizyen and Imam Wajdi Hamza Al-Ghazzawi, who has been instrumental in providing me with the teachings of *Umrah*, according to the Qur'an and *Sunnah*.

Imam Wajdi Hamza Al-Ghazzawi did the Islamic editing of the *Hajj* book hence the same acknowledgement applies here, as much of the same data was used. For all the additional *Fiqh* issues, including the Ramadaan chapter, Imam Said Al-Mizyen did the Islamic editing.

All the people that contributed to the *Hajj* book are acknowledged here as well, as that book was used as the base for this one. *Jazakallahu Khairan.*

Once again I would like to thank my wife and children for their patience and understanding, as this book again took many hours of precious time that could have been spent with them.

If by chance I failed to thank someone who contributed to this project, please forgive me. May Allah reward all those who have contributed, directly or indirectly, in compiling this book. *Aameen.*

Preface

Praise be to Allah, Lord of the Universe. May peace and blessings be upon Prophet Muhammad, the last of the Prophets and Messengers, and upon his family and esteemed Companions.

Allah, Your help we seek, Your forgiveness we ask, and we seek Your refuge from the evil of our own selves and from our sinful deeds. Whosoever Allah guides, there is none to misguide him. And whosoever He leaves astray, none can guide him. I bear witness that there is no god worthy of worship besides Allah, and I bear witness that Muhammad (ﷺ) is His servant and Messenge.

There are hardly any books in English language that covers the subject of *Umrah* only. There is a definite need for such a book, as with *Hajj*, you see so many Muslims during *Umrah*, not knowing how to perform the rites properly. Since the publishing of the *Hajj* book, due to popular demand, I completed and published an *Umrah* pocket guide; a *Hajj* pocket guide; a *Hajj* pocket fold-out card and a pocket size supplication (chapter 11 of the *Hajj* book) booklet. These pocket guides have been extremely popular and useful. So if *Umrah* is new to you and you were hoping to go on a quick trip and perform *Umrah*, but feel overwhelmed by the size of this book, don't! Use the small *Umrah* pocket guide or just look at the few pages in chapter eight that covers the actual *Umrah* itself. However I advise that you do read the rest of the book as it helps you to plan, and get the best out of the trip.

So by using my *Hajj* book entitled, *Getting the Best out of Hajj* as the base, I made the necessary modifications to emphasise on the *Umrah* aspects only. Hence all the *Fiqh* rulings and the general style of this book is the same as that of the *Hajj* book.

I added a special chapter on *Umrah* in Ramadaan. Having been blessed to have spent Ramadaan in Makkah over the last fourteen years, I felt it was important to share it with you. I have also included a short '*Hajj* Chapter' as a reminder to my fellow Muslims about their duty they owe unto Allah, to perform their *Hajj*!

As with the *Hajj* book, I maintained the 'down to earth approach' to this book, so you may find the style of writing informal and chatty in some places. I also did this, as so many comments from the *Hajj* book were that the readers enjoyed this style. At the time of writing, the second edition of the *Hajj* book was being prepared for publishing. I have found such a great deal of satisfaction when I found what a positive difference the *Hajj* book has made for the pilgrims who chose to use it. So if you have taken the decision to visit the House of Allah, then I sincerely hope that this work will assist in making your journey a more pleasant and rewarding one.

﴿فَإِذَا عَزَمْتَ فَتَوَكَّلْ عَلَى اللَّهِ إِنَّ اللَّهَ يُحِبُّ الْمُتَوَكِّلِينَ﴾

"Then, when you have taken a decision, put your trust in Allah. For Allah loves those who put their trust (in Him)."
[*Surah Al-Imran (3), part of Ayah* 159]

As with any other trip, there may be some anxious moments, try to be patient. Especially when it comes to obtaining visas for *Umrah*, as from experience this process can be extremely vexing.

I ask Allah's forgiveness for my own shortcomings and any mistakes I may have made in writing this book. I encourage the readers, if they have any suggestions or come across any mistakes, to share them with me, for indeed the believer is strengthened by the help of others.

All praise is due to Allah, our Creator and Sustainer, Lord of the Worlds.

Abu Muneer Ismail Davids
Muharram 1425 (March 2004)
Jeddah, Saudi Arabia.

Chapter 1
About *Umrah*

What is *Umrah*?

In Arabic the word *Umrah* is derived from *Al-I'timar* which means a visit. Here it means paying a visit to the Ka'bah, performing *Tawaaf* around it, walking between Safaa and Marwah seven times, and then shaving one's head or cutting one's hair short.

Why should one perform *Umrah*?

There is consensus among scholars that it is a prescribed worship.

Ibn 'Abbas reported that the Prophet (ﷺ) said:

«عُمْرَةٌ فِي رَمَضَانَ تَعْدِلُ حَجَّةً».

"An Umrah in the month of Ramadaan is equal (in reward) to performing a Hajj."

(This does not, however, remove from one the obligation of performing the obligatory *Hajj*)

(*Ahmad*: 2808 and *Ibn Majah* : 2994)

Abu Hurairah reported that the Prophet (ﷺ) said:

«العُمْرَةُ إِلَى العُمْرَةِ كَفَّارَةٌ لِمَا بَيْنَهُما، وَالحَجُّ المَبْرُورُ لَيْسَ لَه جَزاءٌ إِلَّا الجَنَّةُ».

"From one 'Umrah to the next is an atonement for any sins committed in between and the reward for an accepted Hajj is nothing but Paradise."

(*Bukhari* : 1773, *Muslim* : 1349 and *Ahmad* : 9948)

Umrah before *Hajj*?

Bukhari has reported from 'Ikrimah bin Khalid that he said, "I asked Abdullah bin Umar about performing *Umrah* before *Hajj*, whereupon he said, 'There is no harm in doing so, because the Prophet (ﷺ) himself performed *Umrah* before the *Hajj*.''

Needless to say that one should give priority to perform one's *Fardh Hajj*. However if the opportunity arises to perform *Umrah* and one has not performed *Hajj* yet, then it is quite acceptable to do so. There are also many other misconceptions about performing *Umrah* prior to performing *Hajj*:

Some of the INCORRECT statements some people ascribe to:

☒ If you perform *Umrah* in the *Hajj* months, you must perform *Hajj* in the same year.

☒ If you perform *Umrah*, you must perform *Hajj* in the same year.

☒ You are not allowed to perform *Umrah* in the *Hajj* months if you are not going to perform *Hajj* also.

☒ You are not allowed to perform *Umrah* in the *Hajj* months.

☒ You cannot (should not) perform *Umrah* only, if you have not performed your *Fardh Hajj* yet.

There is no instruction from the Qur'an or the *Sunnah* that one MUST perform *Umrah* and *Hajj* in the same year. There is also nothing to substantiate that you cannot perform *Umrah* in the *Hajj* months. This is a belief from the days of polytheism and there is plenty of evidence proving the contrary.

If a person performs *Umrah* in the *Hajj* months followed by performing *Hajj*, the person automatically opts for the *Tamattu* method of *Hajj*, meaning that a sacrifice (to THANK Allah for being able to perform *Umrah* and *Hajj*) becomes compulsory.

> # The Prophet (ﷺ) performed three *Umrahs* in Dhul-Qada, without performing *Hajj* also!

حَدَّثَنَا قَتَادَةُ أَنَّ أَنَسًا [رَضِيَ اللهُ عَنْه] أَخْبَرَهُ أَنَّ رَسُولَ اللهِ ﷺ
اعْتَمَرَ أَرْبَعَ عُمَرٍ، كُلُّهُنَّ فِي ذِي الْقَعْدَةِ إِلَّا الَّتِي مَعَ حَجَّتِهِ:
عُمْرَةً مِنَ الْحُدَيْبِيَةِ، أَوْ زَمَنَ الْحُدَيْبِيَةِ، فِي ذِي الْقَعْدَةِ، وَعُمْرَةً
مِنَ الْعَامِ الْمُقْبِلِ، فِي ذِي الْقَعْدَةِ، وَعُمْرَةً مِنْ جِعْرَانَةَ، حَيْثُ
قَسَمَ غَنَائِمَ حُنَيْنٍ فِي ذِي الْقَعْدَةِ، وَعُمْرَةً مَعَ حَجَّتِهِ.

"Qatadah said that Anas (ﷺ) had informed him that the Prophet (ﷺ) performed four Umrahs, all during the month of Dhul-Qada including the one he performed along with Hajj (and these are): The Umrah that he performed from Al-Hudaibiyah or during the time of (the truce of) Hudaibiyah in the month of Dhul-Qada, then the Umrah of the next year in the month of Dhul-Qada, then the Umrah for which he had started from Ji'raanah, the place where he distributed the spoils of (the battle of) Hunain in the month of Dhul-Qada, and then the Umrah that he performed along with his Hajj (on the occasion of the Farewell Pilgrimage)."

(*Muslim*: 1253)

When should one go?

There is no need to defer *Umrah* or *Hajj* until later in life. Many Muslims tend to do this, but this is a major error. Go as soon as an opportunity avails itself and go as often as possible if you are by the means to do so. *Umrah* can be performed as many times in one's life as one is physically and financially able.

If you have performed *Hajj* or *Umrah* before and you feel complacent about it, or if you are not convinced about the benefits of *Umrah*, ponder over the following *Hadith Qudsi*:

Narrated Abu Sa'id Al-Khudri, the Prophet (ﷺ) said:

«قَالَ اللهُ: إِنَّ عَبْدًا صَحَّحْتُ لَهُ جِسْمَهُ وَوَسَّعْتُ عَلَيْهِ فِى
الْمَعِيشَةِ يَمْضِي عَلَيْهِ خَمْسَةُ أَعْوَامٍ لَا يَفِدُ إِلَيَّ لَمَحْرُومٌ»

"Allah said: Any of My slaves who is healthy and is by the means, and for five years did not visit My house, he is Mahroum."[1]

(*Ibn Hiban*: 3703 and *Musnad Abu Ya'laa*: 1031)

For details on the 'best times' and visa issues for *Umrah*, see in chapter two under visas.

Should you take children?

Unlike *Hajj* where it is not recommended to take small children, *Umrah* is different and it is definitely advisable to take your children to the house of Allah if you are able to afford it. See in chapter 3 for more details about children.

Umrah in Ramadaan

Due to the numerous benefits of performing *Umrah* in Ramadaan, I have dedicated an entire chapter to it. See chapter 9.

Ibn 'Abbas reported that the Prophet (ﷺ) said:

«عُمْرَةٌ فِي رَمَضَانَ تَعْدِلُ حَجَّةً» .

"An 'Umrah in the month of Ramadaan is equal (in reward) to performing a Hajj."

(*Ahmad*: 1/308 and *Ibn Majah*: 2994)

Umrah according to Qur'an and *Sunnah*

Any form of worship (*Ibadah*) in Islam must be performed according to the Qur'an and *Sunnah* for it to be acceptable to Allah. One's true intention (*Niyah*) must be for Allah alone

---

[1] *Mahroum*: The direct translation of the word is 'deprived'. Meaning that a person who is able and does not do so, has certainly deprived himself of something good, which he may regret it on the Day of Judgement.

and a desire for the Hereafter. It cannot be done with the intention of being seen among men for worldly gain. Strict care should be taken to perform all actions with *Ikhlas* (to perform any act solely for Allah) and *Itiba'a* (adherence to the *Sunnah*). This means performing *Umrah* as performed by the Prophet (ﷺ) without adding to or deleting from the rituals. Also, the money required for *Umrah* MUST be earned by lawful (*Halal*) means. One should start on this journey with the exclusive intention of carrying out the commands of Allah and to seek Allah's guidance and pleasure.

There is only one way of performing *Umrah*, that is, according to the Qur'an and *Sunnah*!

﴿وَمَا كَانَ لِمُؤْمِنٍ وَلَا مُؤْمِنَةٍ إِذَا قَضَى ٱللَّهُ وَرَسُولُهُۥٓ أَمْرًا أَن يَكُونَ لَهُمُ ٱلْخِيَرَةُ مِنْ أَمْرِهِمْۗ وَمَن يَعْصِ ٱللَّهَ وَرَسُولَهُۥ فَقَدْ ضَلَّ ضَلَٰلًا مُّبِينًا﴾

"It is not for a believer, man or woman, when Allah and His Messenger (ﷺ), have decreed a matter that they should have any option in their decision. And whoever disobeys Allah and His Messenger (ﷺ), he has indeed strayed into a plain error."

[*Surah Al-Ahzab* (33), *Ayah* 36]

The Golden Rule

With so many opinions and interpretations on certain issues it is not uncommon for the people to find themselves in a state of confusion. If there are any disagreements on any issues, always ask yourself the following question:

**What did the Prophet (ﷺ)
say, do or didn't do?**

Adopt this simple rule and it will make 'your life much easier'.

Umrah at a Glance:

Below I have listed the actions as the Prophet (ﷺ) performed them or advised us to do. I have called them the "best actions." There are various allowable deviations/options, depending on one's condition or circumstances. If you are able to perform the *Umrah* by abiding as close as possible to these actions listed, then you should.

Many Muslims are not aware that same rules for *Ihraam*, *Tawaaf* and *Sa'ee*, etc. apply to *Umrah* as it does for *Hajj*. Also they are not aware that the *Talbiyah* applies to *Umrah* also.

The "Best Actions" are:

☑ Prepare for *Ihraam* (cut nails, pubic hair, underarm hair, *Ghusl*, etc., if needed. Remember as per the *Sunnah*, one should not exceed 40 days without trimming one's nails and pubic hair).

☑ Adopt *Ihraam* at the *Meqaat* with the *Niyah* for *Umrah*.

☑ Recite the *Talbiyah*.

☑ Men expose their right shoulder prior to *Tawaaf*.

☑ Perform *Tawaaf* (seven circuits) for *Umrah* upon reaching Makkah starting at the *Hajr-al-Aswad*.

☑ Perform two *Rak'at* at the *Maqaam* Ibraheem upon completion of the *Tawaaf*.

☑ Recite *Suratul-Kafirun* (109), in the first *Rakah* and *Suratul-Ikhlas* (112) in the second *Rakah*.

☑ Drink *Zamzam* and kiss the *Hajr-al-Aswad* if possible. If not, proceed to Safaa.

☑ Perform *Sa'ee* for *Umrah*, starting at Safaa and finishing at Marwah (seven laps).

☑ Shave your head (men), ladies cut about one inch of hair from one place.

☑ You are now out of *Ihraam*.

☑ Always perform the two *Sunnah Rak'at Salah* before *Salatul-Fajr*.

☑ Always perform *Salatul-Witr*.

☑ Perform *Tawaaf-al-Wadaa* as your last rite in Makkah before you proceed for home.

Some common MISTAKES people make:

In my experience, I found the following to be some of the most common actions many Muslims opt to do, which does not conform to the *Sunnah*:

☒ Pass the *Meqaat* without adopting *Ihraam*.

☒ Adopting the *Ihraam* in Jeddah and refusing to perform the expiation.

☒ Women refusing to enter into *Ihraam* while in their menses.

☒ Women insisting on wearing white clothes for *Ihraam*.

☒ Not believing or understanding the same *Ihraam* rules apply as that for *Hajj*.

☒ Not reciting the *Talbiyah* as they believe it is for *Hajj* only.

☒ Men wearing an *Ihraam* with studs to keep it closed.

☒ Performing a special prayer after putting on the *Ihraam*.

☒ Keeping the right shoulder uncovered for the entire *Umrah*

☒ Performing multiple *Umrahs* and missing the *Fardh Salah* due to tiredness.

☒ Performing *Salah* outside the *Haram* even though there is space inside.

☒ Men and women standing next to each other while performing *Salah*.

☒ Women standing in front of men during *Salah*.

☒ Insisting on entering the *Haram* from Baab-as-Salam.

☒ Uttering a special *Niyah* and also loudly for *Tawaaf* and *Sa'ee*.

☒ Kissing the Rukn-al-Yamani Corner.

☒ Kissing and touching/rubbing the Maqaam Ibraheem.

☒ Pushing and hurting fellow Muslims, in order to kiss the Black Stone.

☒ Performing *Tawaaf* in large groups.

☒ Reciting in loud voices while performing *Tawaaf* and *Sa'ee*.

☒ Adhering to special booklets that contain specific *Du'a'* for each circuit.

☒ Hiring a special guide for *Tawaaf* to read aloud for you to follow.

☒ Reciting the Verse: *Inna Safaa Wal-Marwatta* at the beginning of each round in *Sa'ee*.

☒ Men cutting only a few strands of hair.

☒ Omit *Tawaaf-al-Wadaa*, prior to departing for home.

Chapter 2
Planning and Preparation

Like any other trip, be it business or vacation, *Umrah* requires planning and preparation; tickets, visas, money, accommodation, etc.

Debts:

☐ Being debt free is not a precondition for performing *Umrah*.

☐ If you have any debts, make arrangements for their payment during your absence, or in the event of your death.

☐ Ensure that family members are aware of any outstanding debts (money owed to someone is something many people treat very lightly, even though it is a very serious matter in Islam. It may keep you from entering *Jannah*).

☐ Have a 'Will' drawn up. Ensure that it conforms to the Islamic rules.

Dates/Bookings/Passport/Visas:

☐ It is commendable to visit the Prophet's (ﷺ) mosque in Madinah if you are able to.

☐ There is no *Sunnah* requirement to spend a minimum of 8 days in Madinah. See chapter 10 for more details about this misconception.

* The Islamic Months are (each month has a maximum of 30 days):

1. Muharram
2. Safar
3. Rabi-al-Awwal
4. Rabi-ath-Thaani (Rabi-al-Aakhir)
5. Jumada-ul-Awwal
6. Jumada-ul-Thaani (Jumada-al-Aakhir)

7. Rajab

8. Sha'ban

9. Ramadaan

10. Shawaal

11. Dhul-Qada

12. Dhul-Hijja

* Since 1422 (2001) new *Umrah* visa rules have been implemented with the objective of increasing the *Umrah* period as well as the length of stay. Prior to this, the *Umrah* period was restricted to certain times of the year and the visa validity was for 2 weeks only. As an example no *Umrah* visas were issued from about the last week in Ramadaan until almost the end of Muharram. With the new rules it is envisaged that *Umrah* visas will be issued in *Shawaal* as well and the period of stay is for one month. One other feature of the new rules is that one can visit other cities such as Riyadh and Taif, which was not allowed before.

* Unlike before when you could book a flight and get on an aeroplane and arrange your accommodation when you get to Makkah, the new rules are:

1. You must book through an appointed agent.

2. The agent will arrange your flight, transport, accommodation in Makkah and Madinah.

3. You must pay for everything prior to leaving.

4. The agent will provide all your details and proof of payment and itinerary to the Saudi Arabian Embassy in your country, who will then issue a visa.

5. The agent in Saudi Arabia will meet you upon arrival and will take your tickets from you. They return it prior to your departure. The reason for this is to avoid 'overstayers'. There are obvious problems associated with this process, such as losing your tickets, turning up

late for your departure, etc. I have experienced both instances already during the first few years. Also, the authorities do not seem to realize that those that wish to overstay (to work), don't need their tickets. So don't be surprised when they decide to take your passport instead, as they do with *Hajj*.

* There are obvious benefits as well as drawbacks with these new rules. The benefits I will leave for you to decide. The main drawback being that one is 'forced' into specific timings and packages. The idea is to make it easier and less expensive, but I personally cannot see how it can be less expensive, when there are at least three new 'players' involved (i.e. the local agent, the agent in Saudi and the companies such as Labbayk, Al-Qaswa and Tawaaf which provides the computer systems that facilitate the hotel and transport bookings.

* The Saudi Arabian Embassy may have some additional requirements before issuing you with an *Umrah* visa. This may vary from country to country:

   o marriage certificate (if applicable);

   o birth certificate for children (if applicable);

   o letter from your local Islamic society stating that you are a Muslim;

   o proof of money (copy of travellers cheques);

   o vaccinations certificates (this vary from country to country;

   o proof of *Mahram* for females.

* If your flight bookings are not confirmed, they will not issue a visa.

* If you are fortunate to travel to Makkah more than once in the same year, be aware that in some countries they will only issue you with an *Umrah* visa once a year.

* In general, the Saudi Arabian Embassy will not issue

Umrah visa for women without a *Mahram*. Women over the age of 45, that have no *Mahram*, may obtain a *Hajj* visa if they are travelling with an organised *Hajj* group. For *Umrah* this may also apply, depending on the group and the country you apply in.

* The visa rules and requirements may change from year to year.

* All females and dependants are 'attached' to the *Mahram/* Father's visa, meaning they MUST all enter and depart at the same time.

* You can only get an *Umrah* visa from a country if you are a resident or have a work permit in that country. Meaning you cannot get a visa in a place where you are merely vacationing, and you decide to include an *Umrah* in your trip.

* Simply stated, getting a visa is not as easy as you might expect. On many occasions people had to cancel their trip due to non-issuing of visas or for not getting it in a timely manner. So expect the unexpected!

→ When is the best time to go?

- As mentioned before, there are no *Umrah* visas issued from the middle of Ramadaan until the middle or end of Muharram and sometimes even until the end of Safar. Even though the 'advertised' new rules stated that *Umrah* will be allowed all year, including Shawaal, I do not believe it will feasible as it will be extremely difficult to control, with pilgrims already arriving in Shawaal. So do not plan to perform *Umrah* (only) in Shawaal. The best time (least busy) is as close to after *Hajj* as possible, meaning Muharram or Safar (if you can get a visa).

- The busiest periods for *Umrah*, in descending order are:

    ☾ Last 10 days of Ramadaan

    ☾ 10th to 20th Ramadaan

ᏉᏛ First 10 days of Ramadaan

ᏉᏛ Second week of Rabi-ul-Awwal (especially in Madinah). Though there are no celebrations in Madinah (or Saudi Arabia for that matter) for the birthday of the Prophet (ﷺ).

ᏉᏛ Apart from the above, if Ramadaan or *Hajj* does not coincide with the following months, then from experience they are the busiest months for Umrah (descending order):

- December

- January

- August

- July

- June

- September

- November

- Without a doubt, Ramadaan is the busiest period other than *Hajj*. Followed by December/January (if it is not Ramadaan, being school holidays in many Western countries. June to September it is very busy with locals and Muslims from the Gulf areas, as it is school break for this region. November is busy mainly with people from Malaysia as it is also school break for them.

- Having said the above, it seems that most of the year (other than *Hajj*) has become busy with people on *Umrah*. I guess busy is a relative term, depending on what you are used to. If you are 'first timer' then Makkah, even at the least busy times (by my standards), will appear to be very busy for you. So the bottom line is: Come when it is convenient for you, as it is always busy.

- See chapter 9 in this book for more details about *Umrah* during Ramadaan.

→Bookings:

- With the new *Umrah* rules some of the points listed may not be necessary as the assigned agents should take care of all these things for you. However I suggest you be aware of them and take some precautions if you feel it is necessary.

- Make your bookings with a reputable travel agent. With the new *Umrah* rules, there are specific appointed agents.

- Ensure that you have a confirmed booking out of Saudi Arabia. The embassy will not issue you with a visa, if your return flights are not confirmed.

- Do not assume that your travel agent knows everything. Double check everything to avoid conflict later.

- Obtain from your agent your booking computer reference number. Using this number makes reconfirmation much easier. It is normally a 6 digit alphanumeric number. Write it down on the cover of your ticket, so it is easily accessible. Use this number during any communication with the airline regarding your booking. Also obtain a computer printout of your booking if possible.

- Request special food, depending on the airline you will be flying with (i.e. Muslim or vegetarian meals). Certain airlines serve only *Halal* food (i.e. Malaysian Airlines, Saudi Arabian Airlines).

→ Passport and Other Visas:

- **Determine all the necessary visas required for en-route stopovers.**

- Make sure your passport expiry date is at least six months after your planned returned date. Visa regulations for some countries require even longer validity dates.

- All females, whose passport contains a photo without a head covering, should endeavour to have it changed prior to the issuing of a visa. The visa will be issued, but this is to avoid embarrassment during the journey. It is a good time to start correcting everything in your life.

- Before leaving home:
  - Make photocopies of your passport and keep them separate from the passport.
  - Obtain the Jeddah, Makkah and Madinah (where applicable) telephone numbers and addresses of the airline (or agent) you are departing from Saudi Arabia with. This is important information, as you may need to call them or visit their offices.

→ Baggage:

- Your ticket will show (in the last column on the right side) your baggage allowance. The standard weight is 20kgs (44lbs) per ticket.

- Most airlines are very strict about excess baggage (weight). Excess baggage charges at airports, including Saudi Arabia, are extremely high. Check this with your agent or airline if you have any doubts. The normal rule for overweight charges is 1% of the 1st class fare, for each kilo. Do your sums and you will be very surprised.

- Most airlines allow only one piece of hand luggage, and it should weigh no more than 5 kg's (11lbs). This is excluding a handbag or a briefcase.

- Keep the size of your suitcase in the normal size range (max. 28"/70cm). It is very difficult to travel with very large suitcases, and your bags will definitely be overweight.

- Do not take your expensive and favourite suitcases. Ensure that your luggage is sturdy as it will be 'well travelled and knocked around' by the time you return.

- Sometimes during check-in the airline may allow you 5 to 7 kg's (11-15 lbs) more, depending on the person checking you in. Do not depend on this.

- If you are leaving home with your bags already weighing 20kg (44lbs), then your bags will most likely be overweight coming back. Unless you do not plan to buy anything, or you have plenty of gifts/parcels for people in Saudi Arabia. (What to take with you is covered later).

- Mark all your luggage clearly, inside and outside. Mark the outside with a unique identifying mark so that it is easily recognizable. Remember there are many bags that look alike. A bright coloured ribbon attached to the carrying handle is a good trick. (Hopefully not everyone reading this will use the same colour ribbon).

- Upon your return you will most likely bring back *Zamzam* water. Check with your customs authorities prior to leaving home, the maximum litres of water you are allowed to bring back with you. (There is no sense in carrying 10 litres of water when the customs in your country will only allow 1 litre per passenger).

- The rules for the *Zamzam* vary from airline to airline. *Zamzam* is not allowed as hand luggage anymore. Also some airlines do not count the weight of the water whereas others do.

- Do not pack the *Zamzam* container (with water in it) inside your suitcase.

→Lost Baggage:

* One of the more unpleasant aspects of travelling is when the airline 'loses' your luggage. This happens on the best of airlines.

* Most airlines have a very good lost baggage tracking system. If your bags have not been stolen (which is unlikely), then in most cases the bags are found and returned to you within a few days.

* Always keep the luggage tags (stickers) that you received during check-in with you, as you will need them in the event of your bags being lost.

* You must have one tag (sticker) for each checked luggage.

* If you did not receive all your luggage, ALWAYS report,

and complete any paperwork, at the first point of arrival.

* Obtain the required file and telephone numbers that you will need for follow-up.

- Under normal circumstances the procedures are in most cases that the airline will endeavour to get your luggage to you (to your hotel). Sometimes you may need to do the 'running around' and you may have to go to the airport a few times to search for your bags. This can sometimes be very difficult, as you may be in Madinah and your bags are in Jeddah.

- Ensure you put the correct local contact number and not your home telephone number on the lost baggage claim forms.

- I have been to numerous 'lost baggage' warehouses around the world. Not because I enjoy going to them, no, I have experienced the agony of lost luggage. I am amazed at the amount of bags in these warehouses. This highlights that in most instances that if you are prepared to do some 'running around', you will find your bags.

- One more reason why you MUST mark your bags inside and outside with your name and contact details. Always include your permanent residence details as well as your Makkah and Madinah contact details.

- Also for this reason you should never pack perishable food items in your luggage.

- Remember or note down the following before you travel:
  - The size of your bags
  - The colour of your bags
  - The make (brand name) of your bags
  - Any other special identification (i.e. black stripes; broken handle)

- This information is very important when you have to complete the required paperwork at the 'lost baggage' counter.

- If you check-in very late (30 minutes before departure), don't be surprised if your bags don't arrive on the same flight as you.

- This is when the group-leader or the travel agent (assuming they are with you) should be of great assistance to you.

- Taking all the above into consideration, I strongly suggest you keep some 'spare' clothes (and underwear) in your overnight bag.

- If you have not been reunited with your luggage prior to your departure for home, make sure you obtain a claim form (file number, contact numbers, procedure to follow etc.) from the airline, in order to pursue the case further once you reach home.

→Accommodation:

- In the past it was possible to find your own accommodation once you arrive in Makkah or Madinah. However since the new rules your accommodation must be selected and pre-paid prior to issuing you with a visa.

- There are many Hotels and apartments. The rates vary a great deal, depending on the time of the year, the location, size and quality.

- Even though there are plenty 5 star hotels, most other accommodation in Makkah is geared to be functional rather than fashionable. Most of the rooms/apartments are sparsely furnished with the bare minimum, yet clean, neat and tidy. Do not expect the same standard 5 or 4 stars, as most are about 2 stars, if not less. Some are minus 2 stars, so be prepared. How you rate the accommodation will depend on what you are used to.

- During the peak periods such as Ramadaan it is more difficult to find suitable accommodation, due to the demand and the rates being much higher. So you may have to settle for the 2 star places. Accommodation during

Ramadaan is in a league of its own. If you plan to perform *Umrah* during Ramadaan, I urge you to review the accommodation section in chapter 9.

- There are various types of packages with a varying range of accommodation. Let your agent explain to you in detail what type of accommodation they provide. If you are told your accommodation is close to the *Haram* (mosque), ask how high up. There are plenty of hilly streets, and although you may be 'close', the hills can be very tiring and strenuous. This is especially important for those with leg or back ailments and for the not-so-young.

- Like most things, the more you pay the better the accommodation.

- Don't let the name of the accommodation (so-and-so palace) 'fool' you.

- Do not take anything for granted, ask questions so you know what you are paying for.

- Ask your agent or any person recommending accommodation at least the following questions. These questions are applicable to both Makkah and Madinah:
  - How far is it from the mosque (by time)?
  - Are there any hills or hilly streets on the way to the mosque?
  - Are there any stairs to climb to get to the building?
  - Do the rooms have telephones, refrigerators, air-conditioning etc.?
  - Do the people who manage the hotel speak English (receptionist)?
  - Do they provide laundry facilities?
  - Are there cooking facilities in the rooms?
  - Who will represent the agent during the trip?

- These questions are repeated in a checklist format for your convenience in chapter 12.

- In the checklist section there is also a table that will help you to evaluate different packages. I have listed some criteria as a guide. It is up to you to add your own criteria and decide which ones are more important, and rate them accordingly. As an example, if cost is very important, rate it as H (high). Then score each package out of five, the cheapest being five. The best accommodation being five and the worst being one. You may wish to score with a

		Packages:				
		Orient	Hajji	Trilite	Hasans	Ocean
Overall Scores:		20	14	14	12	19
Total for High:	H	8	2	4	2	9
Total for Medium:	M	7	11	8	9	7
Total for Low:	L	5	1	2	1	3
Criteria:		**Scores:**				
Agent Reputation	m	5	1	2	1	3
Agent – other factors	l	5	1	2	1	3
Cost:						
Airfare	h	5	1	2	1	3
Accommodation	h	3	1	2	1	3
Other	h	-	-	-	-	3
Accommodation:						
Location (Makkah)	m	1	5	3	5	2
Location (Madinah)	m	1	5	3	3	2

larger range (10 to 1). You then add up all the scores (high, medium and low), which will give you a better idea of the value of each package.

- The example on previous page shows that the package from Orient is the best value based on the listed requirements.

Personal Behaviour

﴿ٱلْحَجُّ أَشْهُرٌ مَّعْلُومَٰتٌ فَمَن فَرَضَ فِيهِنَّ ٱلْحَجَّ فَلَا رَفَثَ وَلَا فُسُوقَ وَلَا جِدَالَ فِى ٱلْحَجِّ وَمَا تَفْعَلُوا۟ مِنْ خَيْرٍ يَعْلَمْهُ ٱللَّهُ وَتَزَوَّدُوا۟ فَإِنَّ خَيْرَ ٱلزَّادِ ٱلتَّقْوَىٰ وَٱتَّقُونِ يَٰٓأُو۟لِى ٱلْأَلْبَٰبِ﴾

"The Hajj (pilgrimage) is (in) the well-known (lunar year) months. So whosoever intends to perform Hajj therein by assuming Ihraam, then he should not have sexual relations (with his wife), nor commit sin, nor dispute unjustly during Hajj. And whatever good you do, (be sure) Allah knows it. And take a provision (with you) for the journey, but the best provision is At-Taqwa (piety, righteousness, etc.). So fear Me, O men of understanding!"

[*Surah Al-Baqarah* (2), *Ayah* 197]

☐ Although the above *Ayah* is in relation to *Hajj*, we can take the meaning from it to be for anytime we visit the House of Allah.

☐ So what are the key warnings/guidance in the *Ayah* :

  ○ No sexual relations while in *Ihraam*

  ○ Not to commit sin

  ○ Not to dispute unjustly

  ○ Whatever good you do, Allah knows

  ○ The best provision is *Taqwa*

☐ It is very important that you adopt very good behavior during *Umrah*. Always act and behave in a manner that will please Allah.

☐ **Remember Allah at all times** (following are a few of the basics):

When:	Say:	Translite-ration:	Meaning:
Starting to do something	بِسْمِ اللهِ	"Bismillah"	In the Name of Allah
Intending to do something	إِنْ شَاءَ اللهُ	"In Sha Allah"	If Allah wills
Something is being praised	سُبْحَانَ اللهِ	"Subhan-Allah"	How perfect Allah is
Expressing appreciation	مَا شَاءَ اللهُ	"Maa Sha Allah"	By the will of Allah
Thanking someone	جَزَاكَ اللهُ خَيْرًا	"Jazak-Allahu-Khairan"	May Allah reward you with good
Thanking Allah	الْحَمْدُ للهِ	"Alhamdu-lillah"	All praise is for Allah
Sneezing	الْحَمْدُ للهِ	"Alhamdu-lillah"	All praise is for Allah
Repenting of a sin	أَسْتَغْفِرُ اللهَ	"Astaghfir-ullah"	I seek Allah's forgiveness
A death message is received	إِنَّا للهِ وَإِنَّا إِلَيْهِ رَاجِعُونَ	"Inna-Lillahi-Wa Inna Ilayhi Raji'un"	We belong to Allah and to Allah we return
Someone sneezes (and he says "Alham-du-lillah")	يَرْحَمُكَ اللهُ	Yar hamuk-Allah"	May Allah have mercy upon you

☐ It is very common for people to perform certain 'good deeds' that have no basis in the *Sunnah* and also they have no proof of its origin. They are merely following traditions and cultures. They also say, " There's nothing wrong with doing so and so...

"Aishah (may Allah be pleased with her) narrated that the Prophet (ﷺ) said:

«مَنْ أَحْدَثَ فِي أَمْرِنا هذَا ما لَيْسَ فِيهِ فَهُوَ رَدٌّ».

"Whoever performs a (good) deed which we have not ordered (anyone) to do (or is not in accord with our religion of Islamic Monotheism), then that deed will be rejected and will not be accepted."

(Bukhari : 2697)

- When I was preparing for *Hajj*, a friend told me that for every dollar I save for *Hajj*, I should save ten bags of patience. Meaning that if you are generally an impatient person, train yourself to be more patient. For *Umrah*, there are less people and generally less stressed, but you will still require patience. Maybe not as much ....

- Mentally prepare yourself:
  - to maintain a positive attitude;
  - to say *"Alhamdulillah"* for everything, be it good or bad;
  - to think of those who are possibly in a worse situation, when your situation is not to your liking;
  - to make *Dhikr* and make *Istighfaar* (seek Allah's pleasure and forgiveness) when you get impatient with people or situations;
  - to 'cope' with crowds.

- It is quite natural for a person to be upset when he does not get what he has paid for. (i.e. the accommodation does not meet his or her expectations). Avoid making a big fuss when you feel that you are being 'short-changed'. Ask yourself instead, am I getting my money's worth of *Ibadah*? Don't 'short-change' yourself, by not fulfilling all the duties of *Umrah*, or by being lazy to go to the mosque. This is the real tragedy of money wasted!

- Make this journey a reformation for yourself by ensuring that the entire trip is an act of *Ibadah* and not only a mere performance of the *Umrah* rituals.

- Always smile, and be polite

- Try to greet first when you meet or see fellow Muslims, even if you don't know them. Always return a greeting with equal or better. (i.e. If your fellow Muslim greeted you with *Asalamu Alaykum*, return his greeting with *Wa-Alaykum-Salaam Wa-rahmatullahi-wa-barakaatu*. This is his/her right!)

Money & Banking:

* Needless to say that the money used for *Umrah* MUST be earned or obtained by *Halal* (lawful by Allah) means.

* The Saudi Arabian monetary unit is the Riyal, which is divided into 100 Halalahs. Notes are in 1, 5, 10, 20, 50, 100, 200 and 500 Riyal denominations. The coins are in 10, 25, 50 and 1 Riyal denominations.

* The Riyal is quoted in US dollars but is based on Special Drawing Rights (SDR). As the SDR/Dollar rate varies, so the official Riyal/Dollar rate is revalued at intervals to keep within a narrow band around the Dollar (Dollar = SR3.75). This fixed rate has been in place for many years, but may change in future.

* The rate of exchange you will obtain in Saudi Arabia for USD will vary between 3.70 - 3.75, depending on where you change your money (bank or money changers). It also depends on whether you have cash or traveller's cheques.

* There are many banks and money exchangers in Makkah, Madinah and Jeddah. The banks do not deal with all currencies. They deal mainly with the mainstream currencies (i.e. American dollar, British pound, French franc, etc.).

* Saudi Arabia has an excellent ATM (Automatic Teller Machine) network called SPAN. If your bank subscribes to Cirrus or Maestro you should be able to withdraw money

from the ATM using your debit card. (I say should, as there is no guarantee that it will work, so do not depend on it).

* All major credit cards are widely accepted in the larger stores, and you can obtain a cash advance at certain banks on your card.

* To exchange some of the 'less commonly used' currencies you need to go to a money exchanger. (How does one know if the bank will change it or not? Well, it's a kind of 'trial and error' situation).

* The banks require lots of proof in order to change your traveller's cheques. They need your passport (or a copy), and proof of purchase of the cheques (the receipt showing the serial numbers).

* The queues in the bank can be very long. The money exchangers normally don't require lots of details (proof), and their queues are generally shorter.

* As you read this, check the expiry dates on all your cards and make sure they do not expire during the duration of your trip. (A friend was unable to withdraw cash from the Cirrus ATM at a critical time, as his card had expired the previous day).

* It is much easier to change your money at the money exchanger, so avoid the banks wherever possible.

* The 'best' money to take with you is American dollars - traveller's cheques as well as some cash notes. It is much easier to change notes than it is traveller's cheques, during the busy periods. Some shops will accept cash dollars.

* Take some small denominations of US dollars (i.e., 10 & 50). These are useful if you need to change a small amount of money for food or departure tax at an airport.

* Also take a small amount of money in the currencies of countries you will be visiting or passing through. Transit delays are common, and you may need to buy something to eat or drink.

* Budget for any departure taxes that you need to pay. Most countries now include the departure tax in the price of the airline ticket. Since 1/6/99 a SR50.00 per passenger departure tax was introduced in Saudi Arabia. However passengers with *Hajj* or *Umrah* visas are exempted. This may change in future, so check with your agent.

* Do not make all the traveller's cheques in your name. Make some in your partner's name.

* Consider budgeting some money for *Sadaqa* (voluntary charity).

* Make a list of all the people for whom you plan to buy a gift. Estimate the amount you plan to spend on each person. Budget, and put the money aside. This is essential as the shopping in Makkah and Madinah is very enticing, and you do not want to run out of money. (See the checklist in chapter 12).

* If you plan to do plenty of shopping, budget for excess baggage charges and possibly customs duties.

* Do not carry all your money with you all the time. Give some to your partner to keep (spend) and keep some in some other 'safe' place. This way you are 'covered' if you happen to lose your wallet.

* Write down in a small pocket size note book all your traveller's cheque numbers and their respective values. Alternatively you may note down all the above details in the checklists provided in chapter 12 of this book.

* Unfortunately and sadly I need to mention that there are pickpockets. As with any other trip, you need to take care of your money. Do not be careless because you are in Makkah.

* Buy yourself a good money belt. Good belts (canvas type) are available in Makkah and Madinah.

Health and Medicine:

- There are many general and specialized hospitals in the Kingdom, as well as clinics, infirmaries and private clinics offering their services.

- Medicines and drugs are easily obtainable in pharmacies, but sometimes prescriptions with generic names are needed, since brand names in the Kingdom may differ from elsewhere.

- There are wheelchair facilities available. (See in the 'Makkah' section under Wheelchair Facilities for more details, chapter 7).

- If you are allergic to certain antibiotics, get your doctor to prescribe an antibiotic for flu and throat infections and have it dispensed in order to take with you.

- If you are carrying any medicine with you, also keep a doctor's letter regarding this medicine.

- Take a pair of sunglasses, especially if you have sensitive eyes.

- Ensure that all the medicine taken along with you is clearly labelled to avoid problems at customs.

Clothes:

☐ *Ihraam:* For men it is two clean, unfitted pieces of cloth, preferably white, while women are free to wear what they please except clothes that are attractive to or imitating men. (More details about *Ihraam* conditions and restrictions are covered in chapter 5 of this book)

☐ Women should not wear perfume when going to the mosque or in the company of strange (non-*Mahram*) men. (This rule applies at all times and not only during *Umrah*).

☐ Many Muslims are confused about the issue of stitched clothes and shoes while in *Ihraam*. It is not a matter of stitches, rather it should not be fitted clothes, such as a shirt or trousers, and the shoes or sandals must not cover the ankles.

Men

Women
(Guideline only)

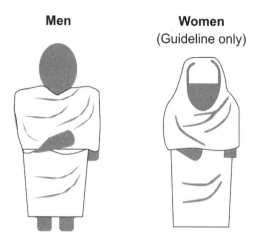

- **Normal:** Take comfortable, loose-fitting clothes.

- You do not need lots of clothes. Take clothes that are acceptable to wear to the mosque, and are easily washed and ironed.

- Take clothes with material that require little or no ironing.

- Keep packets of hand tissues (for the toilet, sweating, etc.). Some tissues are perfumed so avoid using them while in *Ihraam*.

- Washing powder is available in the supermarkets, if you plan to do washing. A bar of washing soap is also very handy.

- Take appropriate clothes with you. (Tight jeans and T-shirts with fancy slogans or figures/photos on them are not appropriate for this trip).

- Take a comfortable pair of sandals to wear with your *Ihraam* and for going to and from the mosque. Take a flat, soft pair if possible, as these are much easier to carry in your hand when you are in the *Haram*. Leave the expensive slippers for another trip, as you may 'lose' them in the *Haram*.

- Carry a small plastic bag or a small cloth string bag with you, to place your sandals/shoes in when you are inside the mosque.

  * Some accommodation packages provide washing facilities for clothes. (i.e. washing machines).

  * There are dry cleaning services available at a very reasonable cost.

Is this your FIRST trip overseas?

- I am assuming that you will be travelling by aeroplane. The requirements are different if you are travelling by bus or by ship.

- Wear loose fitting clothes and a comfortable pair of shoes.

- Swollen feet are a common complaint when flying. To avoid this discomfort, try the following:

  o When travelling take off your shoes and wear socks (preferably made of a natural fibre). Also ensure the shoes you wear while travelling are a good fit and preferably lace-ups so the lacing system can be loosened if your feet swell.

  o Use a pillow to rest your feet on. By raising your feet a little it will help the circulation.

  o Drink plenty of water.

- Do not sit throughout the journey. Get up and walk around a little bit to allow proper blood circulation.

- You may suffer from some earache or your ears may 'close-up' during the landing of the aeroplane. Chew on some gum or a sweet or 'force' a yawn. This will 'open' your ears.

- If you are suffering from a cold, then your earache may be very severe. Carry some pain tablets with you and take them at least ten minutes prior to the landing.

- Most travellers suffer from jetlag after arriving at their destination. This is when your biological clock is out of synch with the local time, meaning you either travelled forward or back in time. There are various methods proposed to overcome jetlag. Each person is different, so there is no clear, uniform method that I know of.

- Do not take many heavy items of hand luggage. It can become a burden on the aeroplane and many airlines do not allow more than one bag.

- Drink plenty of liquids while travelling to avoid dehydration. The drawback is that you may need to frequent the toilet. Try to use the toilets as 'early' as possible during the flight, while they are still clean.

- Perform *Wudhu'* before travelling and put on your socks. This way you can wipe over your socks if you need to perform *Wudhu'* again in the aeroplane.

Other essential items you should take with you:

- In the checklist section of this book (chapter 12) all the suggested items to take with you are summarized. Some items are obvious ones that a person normally takes on a trip; however I have listed them for the less-experienced travellers.

- A small pocket-size Qur'an. There are many Qur'ans available in the mosque however it is much easier to have your own. Also you won't have to get up to get it or take it back, as you may 'lose' your valuable spot in the mosque. (Remember not to enter the toilet with the Qur'an in your pocket).

- Compass for *Qiblah* direction. This will be needed while travelling.

- A Pen. This is always a handy item.

- Scissors (for the women to cut their hair).

- Hairbrush or comb.

- Toothbrush.

- Alarm clock.
- Money belt.
- Umbrella (avoid a black one, as it draws the heat).
- A hat/cap/*Koefia* or scarf to protect your head from the sun if you plan to shave (men only) it after *Umrah*.
- Take the necessary items if you are travelling with children, especially toddlers, as they get bored easily (see chapter 3 for more details).

What is useful to take with you:

- Shoe bag for your shoes while you are in the mosque.
- Some string. (This is useful to hang clothes or to tie a damaged suitcase)
- Some clothes pegs for hanging washing.
- A blow-up travelling neck-pillow. This is very useful during the long journeys (plane or bus).

What NOT to take with you:

- Taking photos and video taping are discouraged in Makkah and Madinah near or around the *Haram* areas. You may have trouble (delays) with the video camera at customs upon entry.
- Lots of clothes.
- Expensive jewelry.
- Any political books.
- Any fashion magazines.
- Any video cassettes. This may delay you considerably at customs upon arrival.

What you should Study:

- Apply the golden rule to every aspect of *Umrah* :

What did the Prophet (ﷺ) say, do or didn't do?

- Needless to say, you should understand all the rites of *Umrah*.

- There is absolutely no need to memorise any of the long and short *Du'a's* you find in many books, for the different rounds of *Tawaaf* and *Sa'ee*. Most of these *Du'a's* have no basis in the teachings of our beloved Prophet (ﷺ).

- There is no specific *Du'a'* except between the Yamani and Black Stone Corner.

- Instead learn the *Du'a's* from the Qur'an and *Sunnah*.

- I suggest you memorise the few supplications related to the *Tawaaf* and *Sa'ee*. This will make your *Tawaaf* and *Sa'ee* much easier as you won't need to keep any books in your hand.

- Memorise the **Talbiyah** and its meaning:

«لَبَّيْكَ اللَّهُمَّ لَبَّيْكَ، لَبَّيْكَ لَا شَرِيكَ لَكَ لَبَّيْكَ، إِنَّ الْحَمْدَ وَالنِّعْمَةَ لَكَ وَالْمُلْكَ، لَا شَرِيكَ لَكَ».

Labbayk Allahumma labbayk. Labbayka laa shareeka laka labbayk. Innal-hamda wan-ni'mata laka wal mulk. Laa shareeka lak.

(Here I am Oh Allah, here I am. You have no partner, here I am. Surely all praise, grace and dominion are Yours, and You have no partner.)

(Muslim: 1184)

- Many people think that the *Talbiyah* is only for *Hajj*. No it is for anyone that is in the state of *Ihraam*, be it for *Hajj* or *Umrah*.

- Study authentic references and discuss any unclear issues with a learned scholar.

- *Wudhu'*: Learn the *Fardh* and *Sunnah* requirements for *Wudhu'*.

- *Salah*: As you will be performing many prayers in the *Haram* in Makkah (where the reward is 100,000 time for each *Salah*) and in the *Haram* in Madinah, (where the reward is 1,000 for each *Salah*), it is imperative that you perform the prayers correctly in order to obtain the highest reward.

- Learn about: What is *Fardh*, what is *Sunnah* and what is *Bid'ah* (innovation).

- Learn about the rewards of using a *Miswak* (tooth-stick) before every *Salah* (sold in and around the *Haram* areas in Makkah and Madinah).

- I recommend the following reading:
  - *Book of Salah* in *Sahih Muslim*
  - *Book of Salah* in *Sahih Al-Bukhari*
  - *The Prophet's Prayer* by Shaikh Muhammad Naasir-ud-Deen Al-Albaani, Al-Haneef Publications, Ipswich, Suffolk.
  - *A Guide to Prayer in Islam* by M.A.K. Saqib, Ta-Ha Publishers Ltd, London
  - About *Wudhu'*, a book entitled, *Sifat Wud'u-in-nabee* by Fahd ibn Abdur-Rahman Ash-Shuwaib, International Islamic Publishing House, Riyadh.

- In Makkah and Madinah, it is more than likely that there will be a *Janazah Salah* (*Salah* for the deceased), after the *Fardh Salah*. It is normally announced over the loud-speakers in the *Haram*. The announcement will also indicate whether it is for a male, female or a child, also if it is for more than one person.

- A few important points I would like to mention:
  1. Learn how to perform the *Janazah Salah* as there are many rewards for performing *Janazah Salah*. (see

chapter 7, under *Janazah Salah*, in this book).

2. Do not be in a hurry after the *Fardh Salah* to perform your *Sunnah Salah*. As a *Musafir* (traveller) you are not required to perform any *Sunnah Salah*, except that of *Salatul-Fajr* and *Salatul-Witr*.

3. Obey the *Sunnah* by sitting for a while after *Salah*, making *Istighfaar* and *Dhikr*. This way you will not miss the *Janazah Salah* if it is being performed.

4. Women should not miss this opportunity to perform the *Janazah Salah*, as they are equally rewarded.

- As you will be performing many prayers while en-route to Makkah, acquaint yourself with the rules and laws governing the *Salah* for **the traveller** (*Musafir*).

- Learn about the rules of wiping over your socks/shoes/ *Khufs* during *Wudhu'*, as it is very useful while you are in the aircraft.

- If you plan to visit Madinah:
  o It is good to learn about the history of Madinah.
  o What and where is *Raudat-ul-Jannah*, Quba Mosque, Al-Baqee cemetery, mountain of Uhud, etc.
  o The etiquette of visiting graves and the grave of the Prophet (ﷺ).

- Learn some basic Arabic words [i.e. thank you; please; the numbers (this will help during shopping); hotel; where; clean my room]

- Sometimes only the 'slang' Arabic words are used in shops, so if the shopkeepers do not understand you, try the 'slang' instead of the colloquial Arabic. If they still don't get it, then maybe it is your accent or the way you are pronouncing the words. Do not despair, it is not easy!

- If all else fails, speak English. You will be surprised to find that most of the shopkeepers can speak a variety of languages (i.e., English, Urdu, Malaysian, etc.).

Chapter 3
About Women

This chapter deals with the issues of women as it relates to *Umrah*, such as:

1. The issue of *Mahram*.
2. Covering of the face while in *Ihraam*.
3. Menstruation.
4. Visiting of graves.

As some of the above issues have such varied opinions, I would like to start with the following reminders:

﴿مَن يُطِعِ ٱلرَّسُولَ فَقَدْ أَطَاعَ ٱللَّهَ﴾

"He who obeys the Messenger (Muhammad) has indeed obeyed Allah..."

[*Surah An-Nisa* (4), part of *Ayah* 80]

Abu Hurairah (may Allah be pleased with him) related that the Prophet (ﷺ) said:

«كُلُّ أُمَّتِي يَدْخُلُونَ الجَنَّةَ إِلَّا مَنْ أَبِى»، قَالُوا: يَا رَسُولَ اللهِ، وَمَنْ يَأْبِى؟ قَالَ: «مَنْ أَطَاعَنِي دَخَلَ الْجَنَّةَ، وَمَنْ عَصَانِي فَقَدْ أَبِى».

"All my followers will enter Paradise except those who refuse. They said, "O Allah's Messenger! Who will refuse?" He said, "Whoever obeys me will enter Paradise, and whoever disobeys me is the one who refuses (to enter it)."

(*Bukhari* : 7280)

If for some reason you do not agree with the opinions expressed in this chapter or the rest of the book for that matter, then keep in mind the following *Hadith* where we are guided as to what to do about doubtful matters.

Narrated An-Nu'man bin Bashir (may Allah be pleased with him): I heard Allah's Messenger (ﷺ) saying:

«الْحَلَالُ بَيِّنٌ وَالْحَرَامُ بَيِّنٌ، وَبَيْنَهُمَا مُشَبَّهَاتٌ لَا يَعْلَمُهَا كَثِيرٌ مِنَ النَّاسِ، فَمَنِ اتَّقَى الْمُشَبَّهَاتِ اسْتَبْرَأَ لِدِينِهِ وَعِرْضِهِ، وَمَنْ وَقَعَ فِي الشُّبُهَاتِ كَرَاعٍ يَرْعَى حَوْلَ الْحِمَى، يُوشِكُ أَنْ يُوَاقِعَهُ، أَلَا وَإِنَّ لِكُلِّ مَلِكٍ حِمًى، أَلَا إِنَّ حِمَى اللهِ مَحَارِمُهُ، أَلَا وَإِنَّ فِي الْجَسَدِ مُضْغَةً إِذَا صَلَحَتْ صَلَحَ الْجَسَدُ كُلُّهُ، وَإِذَا فَسَدَتْ فَسَدَ الْجَسَدُ كُلُّهُ، أَلَا وَهِيَ الْقَلْبُ».

"Both legal and illegal things are evident but in between them there are doubtful (unclear) things, and most people have no knowledge about them. So whoever saves himself from those doubtful (unclear) things, he saves his religion and his honour. And whoever indulges in these doubtful (unclear) things, is like a shepherd who grazes (his animals) near the Hima (private pasture) of someone else, and at any moment he is liable to get in it.

(O people!) Beware! Every king has a Hima and the Hima of Allah (Azawajal) on the earth is His illegal (forbidden) things. Beware! There is a piece of flesh in the body, if it becomes good (reformed), the whole body becomes good but if it gets spoilt the whole body gets spoilt and that is the heart."

(*Bukhari : 52*)

⇨*Mahram*

- ◆ It is essential that you be accompanied by your husband or some other *Mahram* on the journey for *Umrah*.

- ◆ *Mahram:* A male relative whom you cannot legally marry (at any time in your life), i.e.: brother, father, son, husband's father.

Abu Hurairah (may Allah be pleased with him)

reported that the Prophet (ﷺ) said:

«لا يَحِلُّ لاِمْرَأَةٍ تُؤْمِنُ باللهِ وَالْيَوْمِ الآخِرِ أَنْ تُسَافِرَ مَسِيرَةَ يَوْمٍ وَلَيْلَةٍ لَيْسَ مَعَها حُرْمَةٌ»

"It is forbidden for any woman who has faith in Allah and the Day of Judgement to undertake the distance of a day or more without being accompanied by a Mahram."

(*Bukhari*: 1088, *Muslim*: 1339 & *Ahmad*: 2/420)

♦ Your sister's husband cannot be your *Mahram*, even if your sister is present. Although you cannot marry him, while he is married to your sister, you can actually marry him if they are divorced or she dies.

♦ Below are a few points which are common practice today. Are they acceptable? NO!

1. A man making an agreement with a married woman who is about to perform *Umrah* and has no *Mahram*, that he will be her *Mahram*.

2. A woman taking a non-related man as her brother so that he can be a *Mahram* for her — and then treating him as a *Mahram*.

3. A woman travelling together with a group of women.

4. Also similarly travelling along with a man who is a *Mahram* for one of them - claiming that he is *Mahram* for all of them.

♦ The immediate questions that arise are:

➢ What about unmarried women?

➢ What about women without sons or brothers?

♦ Remember that *Umrah* is not a *Fardh* requirement, so avoid disobeying a clear rule.

♦ I need to add that there are some past and present scholars, which rule that it is acceptable if a woman travels with a group of women.

♦ Read the *Hadith* below and you decide...

The Prophet (ﷺ) said:

«لَا يَخْلُونَّ رَجُلٌ بِامْرَأَةٍ، وَلَا تُسَافِرَنَّ امْرَأَةٌ إِلَّا وَمَعَها مَحْرَمٌ». فَقَامَ رَجُلٌ فَقَالَ: يَا رَسُولَ اللهِ! اكْتُتِبْتُ فِي غَزْوَةِ كَذَا وَكَذَا وَخَرَجَتِ امْرَأَتِي حَاجَّةً، قَالَ: «اذْهَبْ فَاحْجُجْ مَعَ امْرَأَتِكَ».

"No man should be in the company of a woman alone. Unless the woman is accompanied by a Mahram or her husband, she should not undertake a journey." A man told the Prophet (ﷺ) that his wife had gone for Hajj while he had enrolled himself for a particular battle. The Prophet (ﷺ) told the man to accompany his wife on Hajj instead.

(*Bukhari*: 3006, *Muslim*: 1341 & *Ahmad*: 1/222)

♦ In general, the Saudi Arabian Embassy will not issue *Umrah* visas for women without a *Mahram*.

♦ Women over the age of 45, that have no *Mahram*, may obtain a *Hajj* visa if they are travelling with an organised *Hajj* group. For *Umrah* this may also apply, depending on the group and the country you apply in.

⇨ *I'ddah* (waiting period):

• If a woman is in her *I'ddah* period (her husband died), she MUST complete her *I'ddah* period first, even though she may meet all the other requirements (*Mahram*, money, health, etc.), before she can embark on her journey.

⇨ Preparation:

• If you are going for a very short time, ensure that your departure dates from Makkah allow you enough time to complete all your *Umrah* rites in the event of your menstruation starting prior to you having completed it.

• Check what the accommodation packages offer. Shared

rooms; couple rooms; en-suites; food included etc. Prepare yourself physically and mentally.

- If your passport contains a photo of you without a head covering, I suggest you have it changed. It is *Haraam* (forbidden) to have such photos displayed to non-*Mahram* males, apart from it causing you embarrassment during the trip.

- Ensure that you have all the necessary medicines and toiletries. The clothes, toiletries and other items to take with you are covered in chapter two of this book.

- Take some of the traveller's cheques in your name. Also keep some of the cash money with you. Avoid keeping all your money in one place.

⇨ **Personal Behaviour:**

◆ No attractive clothes, perfume or make-up should be worn while going to the mosque or in the company of non-*Mahram* men.

◆ Other points regarding the clothes:
  - The material itself must not be decorative.
  - It must be thick enough to be completely opaque (non see-through).
  - It must be loose enough as not to make clear the shape of your body.
  - It must not resemble the dress of men.
  - Or resemble the dress of disbelieving women.
  - It must not be ostentatious.

⇨ *Ihraam:*

◆ The clothes for *Ihraam* can be of any colour.

Some women refuse to enter into the state of *Ihraam* at the *Meqaat* as they are in their menses. They argue that they should first become clean. However, a woman in menses can and should get into the state of *Ihraam* at the prescribed place, and can perform every religious rite, except *Tawaaf* and *Salah*. See under menstruation in this chapter for more details.

◆ Covering of the face and hands while in *Ihraam*:

- ○ The *Hadith* related in *Bukhari* states that a woman should not cover her face with a *Niqaab* (sewn face cover) or cover her hands with gloves.

- ○ Some people use this *Hadith* to 'prove' that women are not supposed to cover their face and hands while in the state of *Ihraam*. The Prophet (ﷺ) told the men that they should not wear fitted clothes (shirt; trousers), but that did not mean that they should go naked. Similarly the women are instructed not to wear gloves and a *Niqaab*. This does not mean that their face and hands should not be covered.

- ○ The *Hadith* narrated by 'Aishah (may Allah be pleased with her) proves that they did cover their faces while in the presence of non-*Mahram* men while in *Ihraam*:

عَنْ عَائِشَةَ رَضِيَ الله عَنْهَا قَالَتْ: كَانَ الرُّكْبَانُ يَمُرُّونَ بِنَا وَنَحْنُ مَعَ رَسُولِ اللهِ ﷺ مُحْرِمَاتٌ فَإِذَا حَاذَوْا بِنَا سَدَلَتْ إِحْدَانَا جِلْبَابَها مِنْ رَأْسِها عَلَى وَجْهِها، فَإِذَا جَاوَزُونَا كَشَفْنَاهُ.

'Aishah (may Allah be pleased with her) said: "The riders had been passing by us while we were with the Prophet (ﷺ). When they came opposite to us or parallel to us, we (the women) would let our veils down on our faces and heads, and when they had passed away we unveiled our faces."

(*Abu Dawud*: 1833 & *Ibn Majah*: 2935)

- ◆ So if you normally cover your face then it is acceptable to do so while in *Ihraam*, as long as you don't do it with a *Niqaab*. There is also no need to wear a baseball type hat to avoid your scarf from touching your face as many sisters do, as there is no basis for this.

◆ Women should cover their feet (with socks or otherwise), especially during *Salah*. For some unknown reason many women do not cover their feet. It is a requirement as instructed by Allah that their *Aurah* must be covered and the feet are part of a women's *Aurah*.

◆ While in *Ihraam* it is permissible to remove the socks or change one's clothes.

⇨ **About Menstruation:**

The subject of *Tahaara* (purification etc.) is a very large subject and has many viewpoints from many renowned scholars, each having substantial support for his point of view. This makes the rulings on this topic all the more difficult.

While I was gathering the information for this topic, I realised how complicated this matter can be. At one stage I wanted to leave it out, but then I thought, if it is so hard for me to gather the right rulings, and I have plenty of time, what about the women, if they need to find a ruling for their particular situation, with limited time. Hence I spent a great deal of time, researching and checking with my references that I used for the rest of the *Fiqh* related issues in this book, in order to compile the following data. Allah knows best.

◆ A woman MUST adopt *Ihraam* at the *Meqaat*, even though she is menstruating. This applies for *Umrah* as well as for *Hajj*.

◆ If she fails to do so intentionally, and adopts her *Ihraam* only in Makkah once she has completed her menstruation, then she should pay an expiation (sacrificing of one sheep), for violating the *Meqaat* rule.

◆ If a woman enters into the state of *Ihraam* while she is menstruating and she is not sure that her menstruation will be completed prior to her departure from Makkah, then she can make her *Niyah* with a stipulation (*Ishtirat*). (See chapter 5, under *Niyah*). This will save her from having to perform a sacrifice for coming out of *Ihraam* without completing the rites of *Umrah*. See case 3, under the examples listed. On the other hand if she is sure that she will not complete her menstruation in time, then she need not enter into *Ihraam* at all, as she now has no intention of performing *Umrah*. (See case 6). If for some reason her menstruation does complete in time, she can then go to the *Meqaat* at *Tan'ym* and adopt *Ihraam*, and return to Makkah to perform *Umrah*. (See case 7.)

◆ Some scholars agree that it is permissible for a woman to use pills which prevent or delay the menstruation, after she has confirmed the safety of their usage from a doctor. Below are two comments from female pilgrims. Take note of them as they also apply to *Umrah*, if you plan to take these pills.

    ○ The comment I have received from many pilgrims is that they discourage the use of these pills, as it has caused them more 'problems' instead of having helped them.

    ○ Another point they asked me to mention: If you do decide to use these pills, then you should start taking them at least two months before traveling.

◆ Menstruating women and postnatal bleeding women may omit the Farewell *Tawaaf* (*Tawaaf-al-Wadaa*).

عَنِ ابنِ عَبَّاسٍ رَضِيَ اللهُ عَنْهُمَا قَالَ: أُمِرَ النَّاسُ أَنْ يَكُونَ
آخِرُ عَهْدِهِمْ بالبَيْتِ إِلَّا أَنَّهُ خُفِّفَ عَنِ الحائِضِ.

Narrated by Ibn Abbas ﷺ: "The people were ordered to perform the Tawaaf of the Ka'bah (Tawaaf-al-Wadaa) as the lastly thing, before leaving (Makkah), except the menstruating women who were excused."

(*Bukhari : 1755*)

عَنْ طَاوُسٍ قَالَ: كُنْتُ مَعَ ابْنِ عَبَّاسٍ، إِذْ قَالَ زَيْدُ بْنُ ثَابِتٍ: تُفْتِي أَنْ تَصْدُرَ الْحَائِضُ قَبْلَ أَنْ يَكُونَ آخِرُ عَهْدِهَا بِالْبَيْتِ؟ فَقَالَ لَهُ ابْنُ عَبَّاسٍ: إِمَّا لَا! فَسَلْ فُلَانَةَ الْأَنْصَارِيَّةَ؟ هَلْ أَمَرَهَا بِذَلِكَ رَسُولُ اللهِ ﷺ؟ قَالَ: فَرَجَعَ زَيْدُ بْنُ ثَابِتٍ إِلَى ابْنِ عَبَّاسٍ يَضْحَكُ، وَهُوَ يَقُولُ: مَا أَرَاكَ إِلَّا قَدْ صَدَقْتَ.

Narrated by Abdullah bin Abbas: Tawus reported: "I was in the company of Ibn Abbas when Zayd bin Thabit said: 'Do you give religious verdict that the woman who is in menses is allowed to go without performing the last circumambulation (Tawaaf) of the House?' Ibn Abbas said to him: 'Ask such and such woman of the Ansar, if you do not (believe my religious verdict) whether Allah's Messenger (ﷺ) had commanded her this.' Zayd bin Thabit (went to that lady and after getting this verdict attested by her) came back to Ibn Abbas smilingly and said: I did not find you but telling the truth.' "

(Muslim : 1328)

◆ Sometimes a woman gets upset when her menses start while she is in Makkah, as she cannot attend prayer in the *Haram*. Try not to be too upset, as this is a natural process from Allah. Allah in His Mercy will certainly not give you any less reward than what you would have obtained if you did not have your menses. Use this time to indulge in other forms of *Ibadah*, such as *Dhikr*, *Du'a'*, and reading. Read books that will help you increase your knowledge about Islam or books on *Tafseer* in order to increase your understanding of the Qur'an.

سَمِعْتُ القَاسِمَ بنَ مُحَمَّدٍ، عَنْ عَائِشَةَ رَضِيَ اللهُ عَنْهَا قَالَتْ: ... فَدَخَلَ عَلَيَّ رَسُولُ اللهِ ﷺ وَأنا أَبْكِي فَقَالَ: «مَا يُبْكِيكِ يَا هَنْتَاهُ؟» قُلْتُ: سَمِعْتُ قَوْلَكَ لِأَصْحَابِكَ فَمُنِعْتُ العُمْرَةَ. قَالَ: «وَمَا شَأْنُكِ؟» قُلْتُ: لَا أُصَلِّي، قَالَ: «فَلَا يَضُرُّكِ إِنَّمَا أَنْتِ امْرَأَةٌ مِنْ بَنَاتِ آدَمَ كَتَبَ اللهُ عَلَيْكِ ما كَتَبَ عَلَيْهِنَّ،

$$\text{«فكُوني في حَجَّتِك فَعَسَى اللهُ أَنْ يَرْزُقَكِيها»}$$

Narrated by Al-Qasim bin Muhammad "...'Aishah added, "Allah's Prophet ﷺ came to me and saw me weeping and said, "What makes you weep, O Hantah?" I replied, "I have heard your conversation with your companions and I cannot perform the Umrah." He asked, "What is wrong with you?" I replied, "I do not offer the prayers (i.e. I have my menses)." He said, "It will not harm you for you are one of the daughters of Adam, and Allah has written for you (this state) as He has written it for them. Keep on with your intentions for Hajj and Allah may reward you that."

(*Bukhari* : 1560)

♦ Menstruating women should not enter a mosque, including the *Haram* in Makkah and Madinah.

> ## ➤ Let us look at some examples:

I hope that I have managed to cover most of the cases. If your 'condition' is not covered, review the general principals of the examples and I am sure that you will be able to formulate what you are supposed to do.

- **Case 1:**
   - ❖ You arrived for *Umrah* and went to Madinah first. Prior to departing for Makkah your menstruation starts:
      - √ You must adopt your *Ihraam* at the *Meeqaat* (Dhul-Hulaifah) and proceed to Makkah.
      - √ You remain in *Ihraam* for the duration of your menstruation.
      - √ Once your menstruation is completed, you perform *Ghusl*.
      - √ Proceed to the *Haram* to perform *Umrah*.
      - √ Cut your hair and you are relieved from *Ihraam*.

- **Case 2:**
  - ❖ On your way to Saudi Arabia your menstruation starts. You are planning to proceed directly to Makkah from Jeddah:
    - √ You must adopt your *Ihraam* at the *Meeqaat*.
    - √ You remain in *Ihraam* for the duration of your menstruation.
    - √ Once your menstruation is completed, you perform *Ghusl*.
    - √ Proceed to the *Haram* to perform *Umrah*.
    - √ Cut your hair and you are relieved from *Ihraam*.
- **Case 3:**
  - ❖ You have not performed your *Umrah* yet, and your menstruation is not completed and you must leave for home:-
    - √ *Niyah* with *Ishtirat*:
    - √ Cut your hair.
    - √ You are relieved from *Ihraam*.
    - √ You may leave for home.
    - √ *Niyah* without *Ishtirat*:
    - √ You must perform an expiation (sacrifice of one sheep or goat).
    - √ Cut your hair.
    - √ You are relieved from *Ihraam*.
    - √ You may leave for home.
- **Case 4:**
  - ❖ You have completed your *Umrah* and you are about to depart for home, when your menstruation starts:
    - √ You are exempted from performing *Tawaaf-al-Wadaa*.

√   You do not need to perform any expiation.

√   You may proceed for home.

- **Case 5:**

  ❖ Your menstruation starts:

  √   While you are performing *Tawaaf* for *Umrah*:

  √   You cannot continue.

  √   Follow the steps as in case 1.

  ❖ While you are performing the Farewell *Tawaaf* (*Tawaaf-Al-Wadaa*):

  √   You cannot continue.

  √   Follow the steps as in case 4.

  ➢ While you are performing *Sa'ee* for *Umrah*:

  √   You may continue, as you do not need to have *Wudhu'* to perform *Sa'ee*. However you must ensure that you will not 'soil' the mosque. If you have to leave to pad yourself, and there is only a reasonable time elapse, then you need not start the *Sa'ee* from the 1st lap again. However you must redo the incomplete lap, if applicable.

Case 6:

  ❖ You are not in *Ihraam* yet, and your menstruation is not completed and you are sure that it will not complete before you must leave for home:

  √   You need not enter into the state of *Ihraam*.

  √   You may enter Makkah but not the *Haram* (mosque).

  √   You may leave for home, without performing any expiation (sacrifice).

Case 7:

  ❖ You were in the situation as in case 6, and for some

reason your menstruation has completed before your planned departure for home:

√ Adopt your *Ihraam* clothes and proceed to *Tana'ym* (*Meqaat*), where you will make your *Niyah* for *Umrah*.

√ Proceed to the *Haram* to perform *Umrah*.

√ Cut your hair and you are relieved from *Ihraam*.

√ You may leave for home, without performing any sacrifice.

- These examples highlight why meticulous planning is needed.

In all cases you must start the *Tawaaf* or *Sa'ee* from the beginning again, once there is a large time elapse (i.e. day) between the time you stop and the time you restart.

⇨ Pregnancy:

- There are a few considerations pregnant women should take into account before embarking on this journey. As with everything else, each person knows his or her own strengths and weaknesses. Therefore, the information given below is only a general guide and should not be used as definite rules.

- In the early stages (first 3 months) of pregnancy it is more 'risky' as the rituals of *Umrah* can be very strenuous.

- In the last stages of pregnancy it can also be 'risky' and uncomfortable.

- Pregnant women should not take any vaccinations, especially meningitis.

- Most airlines will not allow a woman who is more than seven months pregnant to fly.

- If you happen to give birth in Saudi Arabia, do not forget to obtain all the proper paperwork (birth registration etc.) prior to departing.

- Ensure that you budget for the possible additional cost.

⇨ **Children:**

◆ If the parent wishes for the child to perform *Umrah*, then it is commendable for the child to wear *Ihraam* and the *Niyah* can be made by the parent.

◆ It is commendable if the child is able to complete all the rites, however there is no penalty if certain rites or pillars are missed.

◆ It is acceptable to carry the child on your shoulders during *Tawaaf* or *Sa'ee*.

● Unlike *Hajj*, it is a good idea to take your children with you to the House of Allah.

● Explain to the children the procedure they should follow if they become lost and show them the lost children's section at door no 13.

● Alternatively, teach them to stay (wait) in one place in the event of you 'losing' them.

● At the *Haram* in Madinah they do not allow any boys, regardless of age (infants excluded) to enter the female section of the mosque. Even if they are with their mothers. So, if you have younger boys, send them with their father, otherwise they will be forced to sit outside. I am not sure of the logic of this, but it happens.

Following are some more points to keep in mind for the different categories of children:

Teenagers:

● Same rules as those of adults apply in relation to acts of *Ibadah*.

● Assist them to prepare for the journey, keeping in mind that the needs and interests of teenagers are different from adults.

● A companion, such as a sibling or a friend will be of great value if they can also accompany them.

Ages 7-12 years:

- Don't take too many clothes, as it is easy to wash and dry your clothes in Makkah.

- Despite the heat, it is advisable to dress them modestly, especially when going to the mosque.

- Encourage the girls to wear *Hijab*, even though they may not have reached puberty yet. This is a good chance for you to get them use to it.

- The Prophet (ﷺ) advised us that we should encourage our children to perform *Salah* from the age of 7 and start disciplining/punishing them at the age of 10 if they do not perform *Salah*. So heed this advice and don't let the children be an excuse for not going to the mosque, instead let them frequent the mosque.

- Most airlines have special meals for children. If you are not flying with an airline that normally serves all *Halal* food, and you have booked *Halal* meals for yourself, then double-check with the airline if the children's meals are also *Halal*. Most of the time the children's meals are not *Halal*, hence you may have to take your own food. Take some potato chips, biscuits and some sandwiches for the children, just in case.

- Also take some sweets or chewing gum for them to chew on, during take-off and landing, to minimise earache.

Ages 0-6 years:

- Diapers are readily available, but take enough for the journey and for at least a few extra days. I suggest you take more than what you would normally use in a day, as babies are prone to diarrhea when travelling.

- Take baby food, bottles, milk, and medicine (especially for pain and fever). Do not rely on getting baby food on the plane as it is not always *Halal*.

- Take enough clothes for the baby. Keep at least two sets of clothes for the baby in your hand luggage.

- Also a change of clothes for the toddlers in your hand luggage is a good idea. Pack some brightly coloured clothes.

- For infants it is best to give them some painkiller medicine about half an hour before take-off and landing.

- If you are breastfeeding, wear appropriate clothes that will facilitate easy breastfeeding on the plane.

- Take a stroller, but not a bulky one. Although the stroller can get in the way sometimes in the crowds, most times it is of great value.

- Take toys and books to keep them occupied during the journey. Do not take too many toys, as there are plenty of cheap toys to buy in Makkah. The little ones get bored very quickly on the plane and your nerves will be tested, so be patient.

- Let the children use the bathroom in the plane prior to landing, to avoid toilet trips while queuing at immigration or customs.

- Children also tend to fall asleep at the worst possible times, so you may have to carry them. Meaning you should try to minimise hand luggage.

- Book a bassinet for the baby on the plane, and don't forget to reconfirm it prior to your flight. During check-in make sure that you are allocated the bassinet seats.

In Makkah:

- Once you are in Makkah, I suggest you rest yourself and the children before performing *Umrah*. Remember children also suffer from jetlag, and will make your *Umrah* very stressful if they are tired and miserable. So let them sleep and eat first. There is no rush. The *Umrah* will take in excess of two hours and the distance of *Sa'ee* alone is about 3.5km.

- You can go to the *Haram* with your stroller, but you will have to leave it outside. Put the stroller behind or on top of the shoe racks outside the *Haram* doors.

- You are allowed to rest during *Tawaaf* and *Sa'ee*, and it is acceptable to carry the children on your shoulders.

- You may consider getting a wheelchair, see chapter 7, to push the children in.

- Once you have completed your *Tawaaf*, you and your partner can take turns in performing the two *Ra'kat Salah*, while the other minds the children.

- The mosque gets very crowded, so you should take care of toddlers and babies in the crowds. Babies that crawl should either be watched by a toddler or tied to you, during *Salah*. You may use a harness like belt or just a normal scarf to ensure baby does not crawl too far. Give them some room to move around, otherwise they will cry and cause a bigger distraction.

- Warn toddlers not to wander off during *Salah*.

- If you do plan to take them to the *Haram* often, dress them in their brightly coloured clothes so they are easily recognisable in a crowd.

- Always pin an identification tag on them. The business card of your hotel is also useful to keep in their pocket.

⇨ **General:**

♦ When you are in Makkah and you wish to perform *Tawaaf*, keep track of the *Salah* times to avoid starting your *Tawaaf* very close to *Iqaamah* time. If you do not watch the times, it will result in you getting 'caught' amongst the men during the *Fardh Salah*. It is unacceptable for women to perform their *Salah* in front of men, even though you may see it happen in the *Haram*. You may argue that the *Haram* is exempted due to the crowds. This is definitely not so. Plan your *Tawaaf* times to avoid inconvenience to yourself, and the rest of the people. If for some reason you are caught up in this situation, then it is best for you to stand in one place without performing your salah, and to perform the *Salah* later.

♦ Avoid walking in front of a person performing their *Sunnah Salah*. The *Harams* are not exempted from the prohibition of walking in between a person and his *Sutrah* (wall or item directly in front of a person performing *Salah*). Sometimes it is almost impossible to avoid this. However do your best.

♦ It is also more relevant for women NOT to pass in front of men performing their *Salah*. As per the *Hadith*, this action invalidates the *Salah* of the man (except congregational *Salah*). There is a difference of opinion on this point, but be aware of it and do try to avoid walking in front of the men.

♦ Women should also perform the *Janazah Salah*, as they are equally rewarded.

⇨ Visiting of Graves:

• This is another controversial issue and also the book most commonly used by many people (*Fiqh-us-Sunnah*) contradicts the most commonly held view of the scholars and major reference books I chose to use.

• The visiting of various graves is neither a requirement nor a rite of *Umrah*. My suggestion is to err on the side of caution. Meaning that if there is uncertainty or disagreement on a particular issue, 'stay on the safe side'.

• Take heed of the instruction given to us by our beloved Prophet (ﷺ) as related in the *Hadith* in the beginning of this chapter.

• The strongest view is that it is not recommended for a woman to visit graves.

Chapter 4
What to expect

- More details about Makkah (i.e.: medical, inside the *Haram*, accommodation) are covered in chapter 7 of this book. Details about Madinah are covered in chapter 10.

⇨ **Food:**

* There are various kinds of food available in Makkah and Madinah. You will find food from just about every country you can think of. Some of the more popular ones are: Indonesian, Pakistani, Turkish and Egyptian.

* There are also some 'brand name' foods: Pizza-Hut, Kentucky Fried Chicken, Dairy Queen, etc.

* Cappuccinos, Doughnuts, Cream cakes, Burgers and Chips are all readily available.

- Hungry yet? I guess the diet will have to wait a little bit longer!

- If you plan to do your own cooking, don't forget to check whether your accommodation provides cooking facilities.

- You can also eat at the restaurants located in certain hotels. These are relatively more expensive.

- Try the grilled chicken from 'Al-Tazaj' located in the Makkah Towers (Hilton) building. It is unique and delicious.

- There are many small shops that also sell groceries including essential toiletries and household items, such as detergents and toilet paper. Each shop has different stock. In some cases you can buy milk, cereals, tin foods, fruit, vegetables, cheese etc., from one shop.

⇨ **Diet & Diabetic food:**

* Diet drinks are available in most shops. They are sometimes called Pepsi/Coke light and not diet.

* In the big supermarket (Bin Dawood) in the Makkah Towers (Hilton) building you will find a small variety of diet and diabetic food items.

* Artificial sweeteners are also available in most shops.

* There are many juice shops selling freshly squeezed juice.

• Before you get into the habit of having a fresh mango or strawberry juice every morning, a word of caution. These juices are made with fresh fruit, but they add at least one cup of sugar as well as a small tin of condensed milk. This is to make it sweeter. The only true fresh juice is the orange juice. Do not be disappointed, the supermarkets do stock 100% real fruit juices.

• Take a break from the diet and enjoy the trip.

• Diabetics should take special care, as most things, including most bread, contain sugar.

⇨ **Shopping:**

• Please remember that you have come for *Umrah* and that you should try and gain as much reward as possible. Spend your time in the mosque and try to minimize the time spent shopping.

• If you are one of those who 'shop until you drop' then take lots of money. There are so many things that you can buy. You name it, you will find it.

• If you plan to shop for small children, do not take their clothes or shoe sizes, instead measure them and draw the size of their feet on a piece of paper. This will make it easier to buy by measurement instead of size. Do not forget to take the measuring tape with you. If you plan to buy jewelry such as rings, then measure their finger size with a piece of cotton or string.

• Use your gift list and tick the name off the list as you buy. This will alleviate the stress and worry somewhat.

• Shop wisely and keep an eye on the suitcase weight and

your financial budget. See under checklists (chapter 12) for the tables provided especially for gift shopping.

- If you see something that you like, buy it. Chances are you will not be able to find the same shop again or the item will be sold. Sometimes even the shop is changed within the space of a few days.

- If you bought an item and you find it cheaper at another shop, do not feel cheated, or accuse the shopkeeper of cheating. Just return the item and ask the shopkeeper to give it to you at that price. Most times they are obliging.

- Do not necessarily accept the first price they quote you. Bargaining is the name of the game.

- If you are buying any electrical items, check the voltage. 110v or 220v?

- Do not depend on the shopkeeper to give you the right sizes (i.e. will this fit my 5 year old? Chances are, he will say yes).

- Sometimes you will find the shops extremely busy, so it helps to have the right amount of money available. This way, you will not have to wait for change.

- You will be amazed to see how the shopkeepers deal with so many customers at the same time.

- Having the right change (one and five Riyals) to buy small items (i.e. drinks, fruit) is a great help.

- You may experience the shopkeeper 'throwing' your change 'at you'. Do not become flustered and think that he is rude. This is normal, so don't take it personally. Most shopkeepers are reputable, but do not be surprised when you get some 'bad' service.

- Some people debate whether it is better to buy things (gifts etc.) in Makkah or Madinah. I suggest you buy whenever and wherever it is convenient. The prices are generally the same.

- Shopping in Jeddah is marginally more expensive. You also don't get all the same things that you get in Makkah or Madinah. On the other hand you can get many other things, cheap to very expensive. All types of fashion clothes and perfumes are available. Many varieties of shoes, suites, watches, materials and all the latest toys.

- You can also find the latest electrical gadgets (games, radios, and kitchen utilities).

- Computer software and hardware are also reasonably cheap in Jeddah. Ask the taxi to take you to: Khalid bin Walid Street; Baroom Centre or City Centre (this is not the centre of the city, but a complex called City Centre).

- Gold (jewelry), well, what can I say? There are gold markets everywhere (Makkah, Madinah and Jeddah) just waiting for you...........

- Before you buy your favourite perfume, t-shirt, shoe or watch, make sure that the name (label) is authentic (i.e. Charlie and not Charly, Lacoste and not Locaste, Panasonic and not Pensonic, Citizen and not Citazen).

- If you do visit Jeddah, don't miss visiting the Mosque on the water (built partially into the Red Sea).

- If you are not able to visit Jeddah, there are other shopping areas around Makkah City: Mansour Street, Sitteen Street and Aziziah. Ask the taxi driver.

- Do not lose sight of the purpose of your journey, so avoid getting into arguments with any shopkeepers.

⇨ **Signs:**

- Most of the street and shop signs are in both Arabic and English.

- You will have some fun with the English spelling on some of the shop signs.

- Some of the street and location names vary from sign to sign (i.e. one sign may show Mina and the next one may show Muna; Arafat is spelt Arafah on some signs).

⇨ Telephones:

* The telephone system is fully automatic and you can dial almost all long distance calls without operator assistance.

* There are public telephones from which you can phone.

* There are a few shops that have public telephone facilities.

* There are also 'International Telephone Cabins', where you can make your calls.

* There are coin as well as phone-card phones. The minimum cost is SR50.00 for the phone-card.

* There are also pre-paid access-number phone-cards available. The minimum cost is SR50.00 per card. These cards are useful as you can use any telephone to make an international call, by simply calling the access number on the card.

* Mobile (cell) phones are widely used. If you wish to bring your mobile phone with you, I suggest you check with your local supplier whether the service will work in Saudi Arabia.

* You can buy a local card as there are mobile chip cards available, for temporary use. Minimum cost is SR100.00

* Some hotels provide facsimile facilities.

* The city codes are:
    o   Jeddah - 02
    o   Makkah - 02
    o   Madinah - 04
    o   Riyadh - 01

* You need at least a 25 Halalah coin to make a local (Makkah to Makkah) call or a 50 Halalah coin to make an inter-city (Makkah to Jeddah) call.

* Some emergency telephone numbers are:

    o   Fire - 998

    o   Ambulance - 997

    o   Police - 999

    o   Road Accidents - 993

    o   Telephone dir. - 905

- Avoid using the hotel telephones for international calls, as it can be very expensive, due to the hotel service charges.

- Obtaining coins or a phone-card can be difficult; so if you plan to phone often, buy them at the first opportunity you get.

- The telephone cabins are useful as their charges are based on the exact length of the call (seconds).

- The 'menace' of the mobile phone has reached its peak as you notice some people talking on the phone while performing *Tawaaf*.

⇨ Internet and E-Mail:

* Internet has been available in Saudi Arabia since 1998. For the e-mail junkies, there are Internet Cafés springing up all over the place. There are also some hotels in Makkah and Madinah that provide this service.

⇨ Postal:

- There are post offices available if you wish to post a letter. Posting parcels can be a bit more complicated. Big items will have to be sent via cargo.

⇨ Electricity supply:

* The electricity supply varies:

    o   Jeddah mainly 110v (220v is also available in some places)

    o   Makkah and Madinah are mainly 220v.

* The wall plug holes are mainly the small two-point, round-holed ones.

- Buy an international plug adapter if you plan to use any electrical item.

- If your electrical items are 110v, be very careful when using them in Makkah or Madinah. You may not be able to use it at all, if the hotel does not provide a 110v outlet.

- If the item is dual voltage, 110v and 220v, it is best to keep the switch set at 220v. This will 'save' your item if you plug it into the 'wrong' voltage socket.

- There are frequent power fluctuations. I suggest you leave any expensive electrical items at home.

⇨ **Transport:**

* With the new *Umrah* rules, all your transportation should have been prepaid and arranged by your agent. I have listed the following details, in case you need to find your own transport.

* There are air-conditioned buses and taxis at reasonably cheap prices.

* The Saudi Arabian Public Transport Company (SAPTCO) operates a very efficient bus service. All their buses are air-conditioned and provide an hourly service between Jeddah and Makkah and also between Jeddah and Madinah.

* They also provide transport between Madinah and Makkah.

* SAPTCO also have offices at the Airport where they provide a service to Makkah and Madinah. The service to Madinah is from airport to airport. These offices are not open 24 hours a day, so if you arrive late at night, you will need to go to the bus terminal downtown.

* The locations of the arrival and departure of the SAPTCO buses are (if you have trouble finding it, simply ask someone):

   ○ **Jeddah:**

Downtown - Opposite the "Corniche Commercial Centre" in the city. (This area is known as the Balad or downtown Jeddah).

Saudia Terminal — Office location is the second last office to the extreme right of the exit doors at the airport.

Foreign Airlines Terminal — The last section to your left of the hired car and hotel reservation desk, right in front of the arrival area.

○   **Makkah:** - Next to the Makkah Towers (Hilton) building. This area is known as "Shubaika." facing the front of the building, to the right side. If you exit from the King Fahd door (no 79) it will be directly in front of you.

○   **Madinah:** — It is further away from the *Haram*. It is in between the areas called Baab-ul-Khuma and Baab-ul-Shami (these are referring to areas and not doors). If you are inside the *Haram* near the *Mihrab* (front), stand with your back towards it (*Mimbar*) and walk straight ahead, past the two open areas and exit by the big new door right at the end. You should now be in the new open courtyard area with many new hotels in front of you. Turn to your left and walk until you cross the street where there is a traffic light and a tunnel. You should find the buses in this area. Also, as with Makkah the location may change over time, so please ask somebody before you walk too far.

*   There are also non-air-conditioned buses and taxis, at almost the same prices.

*   The yellow coloured taxis are referred to as taxis, whereas the white coloured taxis are referred to as limousines. Their prices may vary somewhat, with the yellow taxis being marginally cheaper, as they are not always air-conditioned.

* Distances between places:

  o   Jeddah to Makkah — 72 km (45 miles)

  o   Jeddah to Madinah — 424 km (265 miles)

  o   Makkah to Madinah — 447 km (278 miles)

* According to Saudi law, one must have a valid Saudi driver's licence to drive in Saudi Arabia. It is therefore not advisable to even chance it as you will be breaking the law, although there are many car rental places around that will rent you a car. You may 'get away' with an international driver's licence for a short time.

* If you plan to drive, keep in mind that driving is on the right side of the road and not on the left as in the United Kingdom and some other places.

• Most taxis do not 'go by the meter'. You have to negotiate the price. So before you venture off, get an idea from somebody about the approximate distances and cost. These prices are negotiable with the driver. However at the airports the taxis are more controlled and they have fixed prices, and you may have to pay first.

• You can get a taxi for as low as SR 10.00 per person from Makkah to Jeddah. The bus costs about 10-15SR. Then again, if you take a limousine from Makkah to Jeddah by yourself, it could cost you as much as 120SR. A taxi from Jeddah to Madinah could cost you from about 50 to 400SR, depending on the type of car and the number of passengers. As you can see there is a big variation, so be careful!

• If you are a small group of six to eight people, you can also hire a big car (GMC), referred to as a Jimms. The prices vary a great deal, so you need to do some skillful negotiating with the driver.

⇨ **News:**

* There are three English daily newspapers, the *Arab News*,

the *Saudi Gazette* and the *Riyadh Daily* available. They are generally sold in the bookstores, which can be found in the general market areas.

* There are also English radio channels and one English TV channel.

• Now if there is a great time waster and possibly causing one to be involved in sin, then it is the television. Many people waste precious time watching television while in Makkah.

• Use this opportunity to take time out from the worldly issues. It is a great feeling. Besides, your time can be better spent in *Ibadah*.

⇨ **Climate:**

* Seasons:

  ○ June onwards it is summer.

  ○ It gets extremely hot.

  ○ The temperatures can go as high as 55° Celsius (133° F).

  ○ December onwards it is winter.

  ○ The weather during winter is very pleasant

  ○ In Madinah the temperature sometimes falls below zero (32° F).

  ○ The marble tiles on the floor in both *Harams* can be very cold, so take socks with you. (Ever wondered what to do with those socks you receive on the aeroplane?)

* Average temperatures:

Makkah:

May to October	32° - 40° C	90° - 105° F
November to April	28° - 33° C	82° - 92° F

Madinah:

May to October	32° - 48° C	90° - 118° F

November to April   10° - 30° C   50° - 86° F

- Take appropriate clothes, depending on the time that you will be in Saudi Arabia. With all the world temperatures changing it is hard to predict the weather.

- I have experienced very cold weather in Madinah during the month of December.

⇨ **Time & Working Hours:**

* Jeddah, Makkah and Madinah are all in the same time zone, 3 hours ahead of Greenwich Mean Time (GMT).

* The *Salah* times vary by about 5 to 10 minutes between these cities.

* In Saudi Arabia everything (shops, banks, gas stations) are all closed during *Salah* times.

* The weekend in Saudi Arabia is on Thursday and Friday and not on Saturday and Sunday.

* Most government offices and banks are closed over the weekend. Some banks and offices provide services until *Salatul-Zuhr* on Thursdays.

* Official public holidays are one week at *Eid-ul-Fitr*, and ten days at *Eid-ul-Adha*. Most shops are open after about the second day of *Eid*.

* If you plan to visit Jeddah for shopping or for official business, the working hours for shops are normally from 10.00am - 1.00pm and from 5.00pm - 10.30pm.

* There are some supermarkets that are open 24 hours, except for *Salah* times.

- As with all other expensive items, I suggest you leave any expensive watches at home and travel with a less expensive one. (This way you will not be too upset if by chance you lose or forget your watch somewhere).

⇨ **Banking:**

* As mentioned in chapter two, there are many banks and

money exchangers where you can change your cash or
traveller's cheques. They deal in most currencies.

* Automatic teller machines for debit and credit card
  withdrawals are widely available.

> **WARNING!**
> Trafficking in drugs - whether smuggling,
> supplying or receiving - incurs capital
> punishment in the Kingdom of Saudi Arabia.

⇨ **Preparation Review**

→ **Ready to go?**

> ➤ Check passport validity
> ➤ Obtain necessary visas
> ➤ Speak to your doctor about any particular medical problems
> ➤ Arrange extra medication, prescriptions or glasses
> ➤ Arrange vaccinations
> ➤ Arrange traveller's cheques, foreign cash, etc.
> ➤ Write or update your will
> ➤ Arrange for someone to look after your house, pets, pot plants, mail
> ➤ Check if you need adapter plugs for the trip
> ➤ Revise your study notes
> ➤ Cancel newspapers, milk, mail
> ➤ Reconfirm your reservations
> ➤ Recheck your travel documents
> ➤ Leave a copy of your itinerary with your family/ friends
> ➤ Leave a copy of your travel documents, traveller's

cheque numbers, etc.

➢ Label all luggage clearly

➢ Finalise security arrangements for the house — locks, timers, etc.

→ Out by the door?

➢ Passport

➢ Tickets

➢ Money

➢ Keys for suitcase locks

➢ Medicine

➢ Lock-up house

➢ Oh yes, and all that patience that you saved up.....

⇨ Travel Supplications:

♦ Before you leave supplicate for your family and friends and ask them to supplicate for you. The supplications listed below are for all travellers.

♦ Supplication of the traveller for those remaining behind:

«أَسْتَوْدِعُكَ اللهَ الَّذِي لَا تَضِيعُ وَدَائِعُهُ» .

As-tawdi-uk-Allah alladhee
laa tadhee'u wadaa'iuhu.

(I entrust you to Allah, whose trust is never lost.)

(*Ahmad*: 2/403 and *Ibn Majah*: 2825)

♦ Supplication of those seeing off the traveller:

«أَسْتَوْدِعُ اللهَ دِينَكَ وَأَمَانَتَكَ وَخَوَاتِيمَ عَمَلِكَ» .

As-tawdi u'llaha deenaka
wa amaanataka wa khawaatima a'malika.

[I entrust your faith, your trust (i.e., family and property), and your final deeds to Allah.]

(*Abu Dawud* : 2600, *Tirmidhi* : 3443, *An-Nasa'i* : 8806 and
Ibn Majah : 2826)

◆ When the person actually leave, those wishing them
farewell should supplicate the following:

«اللَّهُمَّ اطْوِ لَهُ الْبُعْدَ، وَهَوِّنْ عَلَيْهِ السَّفَرَ» .

*Allahummatwi lahul-bu'da
wa hawwin a'layhis-safara.*

(O Allah, shorten the distance for him and make the
journey easy for him.)

(*Tirmidhi* : 3445)

◆ See under chapter 6, ('The Journey from Home until
Makkah') for further supplications regarding travelling.

Chapter 5
About the *Ihraam*

⇨ **Adopting the *Ihraam*:**

- The rites of *Umrah* begin by entering into the state of *Ihraam*.

- For men it is very apparent as they have a specific garment to wear.

- It is two clean unfitted pieces of cloth, preferably white and should be clean. The lower part of the *Ihraam* is referred to as *Izar* and the top part as *Rida*.

- Shoes/sandals must not cover the ankles (it does not have to be plastic, as stitched leather or other material, sandals or shoes are acceptable).

- Women are free to wear what they please. Needless to mention that it should conform to the Islamic code of dress. It can be of any colour. Some women insist on wearing white or green. There is no authentic basis in the *Sunnah* for this action.

- Wearing the *Ihraam* garments does not mean that you are in the state of *Ihraam*. The state of *Ihraam* means to be in a state of ritual consecration. This is normally done at a specific area called the *Meeqaat* (discussed in chapter 6 of this book).

- A person is in the state of *Ihraam* only once the *Niyah* has been uttered.

- The steps to enter into the state of *Ihraam*:

1. Preparation:

- ○ Trim your finger and toe nails if needed
- ○ Shave under your arms if needed
- ○ Shave your pubic hair if needed

عَن أَنَس بِن مَالِكٍ قال: وَقَّتَ لَنَا رَسُولُ اللهِ ﷺ حَلْقَ الْعَانَةِ،
وَتَقْلِيمَ الأَظْفَارِ، وَقَصَّ الشَّارِبِ، وَنَتْفَ الإِبْطِ أَرْبَعِينَ يَوْماً، مَرَّةً.

"It is narrated by Anas (ﷺ) that the Prophet (ﷺ) set a period during which the moustaches and nails be trimmed, hair under the armpit be removed and those below the navel be cut. He asked us not to leave them unattended for more than forty days."

(*Abu Dawood*: 4200 & *Tirmidhi*: 2758)

- ○ Trim the moustache (leave the beard as it is)
- ○ To perform *Ghusl* (shower) is *Sunnah*
- ○ Apply perfume to your head and beard (men only), and not to the garments. (Women are strictly forbidden to wear perfume in *Ihraam* or while in the presence of men who are not their *Mahram*).

The Prophet (ﷺ) said:

«الفِطْرَةُ خَمْسٌ: الخِتَانُ، والاِسْتِحْدَادُ، وَقَصُّ الشَّارِبِ،
وَتَقْلِيمُ الأَظْفَارِ، وَنَتْفُ الآبَاطِ».

"Five things are part of nature: To get circumcised, to remove the hair below one's navel, to trim moustaches and nails and remove the hair under the armpit."

(*Bukhari*: 5891 & *Muslim*: 257)

- If possible avoid buying the very thin cotton *Ihraam*. It sticks to you if you sweat. The toweling or the thicker cotton ones are much better. One may imagine that it will be hot using a toweling cloth, however this is not normally the case.

- The one piece is wrapped around your waist like you would normally do when coming out from the bath. (This is very easy for those people who are used to wearing a *'Lungi'*/sarong'). The other piece is thrown over your shoulders covering the upper part of your body.

- If you are not used to it, it may be a good idea to practice walking with it, making sure it does not fall off and also that you can move your legs.

- There appears to be a new fashion from some countries. The bottom of the *Ihraam* has the name of the travel agent printed in big bold colours. One of the purposes of the two pieces of cloth and no head gear is so that there is no distinction amongst the people. Advertising where you are from on your *Ihraam* is taking marketing concepts too far, in my opinion.

- While preparing for the journey and for the state of *Ihraam*, it is natural that most men have a haircut and some men clean shave their beards. I guess this is to be 'neat and tidy' for the trip. As mentioned earlier, only the moustache should be trimmed and the beard should not be shaved:

The Prophet (ﷺ) said:

«خَالِفُوا المُشْرِكِينَ، وَوَفِّرُوا اللِّحَى، وأحْفُوا الشَّوَارِبَ».

"Oppose the polytheists. Let your beards grow and trim your moustaches."

(*Bukhari*: 5892 & *Muslim*: 259)

- As for the haircut, save your money, as you will be cutting your hair after having completed your *Umrah*.

2. Put on your *Ihraam* clothes:

- As explained before men wear the lower part by wrapping it around their waist and the top part is thrown over covering both shoulders.

- Your right shoulder is open only during *Tawaaf*. It should be covered at all other times, especially while performing *Salah*. Do not be concerned when you notice that so many males are walking around with their right shoulder exposed.

- It is acceptable to wear a money belt to assist in 'keeping up' the lower part. A safety pin is also very useful, to keep the top part from falling off or constantly opening up.

o Watches, hearing aids, eye-glasses, contact lenses, sunglasses, etc. are all acceptable to wear while in *Ihraam*.

o No head gear (men only).

o No underwear (men only).

o Wear slippers/shoes that do not cover the ankles.

o Women may wear any normal clothes, assuming it conforms to the Islamic guidelines.

o Women should cover their feet. They can wear socks.

o Covering of the face and hands for women is covered in chapter 3 in this book.

o It is acceptable to adopt the *Ihraam* clothes prior to the *Meqaat* if it's more convenient.

3. Recite your *Niyah* out loud:

o The *Niyah* should be uttered at the *Meqaat* or close to it after your transport has started moving towards it.

o Though it is very unlikely in this day and age. There are exceptions allowed for those who do not have the recommended garments or shoes:

The Prophet (ﷺ) said:

«مَنْ لَمْ يَجِدْ إِزَارًا فَلْيَلْبَسْ سَرَاوِيلَ، ومَنْ لَمْ يَجِدْ نَعْلَيْنِ فَلْيَلْبَسْ خُفَّيْنِ» .

"Someone who cannot get Izar (wrap) may put on trousers, and who cannot get shoes may put on the leather socks."

(*Bukhari*: 5804 & *Muslim*: 1178)

o This is the only instance where one's *Niyah* is made aloud. All other times the *Niyah* is to be done by heart only, and not the tongue.

○ To enter the state of *Ihraam* one must make *Niyah* for *Umrah* by saying:

لَبَّيْكَ اللَّهُمَّ عُمْرَةً

Labbayk Allahumma Umrah.

(Oh Allah, here I am performing *Umrah*.)

(*Muslim* : 1251)

○ There is no special *Salah* (2 *Rak'at*) established in the *Sunnah* to be performed after adopting or related to the *Ihraam*.

○ It is preferred that the *Niyah* is done after a *Salah*, if possible. The Prophet (ﷺ), pronounced his *Niyah* after having performed a *Fardh Salah*.

○ Menstruating or post-natal bleeding women MUST wear their clothing, make their *Niyah*, proceed to Makkah and wait until they are able to perform *Ghusl*. After completing their *Ghusl* they perform their *Umrah*. See chapter 3 for more detailed information, including some case examples.

○ So let me stress: There is no *Salatul-Ihraam* as some books teach (to perform two *Rak'at Salah* after adopting *Ihraam*). There is also no other *Niyah* to recite (*Allahumma Innee Oreedu......*). Both these actions have not been established in the *Sunnah* whereas the mentioned method has.

⇨ *Niyah* for *Umrah* on behalf of Someone else:

○ Unlike *Hajj*, all scholars do not agree that one can perform *Umrah* on behalf of someone else. Without delving into all the different rulings, I have decided to list the method, as I have found so many people doing it. The only place where you mention the name of that person is in the *Niyah*. The rest of the *Umrah* rites are the same as if you were doing it for yourself.

(Name of the person) لَبَّيْكَ اللَّهُمَّ عُمْرَةً عَنْ

Labbayk Allahumma Umrah 'an <u>Name of the person.</u>

(Oh Allah, here I am performing *Umrah* for <u>Ismail ibn Talib</u>).

> ## *Niyah* with a stipulation (*Ishtirat*):

♦ If one, while entering the state of *Ihraam*, fears one is likely to be subjected to illness or anything else that might obstruct one's *Umrah*, then one can recite a clause of stipulation to Allah by saying:

«فَإِنْ حَبَسَنِي حَابِسٌ فَمَحِلِّي حَيْثُ حَبَسْتَنِي»

Fa in habasani haabisun, fa mahilli haithu habastani.

(Thus, if I am hindered by any obstacle, then my place of conclusion is where You have held me.)

(*Sunan Al-Bahqi*: 5/223)

○ This is based upon the Prophet's (ﷺ) order to Dhuba'ah bint Al-Zubair (﵂) to pronounce the statement of the ***Ishtirat*** (stipulation) when she complained of being ill. This *Hadith* is related by Bukhari and Muslim. The advantage of this is that if one is faced with an obstacle that prevents one from completing *Umrah*, then it is permissible for one to make **Tahallul**, i.e., to conclude *Umrah* early without offering *Fidyah* (expiation). Shaving (men) the head or cutting the hair (women) must still be done, in order to be released from the state of *Ihraam*.

♦ Men should recite the *Talbiyah* loudly once they are in the state of *Ihraam* as often as possible. A woman raises her voice only to the extent of being heard by the person next to her.

«لَبَّيْكَ اللَّهُمَّ لَبَّيْكَ، لَبَّيْكَ لَا شَرِيكَ لَكَ لَبَّيْكَ، إِنَّ الْحَمْدَ

وَالنِّعْمَةَ لَكَ وَالْمُلْكَ، لَا شَرِيكَ لَكَ» .

Labbayk Allahumma labbayk. Labbayka laa shareeka laka labbayk. Innal-hamda wan-ni'mata laka wal mulk. Laa shareeka lak.

(Here I am O Allah, here I am. Here I am, You have no partner, here I am. Surely all praise, grace and dominion are Yours, and You have no partner.)

(*Muslim* : 1184)

◆ You are now in the state of *Ihraam!* A person in the state of *Ihraam* is a *Muhrim*.

⇨ **Conditions of the *Muhrim* :**

◆ Before uttering the *Niyah*, one is not considered a *Muhrim* (in the state of *Ihraam*) even if one wears the clothes of *Ihraam*. Only after uttering the *Niyah* does one become a *Muhrim* and thus the following **prohibitions** apply. Expiation (*Fidyah*) is due if any of the prohibitions are violated intentionally:

◆ **Prohibitions while you are in the state of *Ihraam* :**

☒ Men must not wear clothes that are tailored to fit parts of the human body, for example trousers, jackets, shirts, etc. Meaning fitted clothes. There is a common misconception that one may not wear stitched clothes or sandals. However, this has no basis in the *Sunnah*, as it as an issue of fitted and not stitches. Hence, the *Ihraam* tops with studs should be avoided as it forms a fitted garment. Also, any sandal or shoe must not cover the ankle.

☒ Men MUST NOT wear any underwear or headgear. Men are not allowed to cover their heads. Note that the face is a part of the head and thus it must not be covered.

☒ Though women can wear normal clothes, they must

NOT wear gloves or a face cover that has openings for their eyes (*Niqaab*). Instead, they can fully cover their faces and hands in the presence of men who are not their *Mahram* (see chapter 3 for more details).

☒ Must not apply perfume, wear perfumed clothes, nor use any perfumed substances (shampoo, soap, etc.). Caution, some tissues are perfumed.

☒ Must not trim his/her nails.

☒ Must not cut his/her hair.

☒ Must neither marry, give anyone else in marriage, nor propose marriage.

☒ Must not perform any act likely to arouse sexual passion or indulge in any intimate marital relations.

☒ Must not hunt or participate in hunting (fishing is allowed).

☒ Must not commit an act of disobedience to Allah, such as smoking.

☒ Must not get involved in idle talk or disputes, i.e. fights, arguments and quarrels.

◆ **Permissible actions while you are in the state of *Ihraam*:**

☑ Wearing a wristwatch, eyeglasses, moneybelt, rings, sunglasses, hearing or speech aid, etc.

☑ Cleansing oneself (including having a bath or shower) with unscented soap and to wash and gently scratch one's head and body, even if hair may fall out.

☑ Changing one's *Ihraam* garments. Removing the *Ihraam* clothes does not nullify the state of *Ihraam*. One's *Niyah* places one in the state of *Ihraam* and cutting of one's hair removes one from this state.

☑ Having a shelter over one's head, whether in a car, under an umbrella, or in a tent or building.

☑ Men may also cover their feet (but not their head) while sleeping, with their *Ihraam* or a blanket.

♦ If a person does not complete his *Umrah* after entering into the state of *Ihraam* or commits an act which is prohibited (while in the state of *Ihraam*), then a sacrifice (expiation/ *Dumm*) is due upon him or her. See chapter 3, for more details about menstruation being the cause for not allowing a woman to complete her *Umrah*.

⇨ **Etiquette for men, while in *Ihraam*:**

• Avoid walking around with only the bottom part of your *Ihraam*.

• Keep your right shoulder covered (except during *Tawaaf*).

• Avoid throwing the 'lose' end of your *Ihraam* over your shoulder, as you may 'hit' the person behind you in the face.

• Keep your *Ihraam* clean and do not use it as a cloth to wipe your hands.

• Take extra care as to how you sit, especially on stairs, to avoid exposing yourself. As it is unusual for you to be without underwear, you can easily expose your private parts. This is very common while sitting on the stairs inside the mosque.

Fidyah **(Expiation):**

♦ The general rule is that if a person committed an act in ignorance of the rule then there is no sacrifice required.

♦ The *Fidyah* (expiation) is a means of compensation (Mercy from Allah) for a missed action or for transgressing a *Hajj* or *Umrah* related law. It is sometimes referred to as *Dumm*.

♦ It is important to note that a violation of the *Meqaat* and *Ihraam* rules apply to *Umrah* as it does for *Hajj*. See *Surah Al-Baqarah, Ayah* (196) for more details.

1. The expiation for passing the *Meqaat* without *Ihraam* :
   C· Sacrifice of one sheep or goat.

2. The expiation (*Fidyah*) for violating the *Ihraam* restrictions (e.g., cutting your hair due to an ailment in your scalp; need to remove a nail due to injury, men: applying perfume, wearing fitted clothes, covering their head):
   C· Fast for 3 days or feed 6 poor persons or sacrifice one sheep or goat.

3. The expiation (*Fidyah*) for hunting:
   C· See *Surah Al-Maidah*, *Ayah* 95 for the details.

❖ **Where and how to perform the Sacrifices:**

♦ Remember the sacrifices MUST be done and the meat distributed in the Makkah area. It cannot be done in your home country.

• Unlike *Hajj*, during *Umrah* it is not that easy to perform any required sacrifices for expiation. However it is possible, but requires some effort on your part.

• You need to go to the animal slaughter house in an area called K'akiah. It is about 15km from the *Haram* area and it is near the big vegetable markets.

• The cost will vary, depending on the time of the year, however the average cost is about SR300.00.

➤ This is what you do:

   ○ Buy some small plastic bags (to make meat parcels for distribution).

   ○ Take a taxi and ask him to take you to
   Maslakh Al-Ka'kiah. مسلخ الكعكية
   (The slaughter house in K'akiah.)

   ○ Do not let the taxi wait, as the whole process will take about one hour.

○ Do not 'hire' any of the slaughterers waiting outside.

○ Select the animal and have it slaughtered. Either do it yourself or 'hire' the slaughterers working at the market. They have a vet that will check the animal for any diseases after it has been slaughtered.

○ Ask them to cut it into small pieces and place it in the plastic bags. This may cost you a few extra Riyals.

○ Distribute the meat in the general area around the market. There are many poor people waiting around this area.

○ You are done!

• If you are unable to do the above, you can try one of the butchers in Makkah. Ask him if he can do it for you. Obviously there is no guarantee that it will be done and that the meat will be distributed to the poor.

• Alternatively you can leave money with a trustworthy person and ask him to do it for you later.

• Whatever you do, ensure that you do not leave for home, without doing it or arranging for it, as you would like to obtain the fullest reward for your *Umrah*. Do not cut corners, after having spent lots of money, time and effort to go for *Umrah* in the first place.

• Many people aren't aware of the importance of this, whereas others treat this subject very lightly. I urge you to be serious about it and not to omit it, if your circumstances require you to do it. Make the effort!

⇨ **Smoking:**

◆ I would like to take this opportunity to discuss the issue of smoking, since it relates to the state of *Ihraam*. Allah states in the Qur'an:

﴿ . . . وَيُحِلُّ لَهُمُ ٱلطَّيِّبَٰتِ وَيُحَرِّمُ عَلَيۡهِمُ ٱلۡخَبَٰٓئِثَ . . . ﴾

"...He will make lawful for them all good things and prohibit for them Al-Khaba'ith as unlawful.

(i.e. all evil and unlawful as regards things, deeds, beliefs, persons and foods)...

[*Surah Al-A'raf* (7), part of *Ayah* 157]

◆ There is no doubt that smoking is harmful to the human body.

◆ Hence **smoking is Haraam** (forbidden). It is therefore a sin to smoke and even worse so whilst one is in *Ihraam*. If you think these are strong words, and you do not agree, than read what is says on the cigarette box:

"Smoking causes lung Cancer."

• You will find many people in *Ihraam* smoking, and it will make you wonder whether it is allowed to smoke a cigarette while you are in the state of *Ihraam* or not.

• I am sure that it is not easy for smokers to give it up while they are in *Ihraam*. However during Ramadaan they seem to cope without a cigarette during the day. I suggest that if you are a smoker to sincerely try to refrain from doing so while in the state of *Ihraam* and also make the intention to give it up permanently (for the sake of Allah).

• You are now a "Guest of Allah" and you should behave accordingly.

Chapter 6
The Journey — From Home to Makkah

⇨ *Salah* during Travel:

* Do not neglect your *Salah* while travelling.

* Yes, it is possible to perform your *Salah* while in the aircraft.

* Below is the preferred method as per the *Sunnah* for travellers:

    ○ For *Salah* one must stand and face *Qiblah*. (If the direction of the aircraft changes during the *Salah*, this is ok).

    ○ For *Nafl Salah* one can sit. Only sit in your seat to make your *Fardh Salah* if it is absolutely impossible to do otherwise.

    ○ While you are travelling you can shorten your *Salah*.

    ○ Joining of the *Salah* is not part of travelling only, but rather as per one's need at anytime. However, during travelling it is acceptable to join and shorten whilst on the journey, and to shorten (not join) once you have reached your destination.

    ○ *Fajr* = 2 *Sunnah Rak'at* and 2 *Fardh Rak'at*. The Prophet (ﷺ) never omitted the *Sunnah* for *Fajr*, even while travelling.

    ○ *Zuhr* = 2 *Rak'at* and *Asr* = 2 *Rak'at*. You can join at *Zuhr* time or at *Asr* time.

    ○ *Maghrib* = 3 *Rak'at* and *Ishaa* = 2 *Rak'at*. You can join at *Maghrib* time or at *Ishaa* time.

    ○ *Witr*. This is another *Salah* the Prophet (ﷺ) never omitted, even while travelling.

* There appears to be great deal of confusion on how to perform or join *Salah* while travelling. On many occasions you will enter a mosque, on your way to Madinah or

Makkah, where you may find more than one congregation performing *Salah*. One group performing *Salatul-Maghrib* and one performing *Salatul-Ishaa*. This is incorrect, as there should only be one *Imam* (congregation) at any given time in the same mosque or prayer area. This phenomena stems from the fact that those performing *Maghrib*, believe that they cannot join the group performing *Ishaa*. Many times you will actually find someone standing there stopping people (coming in late for *Maghrib*) from joining the group performing *Ishaa*. My fellow Muslims, it is so easy. If you enter the mosque to perform *Maghrib*, and the congregation is performing *Ishaa* (2 *Rak'at*), join them and complete three *Rak'at* as you would have normally when they complete the two. If you enter and there are two groups, join the group that started first (they will generally be to the front of the mosque). Another error is, when people wait for the group (performing *Ishaa*) to complete and then do *Maghrib* separately.

⇨ *Meqaat:*

◆ The *Meqaat* boundaries were defined by the Prophet (ﷺ), and anybody (with the intention of performing *Umrah* or *Hajj*) that passes through them without *Ihraam* is liable for an expiation (sacrifice).

The Prophet (ﷺ) said:

«فَهُنَّ لَهُنَّ، وَلِمَنْ أَتَىٰ عَلَيْهِنَّ مِنْ غَيْرِ أَهْلِهِنَّ، مِمَّنْ أَرَادَ الْحَجَّ وَالْعُمْرَةَ»

"They (i.e., the Mawaqit) are for those who come from them and those coming from beyond them who intend Hajj or Umrah."

(*Bukhari*: 1524 and *Muslim*: 1181)

◆ Majority of the scholars agree that Jeddah is not a *Meqaat*. Many people adopt their *Ihraam* at Jeddah airport. This is a violation of the *Meqaat* rules. The person should return to their respective *Meqaat* or the nearest one, or perform an animal sacrifice as expiation.

◆ Only the people who reside in Jeddah can adopt their *Ihraams* from their homes in Jeddah.

◆ If you intend to proceed to Madinah upon arrival in Jeddah, you should adopt *Ihraam* at Dhul-Hulaifah in Madinah, before going to Makkah.

عَنِ ابْنِ عَبَّاسٍ قَالَ: وَقَّتَ رَسُولُ اللهِ ﷺ لِأَهْلِ المَدِينَةِ ذَا الحُلَيْفَةِ، وَلِأَهْلِ الشَّامِ الجُحْفَةَ وَلِأَهْلِ نَجْدٍ قَرْنَ المَنَازِلِ، وَلِأَهْلِ اليَمَنِ يَلَمْلَمَ، فَهُنَّ لَهُنَّ وَلِمَنْ أَتَى عَلَيْهِنَّ مِنْ غَيْرِ أَهْلِهِنَّ لِمَنْ كَانَ يُرِيدُ الحَجَّ وَالعُمْرَةَ، فَمَنْ كَانَ دُونَهُنَّ فَمُهَلُّهُ مِنْ أَهْلِهِ، وَكَذَاكَ وَكَذَاكَ حَتَّى أَهْلُ مَكَّةَ يُهِلُّونَ مِنْهَا.

Narrated Ibn Abbas (ﷺ) that the Prophet (ﷺ) fixed Dhul-Hulaifah as the Meqaat for the people of Al-Madinah, Al-Juhfah for the people of Sham, Qarn-ul-Manazil for the people of Najd, and Yalamlam for the people of Yemen; and these Mawaqit are for those living at those very places, and besides them for all those who come through them with the intention of performing Hajj and Umrah; and whoever is living within these Mawaqit should assume Ihraam from where he starts, and the people of Makkah can assume Ihraam (for Hajj only) from Makkah.

(Bukhari : 1526)

* Some airlines such as Saudi Arabian Airlines, Malaysian Airlines, Emirates Airlines, Kuwait Air and Pakistan International Airlines make an announcement in the aircraft prior to it reaching the respective *Meqaat* boundary. Some display a message on the screen about 10 minutes before the *Meqaat*.

* Some of the *Meqaat* names have changed somewhat over the years:

1. Dhul-Hulaifah, is also now known as Abyar Ali or Abaar Ali (the wells of Ali). It is situated about 10 kilometers (6 miles) outside Madinah. It is for the people of Madinah and those coming from the north.

2. Dhat-Irq is for the people coming from the direction of Iraq. It is about 67 kilometers (42 miles) from Makkah.

3. Qarn Al-Manazil, now known as As-Sayl. This is for the people coming from the Najd and the East. It is situated near the city of Taif.

4. Yalamlam, also known as As-Sadiah. This is for the people coming from Yemen and its direction (south). It is about 48 kilometers (30 miles) from Makkah.

5. Al-Juhfah is today an abandoned village north west of Makkah near the town of Rabigh. People coming from Syria and its direction adopt their *Ihraam* from Rabigh.

- Entering Jeddah without *Ihraam* is the most common mistake made by people coming for *Umrah*. Avoid it!

- As the aircraft facilities are limited, it is advisable to prepare oneself (*Ghusl*, trim nails, etc.) and to put on one's *Ihraam* clothes (if the flight is not a very long), prior to boarding the aircraft, and only utter the *Niyah* at the *Meqaat* boundary. Following is a very general diagram to give you an idea of the boundaries.

- If you need to dress in the aircraft, then try to use the toilet designated for mothers with infants. These toilets are marginally bigger and it has a table (nappy change table) that you can use to put your clothes on while changing.

- Some examples (of passengers arriving by air):

    o People coming from the United Kingdom will adopt *Ihraam* at or over Rabigh❺

- ○ People coming from Australia, Malaysia, Singapore, etc. will adopt *Ihraam* at As-Sayl❸ (assuming that the flight is direct and not via Riyadh).

- ○ People coming from America and Canada will adopt Ihraam at Rabigh❺

- ○ People coming from South-Africa and Nigeria will adopt *Ihraam* at As-Sadiah❹

- ○ People from Egypt will adopt *Ihraam* at Rabigh❺

- ○ People coming from Pakistan will adopt *Ihraam* at As-Sayl❸

- • For pilots or for those who have pilot friends, the *Meqaat* for the air routes are printed in the Jeppesen Jeddah area chart 10-1, note 3.

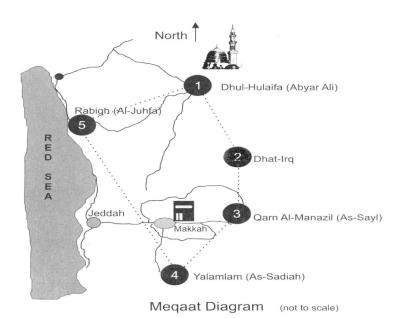

Meqaat Diagram (not to scale)

The Journey:

♦ Once you have boarded your means of transport, supplicate the following:

«اللهُ أَكْبَرُ اللهُ أَكْبَرُ اللهُ أَكْبَرُ سُبْحَانَ الَّذِي سَخَّرَ لَنَا هَذَا وَمَا كُنَّا لَهُ مُقْرِنِينَ، وَإِنَّا إِلَىٰ رَبِّنَا لَمُنْقَلِبُونَ، اللَّهُمَّ! [إِنَّا] نَسْأَلُكَ فِي سَفَرِنَا هَذَا الْبِرَّ وَالتَّقْوَىٰ، وَمِنَ الْعَمَلِ مَا تَرْضَىٰ، اللَّهُمَّ! هَوِّنْ عَلَيْنَا سَفَرَنَا هَذَا، وَاطْوِ عَنَّا بُعْدَهُ، اللَّهُمَّ أَنْتَ الصَّاحِبُ فِي السَّفَرِ، وَالْخَلِيفَةُ فِي الْأَهْلِ، اللَّهُمَّ! إِنِّي أَعُوذُ بِكَ مِنْ وَعْثَاءِ السَّفَرِ، وَكَآبَةِ الْمَنْظَرِ، وَسُوءِ الْمُنْقَلَبِ فِي الْمَالِ وَالْأَهْلِ»

Allahu Akbar, Allahu Akbar, Allahu Akbar. Subhanaladhee sakh-khar-a-lana hadhaa wa maa kunnaa lahu muqrineen, wa innaa ilaa Rabbanaa lamunqaliboon. Allahumma innaa nasaluka fee safarinaa hadhal-birr wa-taqwaa wa minal 'amali maa tardaa. Allahumma howwin 'alaynaa safaranaa hadhaa, wa-tawe'annaa bu'dahu. Allahumma Anta saahibu fissafari, wal-khalifatu fil-ahli. Allahumma inni a'uoodhubika min wa'thaa'issafari, wa kaabatil manthari, wa soo'ilmunqalabi fil-maali wal-ahli.

[Allah is the Greatest, Allah is the Greatest, Allah is the Greatest. How perfect He is, The One Who has placed this (transport) at our service, and we ourselves would not have been capable of that, and to our Lord is our final destiny. O Allah we ask You for *Birr* and *Taqwaa* in this journey of ours, and we ask You for deeds which please You. O Allah, make easy for us this journey of ours and fold up (i.e., shorten) for us its distance. O Allah, You are the companion in travel and the caretaker of the family. O Allah, I seek refuge in You from the hardship of travel and from (finding) a distressing sight or an unhappy return in regard to (my) property and family.]

(*Muslim*: 1342)

(*Birr* and *Taqwaa* = Two comprehensive terms which individually, refer to all good actions and obedience.)

- One advantage of choosing to fly with Saudi Arabian Airlines is that this *Du'a'* is read prior to the taking off of the aeroplane. Apart from the food also being *Halal*, it is good practice to try and support the Muslim countries and airlines, whenever possible.

◆ Supplications during the journey:

➢ Upon ascending and elevation —

Allahu Akbar اللهُ أَكْبَرُ

(Allah is the Greatest.)

➢ Upon descending —

Subahanallah سُبْحَانَ الله

(Glorified is Allah.)

➢ Upon approaching a town during a journey:

اللَّهُمَّ رَبَّ السَّمَاوَاتِ السَّبْعِ وَ مَا أَظْلَلْنَ، وَرَبَّ الأَرَضِينَ السَّبْعِ وَمَا أَقْلَلْنَ، وَرَبَّ الشَّيَاطِين وَمَا أَضْلَلْنَ، وَرَبَّ الرِّيَاح وَمَا ذَرَيْنَ، أَسْأَلُكَ خَيرَ هَذهِ الْقَرْيَةِ، وَخَيرَ أَهْلِهَا وَخَيرَ مَا فِيهَا، وَأَعُوذُ بِكَ مِنْ شَرِّهَا وَشَر أَهْلِهَا وَشَرِّ مَا فِيهَا .

Allahumma rabbis-samaawaatissab'i wa maa athlalna, wa rabbal-ardhainis-sat'i wa maa aqlalna wa rabbash, shayaateeni wa maa adhlalnaa, wa rabbar-riyaahi wa maa dharayna. Asaluka khayra haadhihil qaryati, wa khayra ahlihaa wa khayra maa feehaa, wa a'uoodhu bika min sharri haa wa sharri ahlihaa wa sharri maa feehaa.

(O Allah, Lord of the seven heavens and that which they cover, Lord of the seven earths and that which they carry, Lord of the devils and those they lead astray, and Lord of the winds and that which they scatter, I ask of

You the good of this town and the good of its people and the good of that within it. And I seek refuge in You from its evil and from the evil of its people and from the evil of that within it.)

(*Nasa'i* : 5/256 and *Ibn Habban* : 2709)

♦ When you stop for the night during your journey, supplicate the following:

أَعُوذُ بِكَلِمَاتِ اللهِ التَّامَّاتِ مِنْ شَرِّ مَا خَلَقَ» .

A'uoodhu bikalimaatillahit-taammaati min sharri maa khalaqa.

(I seek refuge in the perfect Words of Allah and from the evil of that which He created.)

(*Muslim* : 2708)

♦ Do not neglect your *Salah* while en-route to Saudi Arabia. If you are travelling during sunset, you will notice that on the one side, looking out of the aircraft, the sun will still be shining, whereas on the other side it will be dark. This makes it difficult to determine the time of *Salatul-Maghrib*. If you will be disembarking prior to 11.30pm, then you can delay and join *Salatul-Maghrib* and *Salatul-Ishaa*. If not, then perform *Salatul-Maghrib* when the sun has set on the side of the aircraft where you are sitting.

♦ If you are going directly to Makkah (not to Madinah first), ensure that you enter into *Ihraam* at the *Meqaat* as explained earlier.

♦ Do not forget to remove your underwear (men only). (This may sound funny, but there are many males who forget to remove their underwear while in *Ihraam*).

♦ Do not forget to remove any headgear you may be wearing (men only).

♦ Make your *Niyah* for *Umrah*, as described previously.

♦ Once you are in the state of *Ihraam*, recite the *Talbiyah* as often as possible.

* Leave home for the airport as early as possible. Most *Umrah* flights are extremely busy. Even though you may hold a confirmed seat, you may find no seats available if you are late (1 hour before departure) to check-in.

* Most airlines operate on an overbooking procedure. Meaning, if everybody that has a confirmed booking turns-up, there will not be enough seats. So be early.

* Reconfirm any special food you may have requested at check-in time.

* The flight attendant or pilot (depending on the airline) will announce the *Meqaat* point prior to you reaching it.

• Carry your small Qur'an and your *Umrah* notes/books with you. Utilize every minute of your time, to seek Allah's pleasure and reward.

• Give the movie (film) on the aeroplane a miss and read Qur'an instead. Start your journey the 'right-way'.

• Most airlines provide the passengers with socks and eye-covers. Take these with you, as the socks are useful to wear if the *Haram* floor is too cold or too hot. The eye-covers are useful, if you will be sharing rooms, and the lights are still on while you are trying to sleep.

• It may be more practical to adopt your *Ihraam* clothes prior to boarding the aircraft for Jeddah. This means that you only have to make your *Niyah* at the *Meqaat* point. (The toilets in the aircraft are extremely small and you might get tangled in your *Ihraam* and get stuck in the toilet. Now wouldn't that be a sight?)

• Men, don't forget your shoes under your seat when disembarking. Sound silly? Ok this is what happens... You decide to adopt *Ihraam* ; you take out your garments as well as your slippers to wear while in *Ihraam*. You take of your shoes as it is easier to go to the toilet with the slippers. You return with your *Ihraam* on and slippers. You put your clothes in your overnight bag, and very likely forget about your shoes... Just recently a friend called me from Makkah and asked how he can go about getting his shoes back that he left under his seat on the plane. He was surprised when I did not ask him how he managed to leave his shoes on the plane.

- Once you are in the state of *Ihraam*, you may experience that suddenly very minor things and issues start to annoy or affect you. Remember, *Shaytaan* will be doing his best to make you violate the rules of *Ihraam*. Be aware and alert!

- Remember, this is a spiritual journey. Don't concern yourself too much with what you see 'wrong' around you. Concern yourself only about whether Allah will accept your *Umrah* performance or not.

⇨ Arrival at Jeddah:

* Jeddah's King Abdul Aziz International Airport has three terminals:

    1. Saudi Arabian Airlines (Saudia) Terminal;

    2. Foreign Airlines Terminal (about 15min by car away from the Saudia Terminal);

    3. Hajj Terminal (located next to the Foreign Airlines Terminal).

* The Hajj Terminal is known as "Tent City". It is constructed with huge tent like structures.

* There is no air transport between Jeddah and Makkah.

* Madinah has its own airport and you are able to go to Madinah by aeroplane.

* The customs at all three terminals are extremely strict and thorough. Be prepared to have all your bags unpacked and checked with a fine tooth comb. (Unlock all your suitcases before you arrive at the customs desk).

* There are certain flights, during the peak *Umrah* period (such as Ramadaan), that arrive at and depart from the Hajj Terminal.

* All three terminals have restaurants, bathrooms, showers, toilets, telephones and *Salah* facilities.

→ Processing:

- When you arrive, you may be tired and exhausted and in a hurry to get to Makkah. Jeddah terminals are very busy at the best of times, so expect delays. For details about arriving in Ramadaan, see chapter 9 of this book.

- Meanwhile, sit, relax, read Qur'an, and make *Dhikr*, *Tasbeeh*, *Istighfaar*, and recite the *Talbiyah*. There is no hurry.

- Also, try to extend your help to others.

- If you plan to travel to other countries after or before *Umrah* and thus have two passports (different countries/ nationalities) with you. Be aware that to enter Saudi Arabia with two valid passports in your possession is illegal. So put the other passport in a 'safe' place.

→ Money:

- Change some money into Riyals at the airport.

- Unfortunately and sadly I need to mention that there are pickpockets. So, like any other trip, you need to take care of your money. Do not be careless because you are on *Umrah*. Buy yourself a good money belt. Good belts (canvas type) are available in Makkah and Madinah.

- When you change your money, obtain some small denominations. (i.e. 1 & 5 Riyals). These are extremely useful when buying small items (such as drinks) when the shops are very crowded. This way you do not have to wait for change.

→ Transport:

* Review chapter 4 in this book for the information about the transport.

⇨ Jeddah to Madinah:

* The distance is 424km (265mi).

* Most of the buses are air-conditioned.

* This journey normally takes about 4 hours.

* The driver may stop at a few places for food and rest.

* If you are going by aeroplane:

    o You will depart from the Saudi Arabian Airlines terminal. If you arrived at the foreign airlines terminal, you need to take a taxi to the Saudi Airlines terminal.

    o The journey to Madinah takes about 45 minutes.

    o Once in Madinah, you will require a taxi to take you to your hotel.

    o The advantage of the new *Umrah* system is that all these transport arrangements should be pre-organised by the agent.

    o More details about Madinah — See chapter 10 in this book.

⇨ Madinah to Makkah:

* The distance is 447 km (278 mi).

* If you are going to Makkah by bus or by taxi (or aeroplane via Jeddah), the procedures are the same.

    o If you do not have the two unfitted pieces of cloth for your *Ihraam* (men), you should purchase them in Madinah.

    o Prior to your departure for Makkah, prepare yourself for the state of *Ihraam* (i.e., *Ghusl*, trim your nails).

    o Attire yourself with your *Ihraam* clothes.

    o The bus or taxi will stop at the *Meqaat* on its way to either Makkah or to the airport.

    o The *Meqaat* is at Abyar-Ali (Dhul-Hulaifah) which is situated about 10 km (6 mi) outside Madinah.

(The mosque at this *Meqaat* has showers and good *Wudu'* and toilet facilities).

○ If you have not put on your *Ihraam*, you need to do so at this stage and make your *Niyah* for *Umrah*. (*Niyah*, see chapter 5)

○ Recite the *Talbiyah* as often as possible. (see chapter 2, for the *Talbiyah*)

• If you are travelling by aeroplane from Madinah, you will need to take a bus or a taxi from Jeddah airport to Makkah.

⇨ Jeddah to Makkah:

◆ You should be in *Ihraam*.

◆ If you had planned to go to Madinah first and for some reason you are unable to go; and you are now going to Makkah first, than adopt your *Ihraam* immediately. You are not liable for expiation for violating the *Meqaat* rule, as it was outside your control.

◆ Recite the *Talbiyah* as often as possible. (see chapter 2, for the *Talbiyah*)

* The distance is 72 km (45 mi).

• This is normally only a one hour journey.

• Remove your passport from your bag, if it is in the trunk of the taxi.

⇨ Checkpoints

• You will stop at the major checkpoint just before entering Makkah.

• At this checkpoint your passport will be checked, so keep it handy.

Prepare yourself, for the great moment.......entering the *Haram* in Makkah and seeing the Ka'bah................

Chapter 7
Makkah Al-Mukarramah:

﴿إِنَّ أَوَّلَ بَيْتٍ وُضِعَ لِلنَّاسِ لَلَّذِى بِبَكَّةَ مُبَارَكًا وَهُدًى لِّلْعَٰلَمِينَ ○ فِيهِ ءَايَٰتٌ بَيِّنَٰتٌ مَّقَامُ إِبْرَٰهِيمَ ۖ وَمَن دَخَلَهُ كَانَ ءَامِنًا﴾

"Verily, the first House (of worship) appointed for mankind was that at Bakkah (Makkah), full of blessing, and a guidance for Al-Alamin (the mankind and the jinn). In it are manifest signs (for example), the Maqaam (place) of Ibraheem; whosoever enters it, he attains security...."

[*Surah Al Imran* (3), *Ayah* 96 and part of 97]

- It is desirable to have a bath (*Ghusl*) before entering Makkah.

- Most people are very anxious to complete their *Umrah*. However, before you go rushing off to the *Haram*, first settle yourself into your accommodation and have something to eat or drink, if you feel hungry or thirsty.

- Keep track of the time. It is not a good idea to perform *Tawaaf* when it is very hot. If you are not used to extreme heat, as is the case in the middle of the day during summer, delay your *Umrah* until later in the day when the weather is a little cooler. Do not be brave, there is no rush.

- Before you leave to go to the *Haram*, ensure that you are familiar with your surroundings and that you know how to get back to your accommodation. Use certain landmarks as a means of directions and locations.

- As in any hotel, check and familiarise yourself with the emergency exits.

- Take an address card of the hotel with you and keep it in your pocket, in addition to some other form of identity (i.e., driver's licence, medical card).

• Before discussing the *Umrah* in detail, there are many other aspects related to Makkah, which I would like to address first.

• Before I explain the layout of the *Haram*, I would like to start with some reminders about personal behaviour as you should be on your best behaviour as you are now a **Guest of Allah!**

Personal Behaviour:

♦ You might be confronted with situations in which many individuals don't know how to handle themselves. They need someone to help them, to guide them, and also advise them. Always try to be first to render your assistance. Try to be 'charitable' in all your actions.

Abu Hurairah (﷽) related that the Prophet (﷽) said:

«كُلُّ سُلَامىٰ عَلَيْهِ صَدَقَةٌ كُلَّ يَوْمٍ، يُعِينُ الرَّجُلَ فِي دَابَّتِهِ، يُحامِلُهُ [عَلَيْها] أَوْ يَرْفَعُ عَلَيها مَتَاعَهُ صَدَقَةٌ، والكَلِمَةُ الطَّيِّبَةُ، وكُلُّ خَطْوَةٍ يَمْشِيها إلى الصَّلاةِ صَدَقَةٌ، ودَلُّ الطَّرِيقِ صَدَقَةٌ».

"Charity is obligatory every day on every joint of a human being. If one helps a person in matters concerning his riding animal by helping him to ride on it or by lifting his luggage on to it, all this will be regarded as charity. A good word; and every step one takes to offer the compulsory congregational prayer are regarded as charity; and guiding somebody on the road is regarded as charity."

(Bukhari : 2891)

♦ Avoid idle talk, arguments and disagreements.

Abu Hurairah (ﷺ) related that the Prophet (ﷺ) said:

«لَيْسَ الشَّدِيدُ بالصُّرَعَةِ، إنَّما الشَّدِيدُ الَّذِي يَمْلِكُ نَفْسَهُ عِنْدَ الغَضَبِ»

"The strong is not the one who overcomes the people by his strength, but the strong is the one who controls himself while in anger."

(Bukhari : 6114)

♦ Take utmost care when quoting *Ahadith* to prove your point. You must be 100% sure that the *Ahadith* are authentic. Do not claim you read or heard from so and so. The responsibility is on you:

Abdullah bin Amr bin Al-'Aas (ﷺ) related that the Prophet (ﷺ) said:

«بَلِّغُوا عَنِّي ولَوْ آيَةً، وحَدِّثُوا عَنْ بَنِي إِسْرَائِيلَ ولا حَرَجَ، ومَنْ كَذَبَ عَلَيَّ مُتَعَمِّدًا فَلْيَتَبَوَّأْ مَقْعَدَهُ مِنَ النَّارِ».

"Convey from me to the people though it may be only one Verse; and you may narrate events from the accounts of Bani Israil, there is no harm in doing so. But a person who

deliberately attributes to me something which is not true shall find his abode in Hell.''

(*Bukhari* : 3461)

◆ There are only three places at the Ka'bah that you can and should touch, if at all possible:

1.   That is the Black Stone (kiss it, if possible) - *Hajr-al-Aswad*.

2.   The South Corner known as the *Rukn-al-Yamani* corner (not to be kissed).

3.   The area known as the *Multazam* (from the Black Stone Corner to the door of the Ka'bah. Also not to be kissed).

◆ There is absolutely no reward and it is contrary to the *Sunnah* to touch the Maqaam Ibraheem, the doors, hanging on to the Ka'bah cloth, etc. Furthermore, refrain from kissing it.

◆ Lower your gaze.....! We are **instructed** in the Qur'an and *Sunnah* to do so:

$$﴿ قُل لِّلْمُؤْمِنِينَ يَغُضُّواْ مِنْ أَبْصَٰرِهِمْ ﴾$$

"Tell the believing men to lower their gaze..."

[*Surah An-Nur* (24), part of *Ayah* 30]

$$﴿ وَقُل لِّلْمُؤْمِنَٰتِ يَغْضُضْنَ مِنْ أَبْصَٰرِهِنَّ ﴾$$

"And tell the believing women to lower their gaze..."

[*Surah An-Nur* (24), part of *Ayah* 31]

عَنْ جَرِيرِ بْنِ عَبْدِ اللهِ، قَالَ: سَأَلْتُ رَسُولَ اللهِ ﷺ عَنْ نَظْرَةِ الْفُجَاءَةِ، فَأَمَرَنِي أَنْ أَصْرِفَ بَصَرِي.

Jarir (ﷺ) says: "I asked the Prophet (ﷺ) as to what should be done when our glance accidentally falls (upon somebody forbidden) to look at." He said: "Turn your eyes."

(*Muslim* : 2159)

♦ Reflect on the meaning of the following *Ayah* :

﴿إِنَّ ٱلَّذِينَ كَفَرُواْ وَيَصُدُّونَ عَن سَبِيلِ ٱللَّهِ وَٱلْمَسْجِدِ ٱلْحَرَامِ ٱلَّذِى جَعَلْنَٰهُ لِلنَّاسِ سَوَآءً ٱلْعَٰكِفُ فِيهِ وَٱلْبَادِ وَمَن يُرِدْ فِيهِ بِإِلْحَادٍ بِظُلْمٍ نُّذِقْهُ مِنْ عَذَابٍ أَلِيمٍ﴾

"Verily! Those who disbelieve and hinder (men) from the Path of Allah, and from Al-Masjid-al-Haram (at Makkah) which He made (open) to (all) men, the dweller in it and the visitor from the country are equal there (as regards its sanctity and pilgrimage). And whoever inclines to evil actions therein or to do wrong, him We shall cause to taste a painful torment."

[*Surah Al-Hajj* (22), *Ayah* 25]

- Maintain a positive attitude and always say *"Alhamdulillah"* for everything, be it good or bad.

- If you get impatient with people or situations, make *Dhikr* and make *Istighfaar* (seek Allah's pleasure and forgiveness).

- If you lose your shoes, or if someone 'takes them', do not take somebody else's shoes. Rather make *Du'aa'* and believe that the person who took it may need it more than you. Buy yourself another pair. They sell for as little as five Saudi Riyals.

- Cleanliness is very important in Islam. Do not spit or litter in the street.

- Some people rush violently in order to touch and kiss the Black Stone. Such behaviour is wrong. Besides exerting effort to the level of fatigue, rushing and pushing in a mixed crowd of males and females may cause harm to someone. It is lawful (*Sunnah*) to touch and kiss the Black Stone when possible. It is sufficient for a person to merely point at it, whereas causing others harm or inconvenience is sinful.

- It is natural that with so many people in one place some confusion, impatience, pushing, etc. will occur. Especially with people with such varied backgrounds. Try your best to perform your activities and movements in a calm and quiet way. Do not push, harm or rush anybody, especially in the crowded areas such as during *Tawaaf, Sa'ee,* at the Maqaam Ibraheem, etc.

- Always smile, be polite and greet the people you know as well as people you do not know. Always return a greeting.

﴿وَإِذَا حُيِّيتُم بِتَحِيَّةٍ فَحَيُّواْ بِأَحْسَنَ مِنْهَآ أَوْ رُدُّوهَآ إِنَّ ٱللَّهَ كَانَ عَلَىٰ كُلِّ شَىْءٍ حَسِيبًا﴾

"When you are greeted with a greeting, greet in return with what is better than it, or (at least) return it equally. Certainly Allah is Ever a Careful Account Taker of all things."

[*Surah An-Nisa* (4), *Ayah* 86]

Narrated Abdullah bin 'Amr (ﷺ): A man asked the Prophet (ﷺ) "What sort of deeds or traits of Islam are good?" The Prophet (ﷺ) said:

«تُطْعِمُ الطَّعَامَ وَتَقْرَأُ السَّلَامَ، عَلَى مَنْ عَرَفْتَ وعَلَى مَنْ لَمْ تَعْرِفْ».

"To feed others, and to greet those whom you know and those whom you do not know."

(*Bukhari*: 6236)

- One of the strangest things I found was that no matter where you are in the *Haram,* there is always somebody trying to go in the opposite direction of the general flow of the people. Avoid walking in the opposing direction of the *Tawaaf.* Rather walk all the way around to the starting point.

- Do not perform *Salah* close to the Maqaam Ibraheem if it's crowded. If you insist, be forewarned that you may get trampled on and somebody may step on your head. Do not even think of standing in front of your wife as protection for her to make *Salah* in this area. You are asking for trouble! It is acceptable to perform your two *Rak'at Salah* after *Tawaaf* anywhere in the mosque.

- Try not to throw the top part of your *Ihraam* (men) over your shoulder as you may hit the person behind you in the face.

- Your behaviour is of the utmost importance at all times. Do not let bad behaviour ruin your good deeds. It is your deeds that you will take with you to your grave, so try and behave well and perform as many good deeds as possible.

Narrated Ibn Abbas (ﷺ) that the Prophet (ﷺ) narrating about his Lord said:

«إِنَّ اللهَ عَزَّ وجَلَّ كَتَبَ الحَسَناتِ والسَّيِّئاتِ ثُمَّ بَيَّنَ ذلكَ، فَمَنْ هَمَّ بِحَسَنَةٍ فَلَمْ يَعْمَلْها كَتَبها اللهُ لَهُ عِنْدَهُ حَسَنَةً كامِلَةً، فإنْ هَمَّ بِها وعَمِلَها كَتَبها اللهُ لَهُ عِنْدَهُ عَشَرَ حَسَناتٍ إلى سَبْعِمائَةِ ضِعْفٍ إلى أضْعافٍ كَثيرَةٍ، ومَنْ هَمَّ بِسَيِّئَةٍ فَلَمْ يَعْمَلْها كَتَبها اللهُ لَهُ عِنْدَهُ حَسَنَةً كامِلَةً، فإنْ هُوَ هَمَّ بِها فَعَمِلَها كَتَبها اللهُ لَهُ سَيِّئَةً واحِدَةً».

"Allah ordered (the appointed angels over you) that the good and bad deeds be written, and He then showed (the way) how (to write). If somebody intends to do a good deed and he does not do it, then Allah will write for him a full good deed (in his account) with Him; and if he intends to do a good deed and actually did it, then Allah will write for him (in his account) with Him (its reward equal) from ten to seven hundred times, to many more times; and if somebody intended to do a bad deed and he does not do it, then Allah will write a full good deed (in his account) with Him, and if he intended to do it (a bad deed) and actually did it, then Allah will write one bad deed (in his account)."

(*Bukhari* : 6491)

⇨ Health:

◆ If you happen to get sick, try to be patient and not to complain too much.

حَدَّثَنَا جَابِرُ بْنُ عَبْدِ اللهِ أَنَّ رَسُولَ اللهِ ﷺ دَخَلَ عَلَىٰ أُمِّ السَّائِبِ، أَوْ أُمِّ الْمُسَيَّبِ، فَقَالَ: «مَا لَكِ؟ يَا أُمَّ السَّائِبِ! أَوْ يَا أُمَّ الْمُسَيَّبِ! تُزَفْزِفِينَ؟» قَالَتِ: الْحُمَّىٰ، لَا بَارَكَ اللهُ فِيهَا، فَقَالَ: «لَا تَسُبِّي الْحُمَّىٰ، فَإِنَّهَا تُذْهِبُ خَطَايَا بَنِي آدَمَ، كَمَا يُذْهِبُ الْكِيرُ خَبَثَ الْحَدِيدِ».

Jabir (رضي الله عنه) relates that the Prophet (ﷺ) visited Umm Sa'ib or Ummul-Musaiyab and asked her: "What has happened to you, O Umm Sa'ib or Ummul-Musaiyab? Why are you shivering?" She answered: "It is a fever; may Allah not bless it." He (ﷺ) said to her: "Do not abuse the fever, because it cleans the sins of the children of Adam as a furnace cleans the dirt of iron."

(*Muslim* : 2575)

- Drink plenty of fluids to avoid dehydration. Drinking very cold drinks after being in the hot sun is **not** very good for your throat (it may cause you to develop a sore throat or cough).
- Drinking yogurt or *Laban* (milky drink) helps in providing the salt your body needs.
- Avoid standing in front of an air-conditioner to cool down.
- Do not sleep with the air-conditioner blowing directly on you.
- One of the most common complaints while travelling is diarrhea. Some steps you should take if you have diarrhea – only eat fruit with a thick skin (i.e. that must be peeled); boil water before you drink it or only drink bottled beverages; don't eat cold meats, shell fish, raw seafood or reheated food; don't drink tap water; don't use ice cubes

unless you know they've been made with purified water; don't eat fried or fatty foods, dairy products, spicy foods or 'acidic' fruits or vegetables (e.g. oranges, tomatoes); try to eat bland food (boiled rice or potatoes), toast (without butter or margarine but with jam or honey) or plain biscuits; drink plenty of fluids (no fruit juices or milk); drink a liquid that will help replace the salt in your body.

- Use sunglasses if you have sensitive eyes. Around the *Haram* areas and inside at the *Tawaaf* areas are marble tiles which cause a very strong glare in the sun. This can be harmful to your eyes. (Try the following: Instead of putting your hand on your forehead to cover your eyes from the glare, put your hand on your nose directly under your eyes. This will stop the glare, which is reflecting upwards).

- Use an umbrella. Buy one without the sharp point as this can be harmful to others whilst you are in a crowd. Also buy a white or green coloured one instead of a black one (the black draws the heat).

⇨ Medical Facilities:

* There are emergency clinics inside the *Haram*. See under "Access to the *Haram*" in this chapter for the locations of these clinics.

* There is a hospital in Makkah very near to the *Haram* in the Ajyad area:

It is a white four-storey building.

> ➢ The sign on the hospital is not in English, only in Arabic.

> ➢ The sign is in gold on a black backing, in front and at the entrance of the building.

> ➢ There are no signs directing you to the hospital area.

> ➢ There is no hospital (Red Crescent) sign.

> ➢ The Arabic word for hospital is:

Mustashfa مستشفى

> ➤ There are trees in front of the building.

> ➤ If you exit from door number 1, you will in the general area called Ajyad.

> ➤ Keep in mind that these things may change over time, so ask before you venture too far. At the time of writing it was rumoured that this hospital will be broken down to make place for a hotel.

* There is a specialist hospital in one of the suburbs of Makkah, quite close to the *Haram* area.

• Most people coming from non-Muslim countries are used to seeing a red cross indicating a medical facility. In the Muslim world it is a Red Crescent (moon).

→ Death of a person in *Ihraam*:

* It is important to always keep some form of identification on you, in case you become ill or die while inside the *Haram* or somewhere alone. This way your family can be contacted.

* In this part of the world burial is extremely quick.

Ibn Abbas (ﷺ) reported that a person fell down from his camel (in the state of *Ihraam*) and his neck was broken and he died. Thereupon the Prophet (ﷺ) said:

«اغْسِلُوهُ بِمَاءٍ وَسِدْرٍ، وَكَفِّنُوهُ فِي ثَوْبَيْهِ، وَلَا تُخَمِّرُوا رَأْسَهُ، فَإِنَّ اللَّهَ يَبْعَثُهُ يَوْمَ الْقِيَامَةِ مُلَبِّيًا».

"Bathe him with water mixed with the leaves of the lote tree and shroud him in his two (pieces of) cloth (Ihraam), and do not cover his head for Allah will raise him on the Day of Resurrection pronouncing Talbiyah."

(*Muslim*: 1206)

⇨ **Money:**

→ **Safety:**

- As with any other trip, keep your money in a safe and secure place. (Keeping it in the refrigerator is not secure).

- Unfortunately there are a small percentage of people who are not here for the same reason you are. So take care of your money and belongings.

→ **Shopping:**

Jabir ♣ says that the Prophet (ﷺ) said:

«رَحِمَ اللهُ رَجُلًا سَمْحًا إِذَا بَاعَ، وَإِذَا اشْتَرَى، وَإِذَا اقْتَضَى» .

"May Allah have mercy on a person who is easy and courteous when he sells, buys or asks for the payment of his dues."

(*Bukhari* : 2076)

- Always keep some small denomination notes with you (one and five Riyal notes). This is very helpful when the shops are very crowded and all you need is a drink. This way you will not need to wait for change.

- You will find the shopkeeper dealing with many customers at the same time. He may give you the wrong change by mistake or even forget totally about you. You may need to give him a gentle reminder that you are waiting. Sometimes you may need to be a bit more forceful.

- Sometimes you may find the shopkeeper 'throwing' your change at you instead of giving it to you in your hand. Please do not feel insulted. This practice is normal and it is definitely not a form of disrespect or otherwise.

→ **Beggars:**

- There are various types of beggars in and around the *Haram*.

- There are the poor, the children, the physically deformed, the 'not so sure' category and the professional beggars.

- The first three categories are easily recognisable, and you can decide on whether you would like to give them any money or not.

- The 'not so sure' are those who do not appear to be poor. Once again this is your call.

- The last category is the most skillful. Be aware of them and do not part with your money unless you are 200% sure the beggar with his 'sad story' is authentic. Do not be fooled by the tears or the medical papers. Remember they are professionals and this is an art for them. Many of them are in *Ihraam* or are very 'well-dressed'. Be careful!

- Don't be fooled by the 'cut money belt'.

- See chapter 9 for more details about beggars in Ramadaan.

⇨ **Sharing Accommodation:**

- If you are sharing accommodation, there are a few basic rules you can apply to make life much more pleasant for everybody.

- Try to accommodate all the cigarette smokers together.

- If you have a snorer in the room, the earplugs from the airlines are very useful.

- If you wish to sleep before 'lights out' time, use the eye covers from the airlines.

- Check the bathroom ensuring that everybody cleans it after using it. If the person entering it finds it dirty, request the previous occupant to clean it (assuming it was clean prior to that). The first clean-up can be done by the group.

- The same clean-up rule can be applied if there are any kitchen facilities involved.

- 'Ban' jumping the bathroom queue. String a line, where people can hang their towels as a means of queuing, instead of waiting outside the bathroom all the time. (One way of avoiding the rush is to wake-up 15 minutes before everyone else).

- Conserve water. (You may notice trucks pumping water into the buildings in Makkah and Madinah). If the water runs out it could take a few hours to refill. Keep some bottles of water in your room for emergencies (*Wudhu'*, toilet). Mark them, for *Wudhu'*. This is in case the building runs out of water at a critical time. It happens!

- If you need to go to the toilet, ensure first that there is water available.

- One of the first things you need to do when you enter your rooms is to turn on the hot water heater. This is if you like to take hot water showers. During the summer months, the cold water taps is sufficient, as the water is quite warm.

- If you wish to take a bath and the bath-tub does not have a rubber plug, some alumunium foil folded as a plug will do the trick.

⇨ **General:**

- Makkah is a very lively and busy city. There are always plenty of activities, cars and taxis blowing their horns, people shopping, people going to and from the *Haram*, day and night. This city does not sleep!

- Cameras and tape recorders are not allowed inside the *Haram*. Do not risk it!

- Do not walk backwards out of the *Haram*. There is no evidence of this practice in the *Sunnah*. As a matter of fact, it is dangerous, as you may trip and fall over somebody.

- Keep a business card of the hotel where you are staying, with you at all times (in your pocket or wallet). In the event of you getting lost, you can show it to the police or taxi driver. As mentioned earlier it is also useful in case you fall ill or end up in hospital.

- Most of the smaller hotels only have one telephone line, which means that it is sometimes impossible to receive any calls, as the line is always busy. This is especially a problem for any family members or friends that are trying to call you from home. Also don't expect to always receive your telephone messages from the reception. If the hotel you live in 'suffers' from this, inform your family, as many times they 'give-up' as they think they have the wrong number or they leave messages and may wait for you to return their call.

- You will notice many stray cats around Makkah. They are all very skinny. If you have a little food left over, don't throw it in the garbage bin, feed it to the cats instead.

⇨ Public Toilet Facilities:

* There are good toilet and *Wudhu'* facilities close to the *Haram*. There are none inside the mosque. Although you may notice many people performing *Wudhu'* at the *Zamzam* taps, they are not there for this purpose.

* If you exit by Marwah (end of *Sa'ee* area) turn to your right, you will be near the big toilet and *Wudhu'* facilities, for both men and women. It is a large marbled structure, light brown in colour.

* Exiting from door no. 1, facing the clock tower, to the right of the tower are toilets for men and to the left are toilets for women.

* If you exit from door no. 62 (*Umrah* door), turn to your right and underneath the road (bridge) there are stairs leading to the road level. Inside to the right of this small tunnel there are toilets, for men only.

⇨ Lost & Found:

* There is a lost and found area near to the Baab-as-Safaa door (door no. 11). It is actually at doors no. 12 & 13.

* This is for lost adults as well as for lost children and lost articles and documents.

* If you are lost, go to this office.

* If you lose an article or your wallet, this office will assist you (or let me rather say, should assist you).

* In the event of loss of identification cards or wallets, certain paperwork needs to be completed at this office. (It helps a great deal if you can take an Arabic speaking person with you, if at all possible.)

• If you have children with you, take them to this area and show it to them. Teach them to wait there (and not to panic) in the event of you 'losing' them.

• Let me highlight that the police taking care of this office does not appear to be trained for this task (taking care of lost crying children).

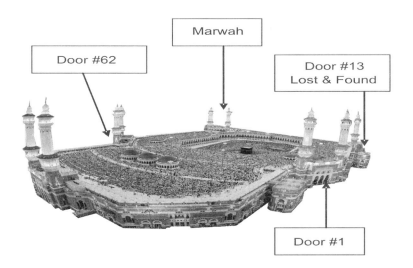

Marwah

Door #62

Door #13
Lost & Found

Door #1

- Put the hotel business card in your children's pockets.

- Dress the children in bright coloured clothes, which make it easier to see them in crowds.

- The police in the *Haram* will take all lost articles and persons to this office.

⇨ **Hairdressers/Barbers:**

- There are many barbers in Makkah. You can pay from between 5 to 50 Saudi Riyals for a haircut, depending on where you go or what you like.

- To have your head shaved will cost only 5 Riyals, and maybe up to 15 Riyals during the peak season.

- A haircut will cost you about 10 Riyals at most barbers. If you choose the hairdresser inside one of the 5 star hotels it will cost you 50 Riyals. The choice is yours.

- There are over a dozen barbers located right outside the Marwah door. If you exit on the ground floor at Marwah, you will find them immediately to your left. If you exit from the middle floor, you will have to turn right, and walk down the road as the barbers are located under the bridge.

⇨ **Shoes:**

- As mentioned previously, use a soft pair of slippers (instead of shoes) as these are easier to carry with you.

- There are shoe racks inside and outside the *Haram*. You may leave them in these racks and for the most part they will be there when you return. On the odd occasion you may find that someone has 'taken' them. It is not always the case of someone taking shoes. If you leave your shoes in the 'wrong' place, the cleaners will sweep them away. (Outside some of the big doors of the *Haram*, you will find a 'mountain' of lost or unclaimed slippers and shoes. You may find a pair that fits you or you could use it as a temporary pair until you get to a shop. You may even find your own shoes).

- It is best to keep your shoes/slippers with you (in a plastic bag, if possible). This is useful as you may 'lose' them or forget where you placed them. Sometimes you may not leave from the same door you entered from.

- If you are keeping them with you, be considerate as to where you place them while performing *Salah*, so that they may not cause any inconvenience to others. Also do not put them flat (with the shoe soles) on the ground. Remember, this is a *Salah* area and your shoes may not be all that clean. (This is why the plastic bag is useful.)

- If you have to leave your shoes in one of the racks, and you are afraid of 'losing' them, then you may consider the following: place your shoes apart from each other, meaning one shoe in one place and the other shoe somewhere else. Now do remember where you put them.

⇨ **About *Salah*:**

→ **The *Adhaan*:**

* About 15 to 20 minutes before *Adhaan* time, you will notice (hear) a 'blowing sound' through the microphones in the *Haram*. They are testing the microphones, and the women can use this as a guide to start moving towards the back, so they can perform their *Salah* in the designated areas for ladies, and not amongst the men.

* The time between *Adhaan* and *Iqaamah* varies for different *Salahs*. Normally the *Iqaamah* is about 15 to 20 minutes after the *Adhaan*, except for *Salatul-Maghrib* which is about 10 minutes.

* There are two *Adhaans* in the morning. One is called one hour before the *Adhaan* of *Salatul-Fajr*, and the second is the *Adhaan* for *Salatul-Fajr*.

It is narrated by Abdullah bin Umar ؓ that the Prophet (ﷺ) said:

«إِنَّ بِلَالًا يُنَادِي بِلَيْلٍ، فَكُلُوا وَاشْرَبُوا حَتَّى يُنَادِيَ ابْنُ أُمِّ مَكْتُومٍ».

"Bilal pronounces the Adhaan at night so that you may eat and drink till Ibn Umm Maktum pronounces the Adhaan (for the Fajr prayer)."

(*Bukhari* : 620)

- What to say on hearing the *Adhaan* :

  It is narrated by Abu Sa'id Al-Khudri (ﷺ) that Allah's Messenger (ﷺ) said:

  «إِذَا سَمِعْتُمُ النِّدَاءَ فَقُولُوا . مِثْلَ مَا يَقُولُ الْمُؤَذِّنُ»

  "Whenever you hear the Adhaan say just as the Muadhdhin is saying."

  (*Bukhari* : 611)

  أَنَّهُ سَمِعَ مُعَاوِيَةَ يَوْمًا فَقَالَ مِثْلَهُ إِلَىٰ قَوْلِهِ : «وَأَشْهَدُ أَنَّ مُحَمَّدًا رَسُولُ اللهِ» قَالَ يَحْيَى : وَحَدَّثَنِي بَعْضُ إِخْوَانِنَا أَنَّهُ قَالَ : لَمَّا قَالَ : حَيَّ عَلَى الصَّلَاةِ ، قَالَ : لَا حَوْلَ وَلَا قُوَّةَ إِلَّا بِاللهِ ، وَقَالَ : هَكَذَا سَمِعْنَا نَبِيَّكُمْ ﷺ يَقُولُ .

  Narrated Mu'awiyah (ﷺ) similar to the above Hadith until 'Wa ash-hadu anna Muhammadan Rasul-ullah' (and I testify that Muhammad is the Messenger of Allah). When the Muadhdhin said, "Haya 'alas-Salah," Mu'awiyah said, "La hawla wa la quwata illa billah (There is neither might nor any power except with Allah)," and added, "We heard your Prophet (ﷺ) saying the same."

  (*Bukhari* : 612 and 613)

- There are five recommended actions in relation to the *Adhaan* :

  1. Repeat after the *Muadhdhin* as described in the first *Hadith*.
  2. Repeat (and I testify) after the *Muadhdhin* as described in the second *Hadith*.
  3. On completion of the *Adhaan*, read the *Du'a'* –

"Allaahumma Rabba hadhihid-da watit-tammati........"

4. Followed by reading *"Allaahumma salli ala Muhammadin wa ala ali Muhammadin......."*

5. Followed by making *Du'a'* for yourself and for your fellow Muslims.

→ *Qiblah* Direction

- For a detailed explanation of the *Qiblah* direction, see in this chapter under "Inside the *Haram*."

→ *Aurah*:

♦ The *Aurah* means that the essential parts of one's body are covered in public, not only for *Salah*.

♦ For the women it is easy as their *Ihraam* clothes ensure that their *Aurah* is covered. However, many women leave their feet uncovered. The feet should be covered! See chapter 3 for more details.

♦ Apart from being dressed correctly, it is essential that your clothes are clean.

♦ For the men it is easy, minimum - from navel to the knees (inclusive).

♦ Would you attend a meeting with an important person with only a pair of trousers and no shirt, or with your shirt open exposing your stomach or in shorts, or with dirty clothes? I am sure most people wouldn't.

♦ Remember you are now in the presence of Allah as well as being a Guest of Allah. Also you would like to obtain as much of the 100,000 reward as possible.

→ *Fardh Salah*:

♦ Perform your *Wudhu'*, apply perfume (men only, and when not in *Ihraam*), put on clean clothes and make a habit of using a *Miswaak* (tooth-stick), prior to going to the *Haram*:

Abu Hurairah ﷺ relates that Allah's Messenger (ﷺ) remarked:

«لَوْلَا أَنْ أَشُقَّ عَلَى أُمَّتِي - أَوْ لَوْلَا أَنْ أَشُقَّ عَلَى النَّاسِ -
لَأَمَرْتُهُمْ بِالسِّوَاكِ مَعَ كُلِّ صَلَاةٍ».

"Had I not feared that it would cause inconvenience to my Ummah (or people) then I would have prescribed the brushing of teeth with a Miswaak before every prayer."

(Bukhari : 887 and *Muslim* : 252)

◆ Always try to be early to start the *Salah* with the *Imam*, and to be in the front row or close to it. Also there is much reward in waiting for the next *Salah* :

Abu Hurairah (ﷺ) states that Allah's Messenger (ﷺ) said:

«خَيْرُ صُفُوفِ الرِّجَالِ أَوَّلُهَا، وَشَرُّهَا آخِرُهَا، وَخَيْرُ صُفُوفِ
النِّسَاءِ آخِرُهَا، وَشَرُّهَا أَوَّلُهَا».

"The best rows of the males in prayer (in congregational prayer) are the first ones and the worst are the last ones, and the best rows among females in prayer are the last ones and the worst are the first ones."

(Muslim : 440)

«لَا يَزَالُ أَحَدُكُمْ فِي صَلَاةٍ مَا دَامَتِ الصَّلَاةُ تَحْبِسُهُ، لَا يَمْنَعُهُ
أَنْ يَنْقَلِبَ إِلَى أَهْلِهِ إِلَّا الصَّلَاةُ».

"As long as you stay in a mosque waiting for prayer (congregation), and are held up there only for the sake of prayer, and only this thing prevents you from returning home, you will be treated as continuously in prayer."

(Muslim : 649)

«لَوْ يَعْلَمُ النَّاسُ مَا فِي النِّدَاءِ وَالصَّفِّ الْأَوَّلِ ثُمَّ لَمْ يَجِدُوا إِلَّا

أَنْ يَسْتَهِمُوا عَلَيْهِ لَاسْتَهَمُوا، وَلَوْ يَعْلَمُونَ مَا فِي التَّهْجِيرِ لَاسْتَبَقُوا إِلَيْهِ، وَلَوْ يَعْلَمُونَ مَا فِي الْعَتَمَةِ وَالصُّبْحِ لَأَتَوْهُمَا وَلَوْ حَبْوًا»

"If the people knew the reward for pronouncing the Adhaan and for standing in the first row (in congregational prayers) and found no other way to get that except by drawing lots they would draw lots, and if they knew the reward of the Zuhr prayer (in the early moments of its stated time) they would race for it (go early) and if they knew the reward of Ishaa and Fajr prayers in congregation, they would come to offer them even if they had to crawl."

(*Bukhari* : 615 and *Muslim* : 437)

- Remember that the reward is 100,000 times more than in any other mosque except the *Haram* in Madinah (1000) and *Masjid-Al-Aqsa* (500) in Jerusalem.
- Ensure that you are facing *Qiblah*, and are standing in straight lines. Join the congregation as soon as the *Iqaama* is called:

  Abu Hurairah (ﷺ) relates that Allah's Messenger (ﷺ) said:

  «إِذَا أُقِيمَتِ الصَّلَاةُ فَلَا صَلَاةَ إِلَّا الْمَكْتُوبَةُ».

  "When Iqaamah (call for beginning the prayer) is called out, no prayer is permissible except the obligatory (Fardh) one."

  (*Muslim*: 710)

- Perform your *Salah* with calmness, humility and concentration. Avoid looking around and raising your head from bowing and prostration ahead of the *Imam*.
- Complete all your actions in a slow and dignified manner. There are numerous *Ahadith* about these points. The Prophet (ﷺ) said that the worst thief is the one who

steals from his *Salah*. Meaning the one who performs the *Salah* actions in a fast and hurried manner. (One should pause for a while in each position.)

◆ Fortunately in Makkah you will notice the practical application of these actions during *Salah*. Some 'differences' (compared to my experiences in many other parts of the world) you will notice in Makkah are:

 ○ It is the only place in the world where there are some circular lines for *Salah*.

 ○ There is no *Dhikr* in congregation after *Salah*.

 ○ There is no *Du'a'* in congregation (except when there is *Qunoot*).

 ○ There is no *Qunoot* (*Du'a'* in *Salah*) in *Salatul-Fajr*.

 ○ The *Salah* is performed in a very slow and calm manner.

 ○ Men and women perform *Salah* intermingled during the busy periods. Often females stand in front of males.

 ○ Most of the time there is a funeral prayer after the *Fardh Salah*.

• It is not my intention to delve into the various opinions about any of these 'differences'. I am merely pointing them out for the reader's awareness.

• After the *Fardh Salah*, it is best not to rush to perform *Sunnah* or *Nafl Salah*. Instead sit and make *Dhikr* as per the *Sunnah*. Also this way you will not 'miss' the funeral prayer, if it is to be performed.

• Do not always follow the crowd through the doors or stairs. Look to your left or right or further ahead, most of the time you may find another door or steps that are less crowded. A large proportion of people tend to follow the crowd.

→ *Jumu'ah Salah* (Friday Prayer):

- For *Jumu'ah* you need to be there early to get a 'good' place as it gets very crowded.

- It is needless to mention the importance of *Jumu'ah Salah*, except to remind you of a few points:

  o It is *Sunnah* to read *Surah Al-Kahf* (18) before *Jumuah* (starting Thursday night).

  o It is *Sunnah* to have a *Ghusl* (shower) before *Jumuah*.

  o To apply perfume (men) and to wear clean clothes.

  o To go to the *Haram* very early.

  o Not to speak during the *Khutbah*.

  o Not to sit with your knees up against your chest:

عَنْ سَهْلْ بِنِ مُعَاذِ بِنِ أَنَسٍ، عن أَبِيهِ: أَنَّ رسولَ الله ﷺ نَهَى
عن الْحِبْوَةِ يَوْمَ الْجُمُعَةِ وَالْإِمَامُ يَخْطُبُ .

"Muadh bin Anas narrates that Allah's Messenger (ﷺ) has forbidden a person with his knees drawn up touching his abdomen while the Imam is delivering the Friday Sermon."

(Abu Dawud: 1110 & Tirmidhi : 514)

→ *Janazah Salah* (Funeral Prayer):

♦ Women should not miss this opportunity to perform the *Janazah Salah*, as they are equally rewarded. Also there are not many other places or instances where they may have this opportunity.

♦ How to perform *Janazah Salah* :

☑ Follow the *Imam*

☑ There are 4 *Takbirs*

☑ After the 1st *Takbir*, read *Surah-al-Fatihah*

☑ After the 2nd *Takbir*, read the *Salawaat* – *"Allaahumma salli alaa Muhammad..."*

☑ After the 3rd *Takbir*, make *Du'a'* for the deceased

☑ After the 4th *Takbir*, make *Du'a'* for the Muslims in general

☑ Make *Istilaam*, to the right only

- Let us see the reward for performing this *Salah* and also for following the bier. So sisters, don't miss out on the *Salah!*

  Abu Hurairah (ﷺ) reports that Allah's Messenger (ﷺ) said:

  «مَنْ صَلَّى عَلَىٰ جَنَازَةٍ وَلَمْ يَتْبَعْهَا فَلَهُ قِيرَاطٌ، فَإِنْ تَبِعَهَا فَلَهُ قِيرَاطَانِ» قِيلَ: وَمَا الْقِيرَاطَانِ؟ قَالَ: «أَصْغَرُهُمَا مِثْلُ أُحُدٍ».

  "He who offered prayer over the dead, but did not follow the bier, for him is the reward of one Qiraat, and he who followed it, for him is the reward of two Qiraats. It was asked what the Qiraats were. He said the smaller amongst the two is equivalent to Uhud." (Uhud is a mountain in Madinah, where the Battle of Uhud was fought.)

  (*Muslim*: 945)

- There are many people that either sit or perform *Sunnah* or *Nafl Salah* during the *Janazah Salah*. (You can always perform your *Sunnah Salah* later). Don't you need the reward?

→ *Nafl Tawaaf:*

- *Tawaaf* is the best *Ibadah* to perform other than the *Fardh Salah* in the *Haram*.
- *Tawaaf* is superior to *Nafl Salah* in the *Haram*.
- There is no fixed time for *Tawaaf*.
- If you plan to perform *Tawaaf*, then you should proceed directly to perform it when entering the *Haram* (*Tahiyatul-Masjid Salah* is only performed if you plan to sit down prior to the *Tawaaf*).

◆ You do not need to be in *Ihraam* to perform *Nafl Tawaaf*.

◆ There is no *Sa'ee* after *Nafl Tawaaf*. (There is no *Nafl Sa'ee*), but you must perform the two *Rak'at Salah* after the *Tawaaf*.

◆ The number of circuits to perform is always seven, regardless of the type of *Tawaaf* (i.e., *Umrah*, *Hajj* or *Nafl*).

◆ There is no *Niyah* to be uttered audibly. The *Niyah* is in the heart as with all other acts of *Ibadah*.

◆ How to perform *Tawaaf* is covered in the next chapter - 'About *Tawaaf*'.

→ *Sunnah* & *Nafl* (voluntary) *Salah*:

◆ Though *Nafl Tawaaf* is superior to *Nafl Salah* in Makkah, it may not always be possible to perform *Tawaaf* due to the excessive crowds.

● We are now at another junction (topic) where people's opinions and understanding differ a great deal. The topic of *Salah* while travelling (*Musafir*).

● The issues are:

1. How long can I stay in one place to be still regarded as a traveller?

2. Why should I shorten my *Salah* when I have plenty of time to do it in 'full'?

● Regarding the first point, the discussion is wide and varied and I do not intend to address it in this book.

● About the second point:

Allah's Messenger (ﷺ) said:

«صَدَقَةٌ تَصَدَّقَ اللهُ بِهَا عَلَيْكُمْ، فَاقْبَلُوا صَدَقَتَهُ».

"It is a gift from Allah which He has bestowed upon you; so you should accept it."

(*Muslim*: 1573)

● The Prophet (ﷺ) did not perform any *Sunnah Salah* (except that of *Salatul-Fajr* and *Witr*) when he was travelling.

- Regardless of the view you hold on this issue, I would like to take this opportunity to remind you of the numerous rewards associated with *Sunnah* and *Nafl Salah*. Implement this in your daily life, if you haven't already done so.

- The 12 *Raatibah Rak'at* (*Sunnah Muakkadah Salahs* associated with the *Fardh Salah*).

Umm Habeebah (أ) related that she heard the Prophet (ﷺ) say:

«مَا مِنْ عَبْدٍ مُسْلِمٍ يُصَلِّي لِلَّهِ كُلَّ يَوْمٍ ثِنْتَيْ عَشْرَةَ رَكْعَةً تَطَوُّعًا، غَيْرَ فَرِيضَةٍ، إِلَّا بَنَى اللهُ لَهُ بَيْتًا فِي الْجَنَّةِ، أَوْ إِلَّا بُنِيَ لَهُ بَيْتٌ فِي الْجَنَّةِ».

"Allah prepares a house in Paradise for every believer who offers twelve Rak'at of Nafl (voluntary) prayer beyond that which is obligatory upon him."

(*Muslim* : 728)

Abu Hurrairah (أ) reported that the Prophet (ﷺ) said:

«إِنَّ اللهَ تَعَالَى قَالَ: مَنْ عَادَى لِي وَلِيًّا فَقَدْ آذَنْتُهُ بِالْحَرْبِ، ومَا تَقَرَّب إِلَيَّ عَبْدِي بِشَيءٍ أَحَبَّ إِلَيَّ مِمَّا افْتَرَضْتُهُ عَلَيْهِ. ومَا زَالَ عَبْدِي يَتَقَرَّبُ إِلَيَّ بِالنَّوَافِلِ حَتَّى أَحْبَبْتُهُ فَكُنْتُ سَمْعَهُ الذي يَسْمَعُ بِهِ، وبَصَرهُ الذِي يُبْصِرُ بِهِ، ويَدَهُ الَّتِي يَبطِشُ بِهَا، ورِجْلَهُ الَّتِي يَمْشِي بِهَا، وإِن سَأَلَني لَأُعطِيَنَّهُ، ولَئِنِ اسْتَعَاذَني لَأُعِيذَنَّهُ».

Allah the Almighty, says: "No servant of mine can seek nearness to Me with anything better than what I have made obligatory upon him; and My servant continues to seek nearness to Me with Nafl prayers until I love him. When I love him, I become his ears with which he hears, his eyes with which he sees, his hands with which he holds, and his legs with which he walks. If he begs Me for anything, I give it to him, and if he seeks My refuge, I give it to him."

(Bukhari : 6502)

- So wouldn't you like Allah to love you?
- Sad as it is, Muslims cannot even agree on the 12 *Rak'at*. So my suggestion is the following: Out of the 12, 10 are generally agreed upon, and they are:
  - 2 before *Fajr*
  - at least 2 before *Zuhr*
  - at least 2 after *Zuhr*
  - 2 after *Maghrib*
  - 2 after *Ishaa*

  That is 10. So you can make the other 2, either before or after *Zuhr*, or before *Asr*.

- Some other *Sunnah/Nafl Salahs* that have great rewards:
  - ○ *Salatul-Tahajjud* - at night, after *Ishaa* until *Fajr*.
  - ○ *Salatul-Duhaa* (also known as *Salatul-Ishraq*. Some books refer to it *Salatul-Chasht*) — from after sunrise until *Salatul-Zuhr*.
  - ○ *Salatul-Wudhu'* — after performing *Wudhu'*.
  - ○ *Salatul-Tahiyatul-Masjid* — Necessary upon entering a mosque prior to sitting down (as mentioned before, if you plan to perform tawaaf then you should proceed directly to do so as this is the *Sunnah*. However if you are not going to perform *Tawaaf*, then *Tahiyatul-Masjid Salah* becomes necessary).

Abu Qatadah (؈) related that Allah's Messenger (ﷺ) said:

«إِذَا دَخَلَ أَحَدُكُمُ الْمَسْجِدَ فَلْيَرْكَعْ رَكْعَتَيْنِ قَبْلَ أَنْ يَجْلِسَ»

"When one of you enters the mosque you should pray two

Rak'at before sitting down."

(*Bukhari* : 444 and *Muslim* : 714)

→ Forbidden Times for *Salah* :

سَمِعْتُ عُقْبَةَ بْنَ عَامِرٍ الْجُهَنِيَّ يَقُولُ: ثَلَاثُ سَاعَاتٍ كَانَ
رَسُولُ اللهِ ﷺ يَنْهَانَا أَنْ نُصَلِّيَ فِيهِنَّ، أَوْ أَنْ نَقْبُرَ فِيهِنَّ
مَوْتَانَا : حِينَ تَطْلُعُ الشَّمْسُ بَازِغَةً حَتَّىٰ تَرْتَفِعَ، وَحِينَ يَقُومُ
قَائِمُ الظَّهِيرَةِ حَتَّىٰ تَمِيلَ الشَّمْسُ، وَحِينَ تَضَيَّفُ الشَّمْسُ
لِلْغُرُوبِ حَتَّىٰ تَغْرُبَ.

Uqbah bin Amir (؎*) said: "There are three times at which Allah's Messenger (*ﷺ*) used to forbid us to pray or bury our dead:*

1. *When the sun began to rise until it was fully up.*

2. *When the sun was at its height at midday till it passed the meridian.*

3. *When the sun drew near to setting till it had set."*

(*Muslim* : 1929)

- Note that it also mentions burying of the dead.

Abu Sa'id Al-Khudri (؎) reported Allah's Messenger (ﷺ) as saying:

«لَا صَلَاةَ بَعْدَ الصُّبْحِ حَتَّى تَرْتَفِعَ الشَّمْسُ، وَلَا صَلَاةَ بَعْدَ
الْعَصْرِ حَتَّى تَغِيبَ الشَّمْسُ».

"No prayer is to be offered after Salatul-Fajr until the sun rises, or after Salatul-Asr until the sun sets."

(*Bukhari* : 586 and *Muslim* : 827)

- Any unintentionally missed *Salah*, due to sleep or forgetfulness, can and should be performed immediately, even if it 'falls' in the forbidden times. Also *Salah* with a purpose, such as the two *Rak'at* after *Tawaaf* and also

Salatul-Tahiyatul-Masjid are also exempted.

Allah's Messenger (ﷺ) said:

«مَنْ نَسِيَ صَلاةً فَلْيُصَلِّ إِذَا ذَكَرَ»

"Who has forgotten the prayer he should pray it whenever he remembers it."

(*Bukhari* : 597 and *Muslim* : 684)

→ **Being late:**

♦ If you are late for the *Salah* do not run towards the mosque or the congregation in order to join it, instead walk calmly and at your normal pace.

♦ Join the congregation immediately in whatever position they are in. Be it *Sujood* or *Tashahud* (even though you need to redo that *Rak'ah*). You will need to complete each *Rak'ah* that you have missed. A *Rak'ah* is considered missed if you did not perform the *Ruku* (and to recite at least once *Subahana Rabbi'al-Adheem*) for that *Rak'ah*.

Abu Hurairah ؓ relates that Allah's Messenger (ﷺ) said:

«إِذا أُقِيمَتِ الصَّلاةُ فَلا تَأْتُوها تَسْعَوْنَ، وَأْتُوها تَمْشُونَ، وَعَلَيْكُمُ السَّكِينَةَ، فَما أَدْرَكْتُمْ فَصَلُّوا، وما فاتَكُمْ فَأَتِمُّوا».

"If the prayer is started, do not run for it. Walk calmly, join the prayer at the point you enter the mosque and make up what you missed afterwards."

The narration in Muslim adds: *"...for once one of you makes the intention to pray, he is considered in prayer."*

(*Bukhari* : 908 and *Muslim* : 602)

→ **General:**

• Some people dispute the validity of performing *Sunnah Salah* before *Salatul-Maghrib*. There are numerous *Ahadith* about its validity. I will mention only one. Instead of disputing or discussing with the person next to you about those that choose to perform it, recite Qur'an, make *Dhikr* or *Du'a*, or perform it.

Abdullah bin Al-Muzani (راضي) relates that Allah's Messenger (ﷺ) asks:

«صَلُّوا قَبْلَ صَلَاةِ المَغْرِبِ». قَالَ فِي الثَّالِثَةِ: «لِمَنْ شَاءَ، كَرَاهِيَةَ أَنْ يَتَّخِذَهَا النَّاسُ سُنَّةً».

"Offer two (Sunnah) Rak'at before Salatul-Maghrib (sunset prayer) and he repeated this direction twice. On the third time he added: One who likes may do so (so that people may not take this direction as muakkadah (essential)."

(*Bukhari*: 1183)

- When you perform your *Salah* and you wish to sit to your side in the last (sitting) *Tashahud* (as per the *Sunnah*), keep in mind that it may not always be feasible due to the sheer number of people. Avoid forcing the issue as you may end up sitting on top of the person next to you, and you may even hurt his or her leg.

⇨ **Other Recommended Actions:**

→ **Reciting Qur'an:**

'Aishah (راضي) says that Allah's Messenger (ﷺ) said:

«مَثَلُ الَّذِي يَقْرَأُ القُرْآنَ وَهُوَ حَافِظٌ لَهُ مَعَ السَّفَرَةِ الكِرَامِ البَرَرَةِ، وَمَثَلُ الَّذِي يَقْرَأُ القُرْآنَ وَهُوَ يَتَعَاهَدُهُ وَهُوَ عَلَيْهِ شَدِيدٌ فَلَهُ أَجْرَانِ».

"A person who recites the Qur'an, and reads it fluently, will be in the company of the obedient and noble angels, and who reads the Qur'an haltingly and with difficulty, will have a double recompense."

(*Bukhari*: 4937 and *Muslim*: 798)

◆ There is no evidence from the Qur'an or the *Sunnah* about kissing or touching the Qur'an with your forehead, before or after reading it.

◆ For those ardent readers, keep the following *Hadith* in mind:

Abdullah bin Amr (⬤) narrated that Allah's Messenger (⬤) told him that:

«لَا يَفْقَهُ مَنْ قَرَأَ الْقُرَآنَ فِي أَقَلَّ مِنْ ثَلَاثٍ» .

"One will not be able to comprehend fully the meaning if one recites the whole Qur'an in less than three days."

(*Abu Dawud* : 1394, *Tirmidhi* : 2949 and *Ibn Majah* : 1347)

• Utilise your time in Makkah to recite as much Qur'an as possible.

• When you are in the *Haram*, do not read aloud, as you may disturb the person next to you, who may be engaged in *Salah* or other forms of *Ibadah*.

• Regarding the print type and positioning of the Qur'ans inside the *Haram* see later in this chapter under 'Inside the *Haram*'.

→ *Du'a'* (supplication):

﴿وَقَالَ رَبُّكُمُ ٱدۡعُونِىٓ أَسۡتَجِبۡ لَكُمۡۚ﴾

"And your Lord said: Invoke Me, I will respond to your (invocation)."

[*Surah Ghafir* (40), part of *Ayah* 60]

◆ A common mistake made by many is that when they supplicate they say *"In Sha Allah"* after it. One should say *"Aameen"* instead.

◆ Also very few Muslims know about *Tawassul*. What is it you may ask? Simply stated, it is a way of seeking nearness to Allah and also how you can 'improve' your chances of your *Du'a'* being accepted. Following is a very brief

explanation, taken from the book: *Tawassul*, its types and
rulings by the late Shaikh Muhammad Naasiruddeen Al-
Albaanee (may Allah have mercy on his soul).

There are three (agreed) means of *Tawassul*, and they are:

1. *Tawassul* by means of the Names of Allah, the Blessed
   and the Most High, and His Attributes. Such as the
   Muslim saying in his supplication: "O Allah I ask You
   by Your being the Most Merciful, the Bestower of
   Mercy, the Most Gracious Knower of all that is hidden,
   the Fully-acquainted: that You grant me safety and well-
   being."

2. *Tawassul* to Allah, the Most High, by means of righteous
   deed which the person supplicating has done. Such as
   the Muslim saying: O Allah by my *Eemaan* in You, and
   my love for You, and my following of Your Messenger,
   forgive me."

3. *Tawassul* to Allah, the Most High, by the supplication of
   a righteous man.

◆ The manner of supplication:

Anas bin Malik (may Allah be pleased with him) relates
that Allah's Messenger (ﷺ) said:

«إِذا دَعا أَحَدُكمْ فَليعْزِم المَسأَلَةَ وَلا يَقُولَنَّ: اللَّهُمَّ إنْ شِئتَ
فَأَعْطِني، فإنَّهُ لا مُستكرِهَ لهُ» .

*"When one of you is to supplicate he should do so with full
confidence and should not say. O' Allah, grant me if Thou
will for there is no power which can force Allah."*

(*Bukhari*: 6338 and *Muslim*: 2678)

﴿ٱدْعُوا۟ رَبَّكُمْ تَضَرُّعًا وَخُفْيَةً﴾

"Invoke your Lord with humility and in secret."

[*Surah Al-A'raf* (7), part of *Ayah* 55]

➤ Sincerity is the most important ingredient, so do it with humility and sincerity.

➤ Face *Qiblah* if possible, though it is not obligatory.

➤ Begin by praising Allah.

➤ Then ask for blessings on the Prophet (ﷺ).

➤ Then supplicate.

➤ Implore Allah by His Names and Attributes which are mentioned in the Qur'an and *Sunnah* (e.g.: O Most Merciful, have mercy on me; O Most Forgiving, forgive me for my sins; O Allah, I ask You O Allah, as You are The One, The Only, *As-Samad* (the Self-Sufficient Master, Possessor of perfect attributes whom all of creation turn to in all their needs).

➤ Plead to Allah and be persistent in the request.

➤ Ask with confidence and do not say: If Allah wills.

➤ Ask for the best (if you ask for *Jannah*, ask for *Janatul-Firdous*).

➤ Finish by saying *Aameen*

◆ Choose the best times when response is more likely. Below are some of the better times (and places) to make supplication:

➤ The last third of the night.

➤ The time between the *Adhaan* and the *Iqaamah*.

➤ At the time of breaking fast.

➤ While travelling (*Musafir*).

➤ During *Salah*:

  o   In the last *Tashahud*, before *Tasleem*.

  o   While in *Sujood*.

➤ On a Friday (special time, hour before *Maghrib*).

➤ During *Tawaaf*.

➢ During *Sa'ee*.

● The above list is definitely not conclusive, but you can see that there are many places where you have a 'better chance' of your *Du'a'* being accepted. Utilise it!

→ Remembrance and mentioning (*Dhikr*) of Allah:

◆ Remember (mention) Allah at all times. *Dhikr* is normally translated as remembering Allah, but in real terms it means remembering as well as mentioning (praising) Allah.

Abu Hurairah (ﷺ) relates that Allah's Messenger (ﷺ) said:

«إِنَّ اللهَ عَزَّ وَجَلَّ يَقُولُ: أَنَا مَعَ عَبْدِي إِذَا هُوَ ذَكَرَنِي وَتَحَرَّكَتْ بِي شَفَتَاهُ».

Allah says, "I am with My servant when he remembers Me and his lips move in My remembrance."

(*Ibn Majah* : 3792)

◆ Make *Dhikr* instead of idle talk.

◆ Do not neglect the *Dhikr* after the *Fardh Salah*.

◆ Allah, the Exalted said:

﴿ فَٱذْكُرُونِىٓ أَذْكُرْكُمْ ﴾

"Therefore remember Me, I will remember you."

[*Surah Al-Baqarah* (2), part of *Ayah* 152]

﴿ وَٱذْكُرُواْ ٱللَّهَ كَثِيرًا لَّعَلَّكُمْ تُفْلِحُونَ ﴾

"And remember Allah much, that you may be successful."

[*Surah Al-Jumu'ah* (62), part of *Ayah* 10]

→ Fasting:

◆ *Nafl* fast has many rewards, so fast as much as you can: Abu Sa'id Al-Khudri (ﷺ) reported that Allah's

Messenger (ﷺ) said:

«مَا مِنْ عَبْدٍ يَصُومُ يَوْمًا فِي سَبِيلِ اللهِ، إِلَّا بَاعَدَ اللهُ، بِذَلِكَ الْيَوْمِ، وَجْهَهُ عَنِ النَّارِ سَبْعِينَ خَرِيفًا».

"He who observes fast for a day in the way of Allah He would remove his face from the Hell to the extent of seventy years distance."

(*Muslim* : 1153)

→ *Sadaqah* (charity):

◆ Perform as many charitable acts as possible and also distribute charity (money, food, etc.) to the poor while you are in Makkah or Madinah.

◆ Remember that helping others and even greeting your fellow Muslim with a smile is an act of charity.

• A suggestion is to give some of your *Sadaqah* to the cleaners in the *Haram* and also the street cleaners.

→ Visiting (*Ziyarah*):

◆ Visit the sick, be it in their hotel or in the hospital.

◆ Visit the cemeteries (graveyards). This is to remind us of death.

◆ There are no places to visit in Makkah as part of *Umrah*. (So, if you do not wish to go anywhere, except spending your time in the *Haram*, then do so).

• However, there are many people who are interested in some of the historical places. Many people save their money over a lifetime to come to Makkah and have learnt about some of these places over the years at school and from *Ahadith* and so on, therefore they are really keen to visit them. Try not to miss your *Salah* in the *Haram* though.

• A trip to Arafat and Mina gives you the opportunity to see these places when they are not crowded.

• One place of interest to visit is the factory where they make the cloth (*Kiswat*) that covers the Ka'bah. You need to make an appointment to visit the factory. Most agents know the procedures to follow to obtain permission for a visit to this factory.

• If you plan to go somewhere and the trip means missing a *Fardh Salah* in the *Haram*, avoid it. Remember the reward is 100,000 times for each *Salah*. Do not 'short-change' yourself.

• Preferably avoid the trips to climb Jabal-Thur or Jabal-Nur (Mountains). This is dangerous and tiring. There is a probability of you hurting your ankles doing this. Furthermore there is no reward for climbing these mountains. If you insist, and are looking forward to see an historical sight, be warned; I think the shops and photographers up on the mountain reduces the spiritual significance of the site.

• DO NOT perform *Salah* on Jabal-Rahmah in Arafat, as many people do.

• Once again, if you decide to go (from an historical point), ensure that you are back in time for *Salah* in the *Haram*.

⇨ **The *Haram*:**

→ **Doors and Levels:**

* For *Salah* there are 4 floor levels inside the mosque:
  ➢ Basement level
  ➢ Ground floor level
  ➢ First floor level
  ➢ Roof level

* The roof area is for men only (no small children either). It is only accessible via the escalators. (Try the roof area in the evening and for *Salatul-Fajr*. It is very comfortable and peaceful. If you get the opportunity, try to view the *Haram*

from the roof. In my opinion the view of the *Haram* and the Ka'bah is spectacular from up there. It also gives you the opportunity to see, how NOT to behave during *Tawaaf*.)

* There are designated *Salah* areas for women inside the *Haram*. (Sometimes during *Jumuah* even these areas are 'taken over' by the men.)

* The only time they allow women on the roof level is during the *Hajj* period.

* There are in excess of 100 doors around the *Haram* to enter from.

* All the doors are numbered. The numbers are inscribed near the door, on the wall tiles on the inside and on the outside of the *Haram*.

* Most of the doors also have a name, in addition to the number.

* The names and numbers are written in Arabic and in English.

* The door numbers go in an anti-clockwise direction.

* Some of the door names and numbers are:

  o King Abdul Aziz Door (Baab-ul-Malik Abdul Aziz)
    - Door no. 1

  o Safaa Door (Baab-us-Safaa)
    - Door no. 11

  o Salaam Door (Baab-us-Salaam)
    - Door no. 24

  o Qarrarah Door (Baab-ul-Qarrarah)
    - Door no. 43

  o Fath Door (Baab-ul-Fath)
    - Door no. 45

  o Shamiah Door (Baab-us-Shamiah)
    - Door no. 52

  o Umrah Door (Baab-ul-Umrah)
    - Door no. 62

  o King Fahd Door (Baab-ul-Malik Fahd)
    - Door no. 79

• The following picture should give you a general idea of some of the door locations.

◆ It is neither a *Fardh* nor a *Sunnah* requirement to enter from Baab-us-Salaam (Door no. 24).

• I have listed the location and door number of **Baab-us-Salaam** only because I have experienced so many times that some people insist on entering from this door. On occasions this door is actually closed as it causes disruption to those performing *Sa'ee*. You will then have to enter at Baab-us-Salaam flyover (Door no. 25). These flyovers are bridges across the *Sa'ee* area. If this door is far from where you are, please be aware that there is no evidence from the Qur'an or the *Sunnah* to indicate or instruct one to enter from this door or any other specific door.

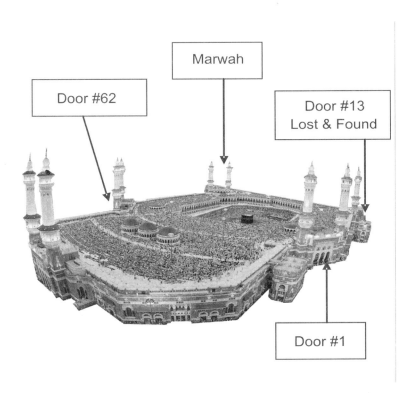

- Both Baab-us-Salaam and the flyover have stairs, so the elderly and people with wheelchairs should definitely avoid them.

→ Access to the Roof, Middle floor and Basement areas:

* The roof area is accessible via the escalators. There is stair access to the roof area, but it is not always open.

* There are escalators at various locations around the *Haram*.

* The escalators can also be accessed from the middle floor inside the *Haram*.

* The escalator entrances are also part of the door number sequence (i.e., the escalator to the right of door no 1 is called the Ajyad Escalator — door nos. 5 and 6; the one to the right of door no 79, Baab-ul-Malik Fahd is named Malik Fahd Escalator, door nos. 91 & 92; Al-Shubaika Escalator, nos. 65 & 66).

* The **middle** floor can be accessed from the escalators and also from the stairs. There are stairs directly inside (to your right and left) of all the major doors (mentioned previously). There are also stairs outside and also at various other locations inside the *Haram*.

* At the Shamiah side of the *Haram* (near Baab-ul-Umrah, door no. 62), you can access the middle floor directly, as it is the same level as the street. The entrances are bridge-like structures. Some of the names and numbers are:
  o Al-Nadwa Bridge   - no. 50
  o Al-Madinah Bridge   - no. 57
  o Al-Mahdi Bridge   - no. 61

* The middle floor is for males and females.

* To get to the middle floor for the *Sa'ee* area there are elevators at door no. 11 in addition to stairs. The stairs are located (standing at Safaa, facing Marwah) to your left, next to the wheelchair ramp.

* The middle floor for *Sa'ee* can also be accessed from the street level at Marwah.

* In the *Sa'ee* area on the bottom floor you will find alluminium stairs. These stairs are not for access to the middle floor. They are the stairs to the 'flyovers'.

* The **basement** area is not very well known to all. There is a huge basement area in the *Haram* and it is for both males and females.

* Access to the basement is via the stairs and some escalators. Most (not all) of the middle floor access stairs also 'go down' to the basement. There are also some other stairs inside the *Haram* that have white metal gates at the entrance. These gates are open during the busy periods and provide direct access to the basement area from inside the *Haram*.

* There are stairs outside the *Haram* that provide access to the basement. The stairs immediately to the right of door no. 1 (there is a sign showing basement); doors no. 75, 76, 77, 81, 82, 83 and 85 are amongst the doors that provide access to the basement.

→ **Wheelchair access:**

* There are various doors around the *Haram* that provide access for wheelchairs. It is important that you are familiar with them as most of the other doors have plenty of stairs. Door no. 11 is the designated area for wheelchair access. Some other entrances that provide wheelchair access are: Door nos. 10, 64, 94.

* Another special door for wheelchairs is at door no. 43, Baab-ul-Qarrarah.

* You can obtain a wheelchair from inside the *Haram*. At Safaa gate, door no. 11, there are elevators that provide access to the middle floor. Entering at door no. 11, to your right are the elevators and to your left you will find the place where you can obtain a wheelchair. If you wish to push it yourself, they are free of charge. You need to leave some form of identification.

* If you require a chair and somebody to push it, it will cost you about 40-60 Saudi Riyals and you can obtain these chairs from outside door no 13 area.

* If you do not find any wheelchairs on the bottom floor, go

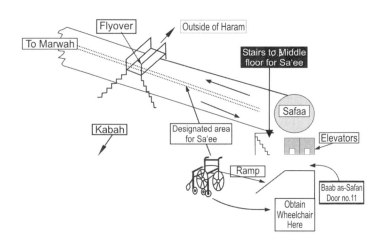

to the middle floor directly above (the location as described
in a previous point), you may find one there.

* If you have your own wheelchair you will need to obtain
  some permit allowing you to enter the *Haram* with it. This
  you can obtain from the office at door no. 12.

* During the busy periods they do not allow wheelchairs in
  the *Tawaaf* area. You will need to hire a *Shubriah* or
  sometimes referred to as a *Kursi*. This is a stretcher like
  chair, which you sit in and is carried by four persons. The
  cost of this service is about 250-350 Saudi Riyals. The cost
  includes the carriers. You are not allowed to carry it
  yourself.

* For *Sa'ee* the wheelchairs are allowed on the ground floor
  (there is a designated area) and also on the middle floor.

* There is also a new office outside door no 1 (nearer to the
  street) where you can obtain a wheelchair free of charge.

* The location inside the *Haram* where you can obtain a wheelchair changes from time to time, so ask one of the guards.

→ Where to meet:

- It is important that you agree beforehand with your partner or group where to meet after *Salah* or in the event of you 'losing' each other.

- If your accommodation is not far from the *Haram* then it may be better to meet back in the room.

- If you plan to meet somewhere inside the *Haram*, avoid the green light area as this is a very common meeting place and it is therefore always very crowded.

- Meeting outside at the clock tower (exit from King Abdul-Aziz Door) is also a very common meeting place. One disadvantage of making this a meeting place is that the clock has four sides and you may spend your time waiting on one side while the other person is waiting on the opposite side (experience talking).

- There are really no 'good' meeting places (other than your hotel) that I can suggest. It all depends on your routine and location. Once you have established a 'good' place, stick to it and try not to change it from day to day.

- The above is important if you are in Makkah during a busy period.

→ If you are lost:

* If you are lost, go to door no. 13 (lost & found section) where you will be provided with assistance.

- If you hire a *Shubriah* for one of the people in your company, make arrangements where to meet again, as the people carrying the *Shubriah* will finish the *Tawaaf* long before you.

- If you have a card of your accommodation, ask any of the policemen for directions. Sometimes the best way is to ask at the reception of another hotel for directions to your accommodation.

- If you come out from the 'wrong' door, do not walk around the *Haram* to try and find your way, instead go back inside the *Haram* and try to find the 'right' door from inside. This method has some distinct advantages:

  ○ You may find someone you know inside.

  ○ It is much cooler inside the *Haram*.

  ○ Find the side of the Ka'bah you entered from.

  ○ Look for the colour coordinated doors (the colours are addressed later in this chapter).

- If all else fails, stay inside the *Haram* until the next *Salah* instead of wandering around outside in the heat or darkness. Move towards the area where you normally perform your *Salah* as you may find someone you know there.

- If you cannot remember the door numbers or names and you are lost, try to remember at least the following one. If you cannot remember the number, think of the name of the author of this book. This door is close to the lost and found; the elevators; the wheelchair access; the medical facilities; the hospital; the roof and basement access and also the toilets:

Baab Ismail (Ismail Door) No 10

⇨ **Entering the *Haram*:**

♦ As with any *Masjid* enter the *Haram* with your right foot and it is *Sunnah* to say:

بِسْمِ اللهِ وَالصَّلَاةُ وَالسَّلَامُ عَلَى رَسُولِ اللهِ، أَعُوذُ باللهِ الْعَظِيمِ

وَبِوَجْهِهِ الْكَرِيمِ وَسُلْطَانِهِ الْقَدِيمِ مِنَ الشَّيْطَانِ الرَّجِيمِ . اللَّهُمَّ
افْتَحْ لِي أَبْوَابَ رَحْمَتِكَ .

Bismillah wassalatu wassalamu ala Rasoolillah. A'oudhu billahil-'Adheem, wa be waj'hihil-Kareem, wa sultanihil-qadeem, minash-shaytanir-rajeem. Allahumma iftahly abwaaba rahmatik.

(In the Name of Allah and blessings and peace be upon the Messenger of Allah. I seek refuge in Allah the Great, and His Honourable face and His ancient authority from the accursed *Shaytaan*. Oh Allah open for me the doors of Your mercy.)

(Abu Dawud : 466)

* There are 'guards' at all the entrances to the *Haram*. All bags including ladies handbags will be searched. You will not be able to take any food or 'dangerous' items inside with you (A simple pocketknife will be confiscated).

* You will not be allowed to take any shopping bags inside with you. So if you did lots of expensive shopping, make sure you have enough time to take it back to your accommodation prior to *Salah*.

* Sometimes you may not be able to take even your umbrella inside with you.

⇨ **Inside the *Haram*:**

* Inside the *Haram* the names of the main doors are indicated by big signs placed across the pillars leading towards these doors. To make it even easier, these signs have different colours. (The big doors are underneath the minarets. There are 9 minarets in case you wondered.)

Name of Door	No	Colour of Sign
King Abdul-Aziz Door (Baab-ul-Malik Abdul-Aziz)	1	Turquoise (light bluish)
Umrah Door (Baab-ul-Umrah)	62	Dark Grey
Fath Door (Baab-ul-Fath)	45	Dark Blue
King Fahd Door (Baab-ul-Malik Fahd)	79	Gold/Yellow
* Some other doors numbers are:		
Safaa Door (Baab-us-Safaa)	11	White
Salaam Door (Baab-us-Salaam)	24	No coloured sign

- If you are entering the *Haram* for your first time, I suggest you spend a few moments to orientate yourself with the surroundings and landmarks. As you should be performing *Tawaaf* as your first rite, you need to proceed directly towards the Ka'bah. (Do not sit down unless you perform *Tawaaf* or two *Rak'at Tahiyatul-Masjid Salah* first.)

- Make a mental note of the name and number (and colour, if applicable) of the door from which you entered. Also observe from which side of the Ka'bah you entered. These signs should help you in finding your way out.

- The sides of the Ka'bah are:

  1. The side of Maqaam Ibraheem

  2. The side of the Hijr (and water spout)

  3. The side where the Rukn-al-Yamani corner is to the right and the Hijr is to your left (facing the Ka'bah).

  4. The side where you

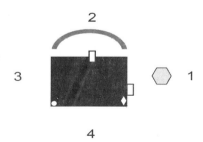

start your *Tawaaf* (Hajr-al-Aswad) is to your right, and the Rukn-al-Yamani corner is to your left (facing the Ka'bah).

- The above landmarks are a mere guideline. You may find other and easier means of remembering where to enter and exit from.

→ A Closer look at the Ka'bah area:

- Let us now take a closer look at the Ka'bah and the immediate area around it followed by the historical significance of some of these landmarks and rites:

☾ **Hajr-al-Aswad** (Black Stone Corner) is where the *Tawaaf* starts and ends.

☾ **Multazam:** This is the area from the Hajr-al-Aswad up to the door of the Ka'bah. It is reported that the Companions (﷽) of the Prophet (ﷺ) used to make *Du'a'* here.

☾ **Maqaam Ibraheem:** This is where one performs two *Rak'at* after *Tawaaf*.

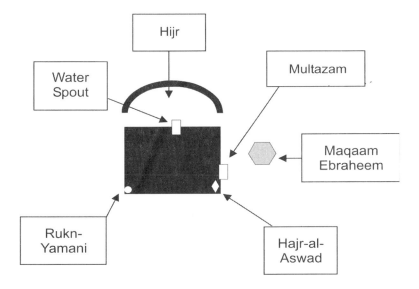

☾ **Hijr:** It is part of the Ka'bah, therefore one should walk around it during *Tawaaf*. Try to perform some *Sunnah/Nafl Salah* in this area. Many books refer to this area as the Hijr-Ismail. Some go as far as to say that the Prophet Ismail and his mother Hagar (﷽) are buried here, hence the name. There is no authentic proof for this or the name. The fact that we are allowed to make *Salah* in this area is proof enough that this cannot be true, as we are not allowed to make *Salah* on graves. Also the Prophet (ﷺ) referred to this area as Al-Hijr.

☾ **Water Spout:** This is located on the roof of the Ka'bah in the middle of the Hijr. Its purpose is to allow any water on the roof to drain down. It has no spiritual or historical significance. Why mention it? Well, some people believe it has certain spiritual significance and fight to perform *Salah* directly beneath it. Also, it is a new addition to the Ka'bah, and did not exist in the time of the Prophet (ﷺ).

☾ **South Corner:** This is also known as Rukn-al-Yamani. During *Tawaaf* one touches this Corner without kissing it. The Rukn-al-Yamani Corner is also referred to as the South Corner. It is between this Corner and the next one (Hajr-al-Aswad) that one recites: "*Rabanaa Aatina, Fidunya........*".

☾ **Different tiled area:** There is no need to stop on this area. The tiles are of a different colour indicating the starting point of *Tawaaf*. There is also a green light on the wall to indicate the starting point. Also the middle floor and the roof both have a green light with a sign indicating the beginning and completion of *Tawaaf*.

☾ **Zamzam Well:** After the two *Rak'at Salah* one proceeds towards this well to drink Zamzam water. Since 2004 the underground Zamzam well area has been closed in order to make more space for *Salah*. The Zamzam water taps are now located against the wall near the green lights (where *Tawaaf* starts and end.)

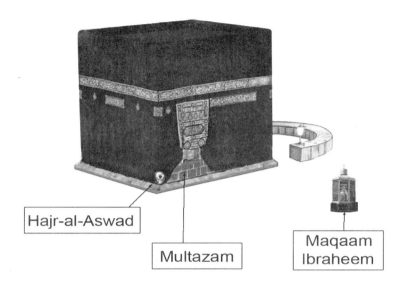

Hajr-al-Aswad

Multazam

Maqaam Ibraheem

G *Tawaaf:* The Hajr-al-Aswad (Black Stone Corner) is where the *Tawaaf* starts and ends. The direction for *Tawaaf* is anti-clockwise. There are also green lights on the wall to help you identify the start and end points (more details about *Tawaaf* are covered in chapter 8).

G *Sa'ee:* The direction for *Sa'ee* is starting at Safaa and finishing at Marwah (more details about *Sa'ee* are covered in chapter 8). The *Sa'ee* area is left from the starting line of the *Tawaaf.*

→ **A brief historical look:**

❖ **Makkah:**

﴿وَإِذْ جَعَلْنَا ٱلْبَيْتَ مَثَابَةً لِّلنَّاسِ وَأَمْنًا﴾

"And (remember) when We made the House a place of resort for mankind and a place of safety."

(*Surah Al-Baqarah* (2), part of *Ayah* 125)

﴿وَإِذْ قَالَ إِبْرَٰهِـمُ رَبِّ ٱجْعَلْ هَٰذَا بَلَدًا ءَامِنًا وَٱرْزُقْ أَهْلَهُۥ مِنَ ٱلثَّمَرَٰتِ مَنْ

$$\text{﴿ءَامَنَ مِنْهُم بِٱللَّهِ وَٱلْيَوْمِ ٱلْأَخِرِ﴾}$$

"And (remember) when Ibraheem said, 'My Lord make this city (Makkah) a place of sanctuary and provide its people with fruits, such of them as believe in Allah and the Last Day."

[*Surah Al-Baqarah* (2), part of *Ayah* 126]

Allah commanded Prophet Ibraheem (عليه السلام) to leave his second wife Haajar and their newly born son Ismail (عليه السلام) alone in the uninhabited valley of Bakkah.

$$\text{﴿إِنَّ أَوَّلَ بَيْتٍ وُضِعَ لِلنَّاسِ لَلَّذِى بِبَكَّةَ مُبَارَكًا وَهُدًى لِّلْعَلَمِينَ﴾}$$

"Verily, the first house (of worship) appointed for mankind was that at Bakkah (Makkah), full of blessing, and guidance for Al-Alamin (mankind and jinns)."

[*Surah Al-Imran* (3), *Ayah* 96]

قالَ ابنُ عَبَّاسٍ: أَوَّلَ مَا اتَّخَذَ النِّساءُ المِنْطَقَ مِنْ قِبَلِ أُمِّ إسْمَاعِيلَ، اتَّخَذَتْ مِنْطَقًا لِتُعَفِّيَ أَثَرَها على سارَةَ، ثُمَّ جاءَ بها إبْراهِيمُ وبابْنِها إسمَاعِيلَ وهيَ تُرْضِعُهُ حتَّى وضَعَهُما عِنْدَ البَيْتِ عِنْدَ دَوْحَةٍ فَوْقَ الزَّمزَمِ في أَعْلى المَسْجِدِ ولَيْسَ بِمَكَّةَ يَوْمَئِذٍ أَحَدٌ، ولَيْسَ بها ماءٌ فَوَضَعَهُما هُنالِكَ، ووَضَعَ عِنْدَهُما جِرَابًا فِيهِ تَمْرٌ وسِقاءً فِيهِ ماءٌ ثُمَّ قَفَّى إبْراهِيمُ مُنْطَلِقًا، فَتَبِعَتْهُ أُمُّ إسْمَاعِيلَ فَقالَتْ: يا إبْراهِيمُ، أَيْنَ تَذْهَبُ وتَتْرُكُنا في هَذا الوَادِي الذِي لَيْسَ فِيهِ أَنِيسٌ ولا شَيْءٌ؟ فَقالَتْ لَهُ ذلِكَ مِرارًا، وجَعَلَ لا يَلْتَفِتُ إلَيها فَقالَتْ لَهُ: آللَّهُ أَمَرَكَ بِهَذا؟ قالَ: نَعَمْ، قالَتْ: إذَنْ لا يُضَيِّعُنا، ثُمَّ رَجَعَتْ، فانْطَلَقَ إبْراهِيمُ حتَّى إذا كانَ عِنْدَ الثَّنِيَّةِ حَيْثُ لا يَرَوْنَهُ اسْتَقْبَلَ بِوَجْهِهِ البَيْتَ ثُمَّ دَعا بِهَؤُلاءِ الدَّعْواتِ ورَفَعَ يَدَيْهِ فَقالَ:

Narrated Ibn Abbas (رضي الله عنه): "The first lady to use a girdle was the mother of Ismail. She used a girdle so that she might hide her tracks from Sarah. Ibraheem brought her and her son Ismail while she was suckling him, to a place near the Ka'bah under a tree on the spot of Zamzam, at the highest place in the mosque. During those days there was nobody in Makkah, nor was there any water. So he made them sit over there and placed near them a leather bag containing some dates, and a small water-skin containing some water, and set out homeward. Ismail's mother followed him saying, 'O Ibraheem! Where are you going, leaving us in this valley where there is no person whose company we may enjoy, nor is there anything (to enjoy)?' She repeated that to him many times, but he did not look back at her. Then she asked him, 'Has Allah ordered you to do so?' He said, 'Yes.' She said, 'Then He will not neglect us', and returned while Ibraheem proceeded onwards, and on reaching the Thaniya where they could not see him, he faced the Ka'bah, and raising both hands, invoked Allah saying the following prayers:

﴿رَّبَّنَآ إِنِّىٓ أَسْكَنتُ مِن ذُرِّيَّتِى بِوَادٍ غَيْرِ ذِى زَرْعٍ عِندَ بَيْتِكَ ٱلْمُحَرَّمِ رَبَّنَا لِيُقِيمُوا۟ ٱلصَّلَوٰةَ فَٱجْعَلْ أَفْـِٔدَةً مِّنَ ٱلنَّاسِ تَهْوِىٓ إِلَيْهِمْ وَٱرْزُقْهُم مِّنَ ٱلثَّمَرَٰتِ لَعَلَّهُمْ يَشْكُرُونَ﴾

'Oh our Lord! I have made some of my offspring to dwell in a valley with no cultivation, by your Sacred House (the Ka'bah at Makkah); in order, Oh our Lord, that they may offer prayers perfectly, so fill some hearts among men with love towards them, and (Oh Allah) provide them with fruits so that they may give thanks.'' '

[Surah Ibraheem (14), Ayah 37]

❖ Running during Sa'ee (between the green lights):

After Ibraheem left them there, Haajar tried to find water for baby Ismail. She left Ismail in the valley and ran between the hills of Safaa and Marwah trying to see if there was an oasis nearby or to find any other people in the area.

وَجَعَلَتْ أُمُّ إِسْمَاعِيلَ تُرْضِعُ إِسْمَاعِيلَ وَتَشْرَبُ مِنْ ذٰلِكَ الْمَاءِ
حَتَّى إِذَا نَفِدَ مَا فِي السِّقَاءِ عَطِشَتْ وعَطِشَ ابْنُها فَجَعَلَتْ تَنْظُرُ
إِلَيْهِ يَتَلَوَّى – أَوْ قَالَ: يَتَلَبَّط – فَانْطَلَقَتْ كَرَاهِيَةَ أَنْ تَنْظُرَ إِلَيْهِ،
فَوَجَدَتِ الصَّفا أَقْرَبَ جَبَلٍ فِي الْأَرْضِ يَلِيها، فَقَامَتْ عَلَيْهِ ثُمَّ
اسْتَقْبَلَتِ الْوَادِيَ تَنْظُرُ هَلْ تَرَى أَحَدًا فَلَمْ تَرَ أَحَدًا، فَهَبَطَتْ
مِنَ الصَّفا حَتَّى إِذَا بَلَغَتِ الْوَادِيَ رَفَعَتْ طَرَفَ دِرْعِها ثُمَّ سَعَتْ
سَعْيَ الْإِنْسَانِ الْمَجْهُودِ حَتَّى جَاوَزَتِ الْوَادِيَ، ثُمَّ أَتَتِ الْمَرْوَةَ
فَقَامَتْ عَلَيها فَنَظَرَتْ هَلْ تَرَى أَحَدًا فَلَمْ تَرَ أَحَدًا، فَفَعَلَتْ
ذٰلِكَ سَبْعَ مَرَّاتٍ. قَالَ ابْنُ عَبَّاسٍ: قَالَ النَّبِيُّ ﷺ: «فَذٰلِكَ
سَعْيُ النَّاسِ بَيْنَهُما»، فَلَمَّا أَشْرَفَتْ عَلى الْمَرْوَةِ سَمِعَتْ صَوْتًا
فَقَالَتْ: صَهٍ، تُرِيدُ نَفْسَها، ثُمَّ تَسَمَّعَتْ فَسَمِعَتْ أَيْضًا،
فَقَالَتْ: قَدْ أَسْمَعْتَ إِنْ كَانَ عِنْدَكَ غُوَاثٌ. . . . .

"...Ismail's mother went on suckling Ismail and drinking from the water (she had). When the water in the water-skin had all been used up, she became thirsty and her child also became thirsty. She started looking at him (i.e. Ismail) tossing in agony. She left him, for she could not endure looking at him, and found that the mountain of Safaa was the nearest mountain to her on that land. She stood on it and started looking at the valley keenly so that she might see somebody, but she could not see anybody. Then she descended from Safaa and when she reached the valley, she tucked up her robe and ran in the valley like a person in distress and trouble, till she crossed the valley and reached the Marwah mountain where she stood and started looking, expecting to see somebody, but she could not see anybody. She repeated that (running between Safaa and Marwah) seven times the Prophet (ﷺ) said, 'This is the source of the tradition of the walking of people between them (i.e. Safaa and Marwah). When she reached the Marwah (for the last time) she heard a voice and she asked herself to be quiet and listened attentively. She heard the *voice again and said, 'O (whoever you may be)! You have made me hear your voice; have you got something to help me?'...''*

❖ Zamzam Well:

Baby Ismail was kicking his feet in the sand, when Allah willed, a spring of water started bubbling forth from the sand. This was the start of the Zamzam water well, and it is still producing water today for the pilgrims and visitors to Makkah. [This well was closed for a while during its history. The Prophet's (ﷺ) uncle, Abu Talib received a dream about digging for the zamzam well, which he did, and the well was reopened.]

فَإِذَا هِيَ بِالمَلَكِ عِنْدَ مَوْضِعِ زَمْزَمَ فَبَحَثَ بِعَقِبِهِ - أَوْ قَالَ:
بِجَناحِهِ - حَتَّى ظَهَرَ المَاءُ فَجَعَلَتْ تُحَوِّضُهُ وتَقُولُ بِيدِها هكَذَا،
وجَعَلَتْ تَغْرِفُ مِنَ المَاءِ في سِقائها وهُوَ يَفُورُ بَعْدَما تَغْرِفُ.
قالَ ابنُ عَبَّاسٍ: قالَ النَّبِيُّ ﷺ: «يَرْحَمُ اللهُ أُمَّ إسمَاعِيلَ لَوْ
تَرَكَتْ زمزم - أَوْ قالَ: لَوْ لَمْ تَغْرِفْ مِنْ زَمْزَمَ - لَكانَتْ زَمْزَمُ
عَيْنًا مَعِينًا»، قالَ: فَشَرِبَتْ وَأَرْضَعَتْ ولَدَها، ....

"...And behold! She saw an angel at the place of Zamzam, digging the earth with his heel (or his wing), till water flowed from that place. She started to make something like a basin around it, using her hand in this way, and started filling her water-skin with water with her hands, and the water was flowing out after she had scooped some of it.' the Prophet ﷺ added, 'May Allah bestow Mercy on Ismail's mother! Had she let the Zamzam (flow without trying to control it) (or had she not scooped from that water) (to fill her water-skin), Zamzam would have been a stream flowing on the surface of the earth.' The Prophet further added, 'Then she drank (water) and suckled her child...' ''

❖ Ka'bah:

فَقالَ لَهَا المَلَكُ: لا تخافُوا الضَّيْعَةَ، فإنَّ هَذَا بَيْتُ اللهِ يَبْني

هذَا الغُلَامُ وأبُوه، وإنَّ اللهَ لا يُضِيعُ أَهْلَهُ، وكانَ البَيْتُ مُرْتَفِعًا مِنَ الأرضِ كالرَّابِيةِ تَأتِيهِ السُّيُولُ فَتَأْخُذُ عَنْ يَمِينِهِ وشِمَالِهِ، فَكَانَتْ كَذَلِكَ حَتَّى مَرَّتْ بِهِمْ رُفْقَةٌ مِنْ جُرْهُمَ - أَوْ أَهْلُ بَيْتٍ مِنْ جُرْهُمَ - مُقْبِلِينَ مِنْ طَرِيقِ كَدَاءٍ فَنَزَلُوا في أَسْفَلِ مَكَّةَ فَرَأَوْا طَائِرًا عَائِفًا فَقَالُوا: إِنَّ هذا الطَّائِرَ لَيَدُورُ عَلى ماءٍ، لَعَهْدُنا بِهَذا الوَادِي وما فِيهِ ماءٌ، فَأرْسَلُوا جَرِيًّا أو جَرِيَّيْنِ فَإِذا هُمْ بالمَاءِ، فَرَجَعُوا فَأخْبَرُوهُمْ بالمَاءِ فَأقْبَلُوا - قالَ: وأُمُّ إِسمَاعِيلَ عِنْدَ المَاءِ - فَقَالُوا: أَتَأْذَنِينَ لَنَا أَنْ نَنْزِلَ عِنْدَكِ؟ قَالَتْ: نَعَمْ، ولكِنْ لا حَقَّ لكُمْ في المَاءِ، قالُوا: نَعَمْ. قالَ ابْنُ عَبَّاسٍ: قالَ النَّبِيُّ ﷺ: «فَأَلْفَى ذَلِكَ أُمَّ إسماعيل وهي تُحِبُّ الأُنْسَ» فَنَزَلُوا وأرسلوا إلى أَهْلِيهِمْ فَنَزَلُوا مَعَهُمْ حَتَّى إذا كانَ بها أهلُ أَبْياتٍ مِنْهُمْ، وشَبَّ الغُلَامُ وتَعَلَّمَ العَرَبِيَّةَ مِنْهُمْ، وأَنْفَسَهُمْ وأعْجَبَهُمْ حِينَ شَبَّ، فَلَمَّا أَدْرَكَ زَوَّجُوهُ امْرَأَةً مِنْهُمْ، وماتَتْ أُمُّ إِسمَاعِيلَ فَجاءَ إِبْرَاهِيمُ بَعْدَما تَزَوَّجَ إِسمَاعِيلُ يُطالِعُ تَرِكَتَهُ فَلَمْ يَجِدْ إِسمَاعِيلَ، فَسَأَلَ امْرَأَتَهُ عَنْهُ فَقَالَتْ: خَرَجَ يَبْتَغِي لنَا، ثُمَّ سَأَلَها عن عَيْشِهِمْ وهَيْئَتِهِمْ، فَقَالَتْ: نَحْنُ بِشَرٍّ، نَحْنُ في ضِيقٍ وشِدَّةٍ، فَشَكَتْ إِلَيْهِ، قالَ: فإذا جاءَ زَوْجُكِ اقْرَئِي عَلَيْهِ السَّلَامَ وقُولِي لهُ يُغَيِّرْ عَتَبَةَ بابِهِ، فَلَمَّا جاءَ إِسمَاعِيلُ كأنَّهُ آنَسَ شَيْئًا فَقالَ: هَلْ جاءَكُمْ مِنْ أَحَدٍ؟ قالَتْ: نَعَمْ، جاءَنا شَيْخٌ كذا وكذا فَسَأَلَنا عَنْكَ فأَخْبَرْتُهُ، وسَأَلَنِي كَيْفَ عَيْشُنا، فأَخْبَرْتُهُ أَنَّا في جَهْدٍ وشِدَّةٍ، قالَ: فَهَلْ أَوْصَاكِ بِشَيءٍ؟ قالَتْ: نَعَمْ، أَمَرَنِي أَنْ أَقْرَأَ عَلَيْكَ السَّلَام ويَقُولُ: غَيِّرْ عَتَبَةَ بابِكَ. قالَ: ذَاكَ أبي، وقدْ أَمَرَنِي أَنْ أُفارِقَكِ، الْحَقِي بِأهلِكِ فَطَلَّقَها، وتَزَوَّجَ مِنْهُمْ امْرَأَةً أُخْرَى، فَلَبِثَ عَنهُمْ إِبْرَاهِيمُ ما شاءَ اللهُ ثُمَّ أَتاهُمْ بَعْدُ فَلَمْ يَجِدْهُ، فَدَخَلَ عَلى

امْرَأَتِهِ فَسَأَلَهَا عَنْهُ فَقَالَتْ: خَرَجَ يَبْتَغِي لَنَا، قَالَ: كَيْفَ أَنْتُمْ؟ وَسَأَلَها عَنْ عَيْشِهِم وَهَيْئَتِهِمْ، فَقَالَتْ: نَحْنُ بِخَيرٍ وَسَعَةٍ، وَأَثْنَتْ عَلى اللهِ عَزَّ وَجَلَّ، فَقَالَ: ما طَعَامُكُمْ؟ قالت: اللَّحْمُ، قالَ: فَمَا شَرَابُكُمْ؟ قَالَتْ: المَاءُ، قالَ: اللَّهُمَّ بَارِكْ لَهُمْ في اللَّحم والمَاءِ. قالَ النَّبِيُّ ﷺ: «ولَمْ يَكُنْ لَهُمْ يَوْمَئِذٍ حَبٌّ، ولَوْ كَانَ لَهُمْ دَعا لَهُمْ فيه». قالَ: فَهُما لا يَخْلُو عَلَيْهِما أَحَدٌ بِغَيرِ مَكَّةَ إلَّا لَمْ يُوَافِقاهُ، قالَ: فإذا جاءَ زَوْجُكِ فاقْرَئِي عَلَيْهِ السَّلامَ ومُرِيهِ يُثبِتُ عَتَبَةَ بابِهِ، فَلَمَّا جاءَ إسمَاعِيلُ قالَ: هَلْ أَتاكُمْ مِنْ أَحَدٍ؟ قالَتْ: نَعَمْ، أتانا شَيخٌ حَسَنُ الهَيْئَةِ – وَأَثْنَتْ عَلَيْهِ – فَسَأَلَني عَنْكَ فأَخْبَرْتُهُ، فَسَأَلَني كَيْفَ عَيْشُنا؟ فأَخْبَرْتُهُ أَنَّا بِخَيرٍ، قالَ: فأوْصَاكِ بِشَيءٍ؟ قَالَتْ: نَعَمْ، هُوَ يَقْرَأُ عَلَيْكَ السَّلامَ ويأْمُرَكَ أَنْ تُثْبِتَ عَتَبَةَ بابِكَ، قالَ: ذَاكَ أبي وأنْتِ العَتَبَةُ، أَمَرَني أَنْ أُمْسِكَكِ، ثُمَّ لَبِثَ عَنْهُمْ ما شاءَ اللهُ ثُمَّ جاءَ بَعْدَ ذْلكَ وإسمَاعِيلُ يَبري نَبْلًا له تَحْتَ دَوْحَةٍ قَرِيبًا مِنْ زَمْزَمَ، فَلَمَّا رَآهُ قامَ إلَيْهِ فَصَنَعا كما يَصْنَعُ الوَالِدُ بالوَلَدِ والوَلَدُ بالوَالِدِ، ثُمَّ قالَ: يا إسمَاعِيلُ، إنَّ اللهَ أَمَرَني بِأمْرٍ، قالَ: فاصْنَعْ ما أَمَرَكَ رَبُّكَ، قالَ: وَتُعِينُني؟ قالَ: وأُعِينُكَ، قالَ: فإنَّ اللهَ أَمَرَني أَنْ أُبْنِيَ هاهُنا بَيْتًا – وأَشارَ إلى أَكَمَةٍ مُرْتَفِعَةٍ عَلى ما حَوْلَها – قالَ: فَعِنْدَ ذْلكَ رَفَعا القَوَاعِدَ مِنَ البَيْتِ، فَجَعَلَ إسمَاعِيلُ يأتي بالحِجارَةِ وإبْرَاهِيمُ يَبْني حتَّى إذا ارتَفَعَ البِناءُ جاءَ بِهذا الحَجَرِ فَوَضَعَهُ لَهُ فَقامَ عَلَيْهِ وهُوَ يَبْني وإسمَاعِيلُ يُناوِلُهُ الحِجارَةَ وهما يَقُولانِ: ﴿رَبَّنَا تَقَبَّلْ مِنَّا إِنَّكَ أَنتَ ٱلسَّمِيعُ ٱلۡعَلِيمُ﴾ [البقرة:١٢٧] قالَ: فَجَعَلا يَبْنِيانِ حتَّى يَدُورَا حَوْلَ البَيْتِ وهما يَقُولانِ: ﴿رَبَّنَا تَقَبَّلْ مِنَّآ إِنَّكَ أَنتَ ٱلسَّمِيعُ ٱلۡعَلِيمُ﴾».

'...The angel said to her, 'Don't be afraid of being neglected, for this is the House of Allah which will be built by this boy and his father, and Allah never neglects His people...' The House (i.e., Ka'bah) at that time was ... and married another woman from amongst them (i.e., Jurhum). Then Ibraheem stayed away from them for a period as long as Allah wished, and called on them afterwards. He saw Ismail under a tree near Zamzam, sharpening his arrows. When he saw Ibraheem, he rose up to welcome him (and they greeted each other as a father does with his son or a son does with his father). Ibraheem said, 'Oh Ismail! Allah has given me an order.' Ismail said, 'Do what your Lord has ordered you to do.' Ibraheem asked, 'Will you help me?' Ismail said, 'I will help you.' Ibraheem said, 'Allah has ordered me to build a house here,' pointing to a hillock higher than the land surrounding it. The Prophet added, 'Then they raised the foundations of the House (i.e. the Ka'bah). Ismail brought the stones and Ibraheem was building, and when the walls became high, Ismail brought this stone and put it for Ibraheem who stood over it and carried on building, while Ismail was handing him the stones, and both of them were saying, 'O our Lord! Accept (this service) from us, Verily, You are the All-Hearing, the All-Knowing'." (Bukhari: 3364)

﴿وَإِذْ بَوَّأْنَا لِإِبْرَٰهِيمَ مَكَانَ ٱلْبَيْتِ﴾

"And (remember) when We showed Ibraheem the site of the (Sacred) House..."

[*Surah Al-Hajj* (22), part of *Ayah* 26]

❖ Hajr-al-Aswad (Black Stone):

A special stone was placed in its eastern corner to mark the starting point for the circling of the Ka'bah. This stone according to the Prophet's (ﷺ) explanation, was originally shining white in colour when it was brought down from Paradise, however due to the sins of man it changed to its present colour of black, hence the name Hajr-al-Aswad (the

Black Stone).

Narrated Ibn Abbas (⌘) that Allah's Messenger (⌘) said:

«نَزَلَ الْحَجَرُ الأَسْوَدُ مِنَ الْجَنَّةِ وهُوَ أَشَدُّ بَيَاضًا مِنَ اللَّبَنِ فَسَوَّدَتْهُ خَطَايَا بَنِي آدَمَ».

"The black stone descended from Paradise whiter than milk, but the sins of the descendants of Adam made it black."

(Tirmidhi : 877)

❖ *Tawaaf:*

Circling of the Ka'bah was performed since the building of the Ka'bah. In the days of ignorance the polytheists used to circle it while naked. The Prophet Muhammad (⌘) stopped this practice.

عَنْ أَبِي هُرَيْرَةَ قَالَ: بَعَثَنِي أَبُو بَكْرٍ الصِّدِّيقُ فِي الْحَجَّةِ الَّتِي أَمَّرَهُ عَلَيْهَا رَسُولُ اللهِ ﷺ، قَبْلَ حَجَّةِ الْوَدَاعِ، فِي رَهْطٍ، يُؤَذِّنُونَ فِي النَّاسِ يَوْمَ النَّحْرِ: لَا يَحُجُّ بَعْدَ الْعَامِ مُشْرِكٌ، وَلَا يَطُوفُ بِالْبَيْتِ عُرْيَانٌ.

Abu Hurairah (⌘) reported: "Abu Bakr Siddiq (⌘) sent me during Hajj before the Farewell Pilgrimage for which Allah's Messenger (⌘) had appointed him an Amir, among a group of people whom he had ordered to make announcement to the people on the day of Nahr: 'After this year no polytheist may perform the pilgrimage and no naked person my circumambulate the House.' "(Muslim : 1347)

❖ Maqaam Ibraheem:

During the building of the Ka'bah, Prophet Ibraheem stood on a large stone block in order to complete the upper part of its walls. He used to move the block around the Ka'bah as it was built, and on completion of the building, it was left outside the Ka'bah near the eastern wall and became known in later years as the Maqaam Ibraheem (the standing place of Ibraheem). Allah refers to it in the Qur'an:

﴿ فِيهِ ءَايَـٰتٌۢ بَيِّنَـٰتٌۭ مَّقَامُ إِبْرَٰهِيمَ ﴾

"In it are Manifest signs (for example), the Maqaam (place) of Ibraheem..."

[*Surah Al-Imran* (3), part of *Ayah* 97]

❖ Area known as the Hijr:

During its history the Ka'bah was destroyed and rebuilt a few times.

عَنْ عَائِشَةَ قَالَتْ: سَأَلْتُ رَسُولَ اللهِ ﷺ، عَن الْجَدْرِ؟ أَمِنَ الْبَيْتِ هُوَ؟ قَالَ: «نَعَمْ» قُلْتُ: فَلِمَ لَمْ يُدْخِلُوهُ الْبَيْتَ؟ قَالَ: «إِنَّ قَوْمَكِ قَصَّرَتْ بِهِمُ النَّفَقَةُ» قُلْتُ: فَمَا شَأْنُ بَابِهِ مُرْتَفِعٌ؟ قَالَ: «فَعَلَ ذٰلِكِ قَوْمُكِ لِيُدْخِلُوا مَنْ شَآءُوْا وَيَمْنَعُوا مَنْ شَآءُوْا، وَلَوْلَا أَنَّ قَوْمَكِ حَدِيثٌ عَهْدُهُمْ فِي الْجَاهِلِيَّةِ، فَأَخَافُ أَنْ تُنْكِرَ قُلُوبُهُمْ، لَنَظَرْتُ أَنْ أُدْخِلَ الْجَدْرَ فِي الْبَيْتِ، وَأَنْ أُلْزِقَ بَابَهُ بِالْأَرْضِ».

'Aishah (⌽) reported: "I asked Allah's Messenger (ﷺ) about the wall, circumpassing the House (i.e. whether the wall on the side of Hijr was included in the Ka'bah)." He said: "Yes." I said: "Then why did they not include it in the house?" He said: "Your people ran short of the means (to do so)." I said: "Why is it that the level of its door is raised high?" He said: "Your people did it so that they should admit one whom they liked, and forbid him whom they disliked, and if your people were not converts to faith, and I did not apprehend that their hearts would feel agitated at this, I would have definitely included (the area of) this wall in the House and would have brought the door to the level of the ground."

(*Muslim : 3249*)

→ Air-conditioned section:

* The newer section of the *Haram* is air-conditioned (including the basement), whereas the older sections only have roof fans as a means of cooling.

→ About *Sutrah*:

◆ What is *Sutrah*? An object like a pillar, wall or stick, spear etc., the height of which should not be less than a foot and must be in front of a person offering *Salah* to act as a symbolical barrier between him and others.

♦ The *Sutrah* rule does not apply to *Fardh Salah* for the *Jama'ah* (congregation), as the *Imam's Sutrah* is valid for the entire congregation.

عَنْ سَهْلٍ قَالَ: كَانَ بَيْنَ مُصَلَّى رَسُولِ اللهِ ﷺ وَبَيْنَ الجِدَارِ مَمَرُّ الشَّاةِ.

Narrated Sahl (bin Sa'd) (ﷺ): "The distance between the Musalla (praying place) of Allah's Messenger (ﷺ) and the wall (Sutrah) was just sufficient for a sheep to pass through."

(Bukhari : 496, Muslim : 508)

أَنَّ النَّبِيَّ ﷺ صَلَّى بِهِمْ بِالبَطْحَاءِ – وَبَيْنَ يَدَيْهِ عَنَزَةٌ – الظُّهْرَ رَكْعَتَيْنِ، وَالعَصْرَ رَكْعَتَيْنِ، يَمُرُّ بَيْنَ يَدَيْهِ المَرْأَةُ والحِمَارُ.

Narrated Abu Juhaifah (ﷺ): "The Prophet (ﷺ) led us and prayed a two-Rak'at Zuhr prayer and then a two-Rak'at Asr prayer at Al-Batha with an Anazah (type of stick) (planted) in front of him (as a Sutrah) while women and donkeys were passing in front of him (beyond the Anazah)."

(Bukhari : 495, Muslim : 503)

Narrated Abu Juhaim (ﷺ) that the Prophet (ﷺ) said:

«لَوْ يَعْلَمُ المَارُّ بَيْنَ يَدَيِ المُصَلِّي مَاذَا عَلَيْهِ لَكَانَ أَنْ يَقِفَ أَرْبَعِينَ خَيْرًا لَهُ مِنْ أَنْ يَمُرَّ بَيْنَ يَدَيْهِ». قَالَ أَبُو النَّضْرِ: لَا أَدْرِي قَالَ: أَرْبَعِينَ يَوْمًا أَوْ شَهْرًا أَوْ سَنَةً.

"If the person who passes in front of another person in Salah knew the magnitude of his sin, he would prefer to wait for 40 (days, months or years) rather than to pass in front of him."
Abu An-Nadr said, "I do not remember exactly whether he said 40 days, months or years."

(Bukhari : 510)

«إِذَا صَلَّى أَحَدُكُمْ إِلَى شَيْءٍ يَسْتُرُهُ مِنَ النَّاسِ فَأَرَادَ أَحَدٌ أَنْ
يَجْتَازَ بَيْنَ يَدَيْهِ، فَلْيَدْفَعْهُ فَإِنْ أَبَىٰ فَلْيُقَاتِلْهُ فَإِنَّمَا هُوَ شَيْطَانٌ» .

*"When one of you prays behind anything which screens from
the people, then if someone wants to pass between him and the
Sutrah, he should repel him by pushing at his chest. And if
he refuses to defer then fight him, for he is a devil."*

(Bukhari : 509)

♦ This authentic *Hadith* which warns against passing in front
of a praying person includes the *Haram* in Makkah and in
Madinah, as it is a general statement. The Prophet (ﷺ) said
it either in Makkah or Madinah. Further proof as per the
Hadith in *Bukhari* about 'Ibn Umar repelling a person in
front of him while he was in *Tashahud* in front of the
Ka'bah.

• Many people believe that the two *Harams* are exempted
from the above *Ahadith* about not walking in front of a
person performing *Salah*. Unfortunately there is also no
unanimous opinion by the scholars on this issue that I
could find. Some scholars say it is acceptable due to the
crowds while others say, it's not.

• During the very busy periods it becomes almost impossible
to avoid performing *Salah* with women next to or in front
of you, let alone being able to avoid 'breaking' a person's
Sutrah. **The most sensible advice I heard on the issue is to
try and avoid both actions and to make it the exception
rather than the rule.** Meaning that one should try and
avoid walking in front of a person performing *Salah* unless
it is absolutely necessary. About making *Salah* next to or
behind women, one should endeavour to move closer to
the front or to an area where there are only men and not
merely stop where everybody else does. On many
occasions I have experienced that there are plenty of
spaces inside the *Haram* or in the front male areas, whereas
people perform *Salah* (mixed) in the street.

- Do your best and ensure that your *Niyah* is to do the right thing. Being early in the mosque somewhat alleviates this problem.

- Avoid performing your *Salah* in doorways, walkways and the *Tawaaf* areas. People have the right to walk in these areas; therefore you should expect people not only to walk in front of you, but also over you.

- If you do end up performing your *Fardh Salah* in these areas, try to move out of the way immediately after the *Salah* is completed. Do not perform your *Sunnah Salah* here as your *Sutrah* will definitely be "broken". Move to a less obstructive place.

→ *Qiblah* Direction:

- One of the most amazing things in the *Haram* is that the closer you are to the Ka'bah the more likely you are to 'miss' the direction. See diagram.

- It is a condition of *Salah* that one faces *Qiblah* (direction of the Ka'bah) while performing *Salah*.

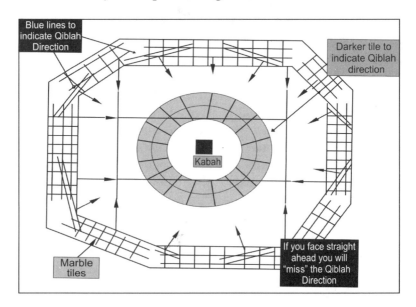

* The marble tiles (in the newer areas) and the ones immediately around the Ka'bah are positioned facing *Qiblah*.

* There is also a thin strip of darker coloured tiles (in a line format) to indicate the *Qiblah* direction.

* The entire courtyard area has the tiles laid facing the *Qiblah* direction.

* In the older areas of the *Haram* where the tiles are laid straight there are two blue lines carved into the marble floor tiles of the *Haram*. This is to indicate the direction of *Qiblah* (also in the *Sa'ee* area).

• The red arrows (in the diagram above) clearly indicate that the person will be 'missing' the *Qiblah* direction. Whereas the green arrows show that the two blue lines carved into the floor tiles guide the person to face *Qiblah*.

• It is almost impossible not to face *Qiblah* when standing closer to the Ka'bah in the circled area. In the courtyard areas the direction is indicated by the tiles and also by a thin strip of a darker coloured tile, serving as a line (guide).

• You will find many people (especially in the women's areas) facing in the wrong direction while performing *Salah* (*Sunnah* and *Fardh*). This is because most people assume that facing straight ahead from wherever they are in the *Haram* is correct. (As soon as one person does it the rest seem to follow).

• Do not necessarily follow the lines of people performing *Salah*. Ensure that they are facing *Qiblah*. I have seen entire rows facing in the wrong direction.

• Around the Ka'bah it is easy and simple. The further back you go the more difficult it becomes to guess the direction. However there is no need to guess, just follow the lines on the floor tiles.

• What shall you do if the entire line is facing the wrong way? Turn as many of them as you possibly can by placing your hands on their shoulders from the back and gently turning them. (Be prepared for resistance and confusion. Do not insist as you may get a slap in the face). After that, you should face the right direction, as those coming after you will follow your lead.

- Around the Ka'bah is the only place in world where you will find people performing *Salah* in a circle. If the *Imam* is standing further back under the covered area (as he sometimes does), where is the first line you may ask? Well, that's another topic all together.

→ Zamzam:

The Prophet (ﷺ) said:

«مَاءُ زَمْزَمَ لِمَا شُرِبَ لَهُ» .

"Zamzam water is for whatever (purpose) it is drunk for."

(*Ibn Majah* : 3062)

«فِيهِ طَعَامٌ مِنَ الطُّعْمِ وَشِفَاءٌ مِنَ السُّقْمِ»

"It satisfies as food and cures illness."

(*At-Tayalisi*)

- There is no particular supplication established in the *Sunnah* when drinking Zamzam, however Abdullah ibn Abbas (﵁) used to recite the following after drinking Zamzam water:

«اللَّهُمَّ إِنِّي أَسْأَلُكَ عِلماً نَافِعًا وَرِزْقًا وَاسِعًا وَشِفَاءً مِنْ كُلِّ دَاءٍ»

Allahumma innee asaluka'ilman naafi'an wa rizqan waasi'an wa shifaa 'an min-kulli daa'in.

(Oh Allah, I ask of You beneficial knowledge, abundant provision, and a cure from all disease.)

- There is no requirement to stand while drinking Zamzam.

- There is also no evidence from the Qur'an or the *Sunnah* about soaking one's *Ihraam* clothes or any other shroud in Zamzam water to be later used for one's burial, as a means of salvation.

* There are plenty of Zamzam taps and drums (beige in colour) all around the *Haram*, with cold Zamzam for your enjoyment.

* Facing the drum the cups in the holder on the right side of the drum are the clean cups and the used ones are in the left cup holder.

* Most of the time the water is cold, however there are a few drums with room temperature water, marked (in Arabic) "Zamzam water not cold".

- Sometimes there are people selling containers of Zamzam outside the *Haram* area. They charge about 5-10 Saudi Riyals for about ten litres. Alternatively you may take a small water bottle or flask inside the *Haram* with you and fill it up at the taps or drums. (Contrary to what many people believe, it is quite acceptable to make tea or coffee, etc., with Zamzam water.)

→ Qur'ans:

- There are many Qur'ans (on stands) inside the *Haram* area.

- The benefits of reading Qur'an are covered earlier in this chapter.

- It is good to keep your own small Qur'an with you all the time. You may 'lose' your sitting place in the *Haram* due to fetching or taking Qur'ans from the stands. Keep in mind that the person has the right to 'claim' his place back, if for some reason you are in his place. (Remove the Qur'an from your pocket, when going to the toilet.)

- There are various 'print styles' of Qur'ans in the stands. The most common one is the style in the first of the two examples shown. These are the green covered Qur'ans as well as the big blue ones. The style in the second example is used in the blue covered (not the big size) Qur'ans. There are not too many of these, so if this is your preferred style you have to be quick, or carry your own. I have noticed that there are also a few green covered Qur'ans in this style. Now this complicates it further. Anyway, as long as you are aware that they are available.

- There are also a few Qur'ans with the meaning in various languages, such as English and French.

→ **First Aid: Emergency medical facilities:**

* At various locations inside the *Haram* there are emergency medical facilities.

* They are located close to certain doors. The clinics can be found:

  ➤ Next to door no. 5 (Ajyad Door) and also in the same location on the middle floor;

  ➤ Next to door no. 64 (no name);

  ➤ Next to door no. 94 (no name).

* Clinics are identified by a white sign with a red crescent.

* There is also an emergency medical station outside door no. 45, Baab-ul-Fath.

→ **Where to sit:**

• During the very busy periods, it is important to choose a 'good' place to sit. The best is to be early for *Salah*.

• Avoid sitting near the doors or walkways. When the mosque gets very crowded people will trample all over you in these areas. If you are forced to sit near a walkway or door, move immediately after the *Salah* is complete.

• Try to sit in the middle or front areas. Directly in front of the Qur'an stands is also a good place.

• Sitting near the Zamzam drums is not such a good idea as this is always busy with people drinking water and the area can sometimes get very wet.

• If you are sitting in the *Tawaaf* area, move immediately after *Salah* has completed to allow people to perform *Tawaaf* comfortably.

• Please keep in mind, that everybody has the right to be inside the mosque so try to accommodate your fellow Muslims wherever possible. Do not try to keep a big and comfortable space for yourself. You will not be able to do so for very long and you will be stressed and creating unnecessary arguments.

• Avoid 'keeping' a place for friends. This will be difficult and you will spend your time 'protecting' this space, instead of making *Ibadah*.

• Even after taking all 'precautions', don't be surprised when you find somebody coming to sit directly in front of you, leaving you no space to make *Salah* properly.

• Some people also give their shoes (space) a higher priority, rather than giving you space to sit. Be patient!

→ **Behaviour:**

- As with everything else, your behaviour inside the *Haram* is of the utmost importance.

- Do not walk backwards out of the *Haram*. This is dangerous, as you could fall and hurt somebody or even yourself. Many people believe that it is showing disrespect to the Ka'bah to turn one's back towards it. The Prophet (ﷺ) was the best of teachers and he did not do this (walk backwards) nor instructed us to do so.

- About shouting and walking in big groups, during *Tawaaf* and *Sa'ee*, don't do it.

- Do not push your hands into the back of the person in front of you while leaving the *Haram* or during *Tawaaf*.

- If somebody else does this to you, politely move their hands from your back.

- Try not to push when the doors are congested. Keep in mind that there are many elderly people and that you could push somebody down the stairs.

- Do not stop or perform *Salah* near the *Tawaaf* starting area. If you need to determine the starting place, look at the people (3 or so levels) in front of you. This way you can tell where the start is as they will be raising their hands.

- You will notice that there are always people going in the opposite direction, no matter where and what time it is. Avoid as best as you can going against the flow of the general traffic.

- One of the more amazing behaviours of certain people, is when they are late, they persist on moving towards the front (even though there is no place), and when the *Salah* is finished they are the first to rush back out again. If you are late, your rightful place is at the back!

→ **Leaving the *Haram*:**

- There is no special supplication upon leaving *Al-Masjid al-*

Haram, however, the one offered upon leaving any mosque should be recited:

«بِسْمِ اللهِ وَالصَّلَاةُ وَالسَّلَامُ عَلَى رَسُولِ اللهِ اللَّهُمَّ إِنِّي أَسَأَلُكَ مِنْ فَضْلِكَ»

Bismillahi wa salaatu wa salaamu alaa rasullillahi, Allahumma innee asaluka min fadlika.

(In the Name of Allah. Blessings and peace be upon the Messenger of Allah. Oh Allah, I ask of You Your favour.)

(*Muslim, Abu Dawud 465, An-Nasa'i* and *Ibn Majah*)

Chapter 8
Umrah

In this chapter we will explain the actual performance of the *Umrah*. However before we address that, I would like to explain some general terms about *Tawaaf* and *Sa'ee*.

⇨ **About *Tawaaf*:**

→ **General Points:**

◆ Types of *Tawaaf*:
  ➤ *Umrah Tawaaf*❶
  ➤ Welcome *Tawaaf (Tawaaf-al-Qudoom)*❷
  ➤ *Tawaaf* for *Hajj (Tawaaf-al-Ifadah* also known as *Tawaaf-as-Ziyarah* or *Tawaaf-al-Hajj)*❸
  ➤ Farewell *Tawaaf (Tawaaf-al-Wadaa')*❹
  ➤ *Nafl Tawaaf*❺

◆ For *Umrah*, only ❶, ❹ & ❺ applies.

◆ ❶ & ❷ You should be in *Ihraam*.

◆ ❶ & ❷ *Ramal* (to walk briskly in the first three rounds) and *Idtiba* (to have your right shoulder open) are required for these *Tawaafs*.

عَنِ ابنِ عَبَّاسٍ رَضِيَ اللهُ عَنْهُما قالَ: قَدِمَ رَسُولُ اللهِ ﷺ وأصحابُهُ فقالَ المُشْرِكُونَ: إنَّهُ يَقْدَمُ عَلَيْكُمْ وَفْدٌ وَهَنَهُمْ حُمَّى يَثْرِبَ، فأَمَرَهُمُ النَّبِيُّ ﷺ أَنْ يَرْمُلُوا الأَشْوَاطَ الثَّلاثَةَ وأَنْ يَمْشُوا ما بَيْنَ الرُّكْنَيْنِ، ولَمْ يَمْنَعْهُ أَنْ يأْمُرَهُمْ أَنْ يَرْمُلُوا الأَشْوَاطَ كُلَّها إلَّا الإبْقَاءُ عَلَيْهِمْ.

Narrated Ibn Abbas (ﷺ): "When Allah's Messenger (ﷺ) and his Companions came to Makkah, the pagans circulated the news that a group of people were coming to them and they

*had been weakened by the fever of Yathrib (Al-Madinah). So
the Prophet (ﷺ) ordered his companions to do Ramal in the
first three rounds of Tawaaf of the Ka'bah and to walk
between the two corners (The Yemenite Corner and the Black
Stone). The Prophet (ﷺ) did not order them to do Ramal in
all the rounds of Tawaaf out of pity for them."*

(*Bukhari* : 1602)

* ❹ This is the last act to be performed before leaving
  Makkah.

* ❺ This *Tawaaf* can be performed at any time and as many
  times as possible.

* ❸ ❹, & ❺ No *Ihraam*, no *Ramal* and no *Idtibah* for these
  Tawaafs.

* There is no *Niyah* to be uttered audibly. The *Niyah* is in the
  heart.

* *Tawaaf* begins at Hajr-al-Aswad (Black Stone) only and
  proceeds in an anti-clockwise direction.

* The *Tawaaf* also finishes at the Hajr-al-Aswad.

* One should encircle (walk around the outside) the area
  called Hijr (the open area, under the roof's waterspout,
  surrounded by a low wall).

* The number of circuits to perform is always seven,
  regardless of the type of *Tawaaf* (i.e., *Umrah*, *Hajj* or *Nafl*).

* When you are in doubt about the number of rounds you
  have made, rely on the lesser number you remember.

* *Du'a'* in your own language, *Dhikr*, and reciting Qur'an are
  all acceptable forms of *Ibadah* while performing *Tawaaf*.

* *Tawaaf* must be interrupted for *Fardh Salah* and
  recommended for *Janazah Salah*. Resume from where you
  have stopped. If you stopped half way through one circuit,
  ensure that you continue at the right place. This is
  important if you stopped for *Salah* and moved positions
  several times before the actual *Salah*. So it is important to

remember exactly where you have stopped, otherwise start again. If you are not sure about the number, choose the lesser number or start again.

♦ It is permissible to talk while performing *Tawaaf*. Most scholars agree that one should only discuss necessary/ required things and not merely engage in idle chat.

♦ Avoid performing *Tawaaf* in groups or following and reciting behind a 'leader'. The Prophet (ﷺ) was the best of teachers and he did not lead anybody, or any group, in *Tawaaf*, nor did he instruct his companions (ﷺ) to do so.

♦ Avoid raising your voice while performing *Tawaaf*.

Narrated Abu Musa: We were in the company of the Prophet ﷺ on a journey, and whenever we ascended a high place, we used to say *Takbir* [(*Allahu Akbar* — Allah is the Most Great) in a loud voice]. The Prophet ﷺ said,

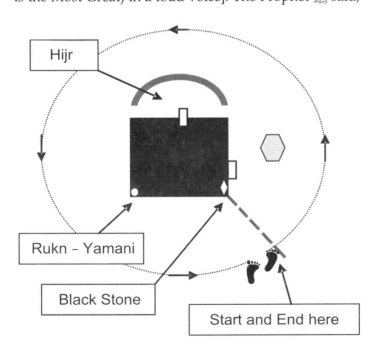

«أَيُّهَا النَّاسُ، ارْبَعُوا عَلى أَنْفُسِكُمْ فإنَّكُمْ لا تَدْعُونَ أَصَمَّ وَلا غَائِبًا» .

"O people! Be kind to yourselves, for you are not calling upon a deaf or an absent one."

(Bukhari : 6384)

♦ Why are we kissing the Black Stone?

عَن ابْنِ عُمَرَ: أَنَّ عُمَرَ قَبَّلَ الْحَجَرَ، وَقَالَ: إِنِّي لَأُقَبِّلُكَ وَ إِنِّي لَأَعْلَمُ أَنَّكَ حَجَرٌ، وَلَكِنِّي رَأَيْتُ رَسُولَ اللهِ ﷺ يُقَبِّلُكَ .

Ibn Umar (ﷺ) reported that Umar (ﷺ) kissed the stone and said : "I am kissing you, whereas I know you are a stone, but I saw Allah's Messenger (ﷺ) kissing you (that is why I kiss you)."

(Muslim : 1270)

- Avoid walking against the flow of people rather walk right around to the starting place.

- There is no need to actually stop at the starting point. This is not a place to stop or make *Salah*. It is a mere indication of where to start. Many people stop at the starting point and make all sorts of gestures towards the black stone, causing a great deal of congestion and confusion.

- It is important to note that if one is unable to reach the Black Stone, one's *Umrah* or *Tawaaf* is not decreased in merit in any way, but if one pushes and shoves his Muslim brethren in order to do so, he risks incurring Allah the Almighty's displeasure.

→ **Some Hints for *Tawaaf*:**

- During the very busy periods the *Tawaaf* area around the Ka'bah is extremely crowded with people performing *Tawaaf*. It is like being in a can of sardines and one can get severely squashed and bruised.

- If you cannot stand being 'pushed and squashed' I suggest you perform your *Tawaaf* on the roof level. It is much easier than the middle floor level as the middle floor has lots of people and pillars to negotiate. The roof can also get very crowded but from experience it is much more comfortable. It may take a while longer due to the bigger area you need to cover. Walking normally, with a fair crowd, one circuit can take about 15 to 20 minutes to complete.

- Apart from the pushing, it is not recommended for women to be in such crowds, if it can be avoided.

- The bottom level around the Ka'bah is the quickest, but it is also for the bravest.

- If you start your *Tawaaf* on the ground level, and find it too 'difficult' to continue, it is acceptable to go to the other floors to complete the seven circuits. It is best to try and complete a circuit prior to going upstairs. If you go halfway through a circuit, then you should redo that circuit. (The distance covered to get upstairs does not count as part of the *Tawaaf*).

- It is also acceptable to go outside the mosque to use the escalators (which is sometimes easier) to get upstairs.

- When the *Tawaaf* area is very crowded adopt the following approach:

  ➢ Start your *Tawaaf* as far out as possible proceed to walk slowly inwards, closer to the Ka'bah.

  ➢ Try to maintain this position and complete the 1st round followed by rounds 2 to 6.

  ➢ On the 7th round start moving slowly towards the outer side again.

  ➢ At the end of the 7th round, walk quickly diagonally along the starting line, in front of the people. Because everybody 'stops' on this line, if you walk quickly, you will find a clear path all the way.

➢ The above method may not work all the time, but it's worth a try.

➢ If you have women with you, I suggest you remain on the outside for all seven circuits.

➢ About getting to kiss the black stone. Sometimes the people actually form a queue. You may wait very long in this queue as there are thousands of others that push in at the front. There is no easy way other than waiting your turn. Do not even consider taking the females to try and kiss the stone. This is looking for trouble. Rather go at a less busy time if possible.

➢ Touching of the Rukn-al-Yamani Corner is also virtually impossible.

➢ You need to complete your two *Rak'at Salah* in another part of the mosque.

⇨ **About *Sa'ee*:**

→ **General Points:**

◆ *Sa'ee* is only performed:

   ➢ After *Tawaaf* for *Umrah*❶
   ➢ After *Tawaaf-ul-Qudoom (Sa'ee* for *Hajj)*❷

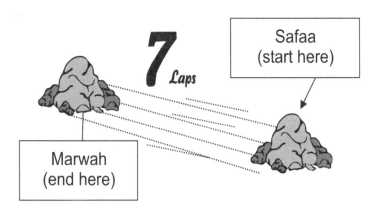

➢ After *Tawaaf-al-Ifadah* for those performing the *Tamattu* method and for the other methods if they did not do it after *Tawaaf-ul-Qudoom*

♦ ❶ & ❷ You should be in *Ihraam*.

♦ For *Umrah*, only ❶ applies.

♦ There is no *Nafl Sa'ee*.

♦ There is no *Sa'ee* after a *Nafl Tawaaf* or after *Tawaaf-al-Wadaa'*.

♦ The *Sa'ee* comprises of seven laps.

♦ Starting at Safaa one proceeds to Marwah. This is one lap.

♦ From Marwah you return to Safaa (this is lap two) and so on, finishing lap seven at Marwah

♦ When you are in doubt about the number of laps you have made, rely on the lesser number you remember. Keep in mind that you should finish at Marwah.

♦ *Du'a'* in your own language, *Dhikr*, *Tasbih*, are all acceptable forms of *Ibadah* while performing *Sa'ee*.

♦ Between the green lights (indicated on the side of the walls nearer to Safaa), the males walk briskly (run). Sometimes due to crowds it is impossible to do so. Also if you are taking care of elderly or females in your company, you can refrain from running between the green lit areas. Some males run all the way from Safaa to Marwah. Maybe they are in a hurry, but this is contrary to the *Sunnah*.

♦ *Sa'ee* MUST be interrupted for *Fardh Salah* and recommended for *Janazah Salah*. Resume from where you have stopped. If you stopped half way through one lap, ensure that you continue at the right place. This is important if you stopped for *Salah* and moved positions several times before the actual *Salah*. So it is important to remember exactly where you have stopped, otherwise start again. If you are not sure about the number, choose the lesser number or start again. *Sa'ee* finishes at Marwah, hence you should take care of the numbers. If you were going towards Marwah, then the count can either be 1, 3, 5 or 7, and if you were going towards Safaa, then it is either, 2, 4 or 6.

- It is permissible to talk while performing *Sa'ee*. Most scholars agree that one should only discuss necessary/ required things and not merely engage in idle chat.

- As with *Tawaaf* avoid performing *Sa'ee* in groups or following and reciting behind a 'leader'. The Prophet (ﷺ) was the best of teachers and he did not lead anybody, or any group, in *Sa'ee*, nor did he instruct his Companions (ﷺ) to do so.

- Avoid raising your voice while performing *Sa'ee*.

- It is preferable but not a requirement to have *Wudhu'* while performing *Sa'ee*.

* **Where is the *Sa'ee* area?** With your back facing the Maqaam Ibraheem, Safaa is located towards your right. There is a big white sign indicating the direction. Also if you proceed straight towards the back of the *Haram* from the green light or brown starting point, you will be going in the right direction.

* *Sa'ee* can also be performed on the middle and roof areas.

- Once again I suggest the roof area to be the best. However the middle floor may be better if you are performing *Sa'ee* during the day and it is hot.

- Sometimes the stairs to the upper floors of the *Sa'ee* area are just as crowded as the *Sa'ee* itself. If this is the case, I suggest you exit from door number 11 (Baab-us-Safaa) and turn right to enter from door 8 (Ajyad Escalator), to go to the roof or middle floor.

- At Marwah, and if you are performing *Sa'ee* on the second floor or on the roof, you will not be able to see the Ka'bah, so you need to ensure that you face the correct direction while supplicating.

- Many people make the mistake of counting from Safaa to Safaa as one round. This means you will end up performing 14 laps.

⇨ **About Cutting your Hair:**

♦ There is more reward in shaving your head (men), instead of just cutting it short.

♦ Shaving is referred to as *Halq* and cutting as *Qasr (or Taqseer).*

♦ It is not enough to cut a small piece of hair from one side only. You should cut from all over your head. In other words, have a haircut.

♦ Women should cut no more than one fingertip length (about one inch) from their hair (one place only).

♦ The Prophet (ﷺ) supplicated to Allah three times to forgive those who had their heads shaved and once for those who had their hair cut short.

عَنِ ابْنِ عُمَرَ أَنَّ رَسُولَ اللهِ ﷺ قَالَ: «رَحِمَ اللهُ الْمُحَلِّقِينَ»
قَالُوا: وَالْمُقَصِّرِينَ؟ يَا رَسُولَ اللهِ! قَالَ: «رَحِمَ اللهُ الْمُحَلِّقِينَ»
قَالُوا: وَالْمُقَصِّرِينَ؟ يَا رَسُولَ اللهِ! قَالَ: «رَحِمَ اللهُ الْمُحَلِّقِينَ»
قَالُوا: وَالْمُقَصِّرِينَ؟ يَا رَسُولَ اللهِ! قَالَ: «وَالْمُقَصِّرِينَ».

Ibn Umar (ﷺ) reported that the Prophet (ﷺ) said: "May Allah have mercy upon those who had their heads shaved'' They said: "Messenger of Allah, what about those who had their hair clipped?'' He said: "May Allah have mercy upon those who had their heads shaved'' They said: "Messenger of Allah, (what about those who had their hair clipped?)'' He said: "May Allah have mercy upon those who had their heads shaved'' They said: "Messenger of Allah, (what about) those who had their hair clipped?'' He said: "(Oh Allah, have mercy upon) those who had their hair clipped.''

(Muslim : 1301)

♦ Do not shave only parts of it. Sometimes people plan to perform more than one *Umrah*, so they shave only part of the head at a time:

عَنِ ابْنِ عُمَرَ؛ أَنَّ رَسُولَ اللهِ ﷺ نَهَىٰ عَنِ الْقَزَعِ، قَالَ: قُلْتُ لِنَافِعٍ: وَمَا الْقَزَعُ؟ قَالَ: يُحْلَقُ بَعْضُ رَأْسِ الصَّبِيِّ وَيُتْرَكُ بَعْضٌ.

Ibn Umar (ﷺ) said that the Prophet (ﷺ) has forbidden Al-Qaza'. He said: "I asked Nāfi': 'What is Al-Qaza'?' He said: 'Shaving only a part of the head and leaving unshaved another part.

(*Bukhari*: 5921 and *Muslim*: 2120)

♦ Start cutting or shaving from the right side:

عَنْ أَنَسِ بْنِ مَالِكٍ أَنَّ رَسُولَ اللهِ ﷺ أَتَىٰ مِنًى، فَأَتَى الْجَمْرَةَ فَرَمَاهَا، ثُمَّ أَتَىٰ مَنْزِلَهُ بِمِنًى وَنَحَرَ، ثُمَّ قَالَ لِلْحَلَّاقِ: «خُذْ» وَأَشَارَ إِلَىٰ جَانِبِهِ الْأَيْمَنِ، ثُمَّ الْأَيْسَرِ، ثُمَّ جَعَلَ يُعْطِيهِ النَّاسَ.

Anas bin Malik (ﷺ) reported that the Prophet (ﷺ) came to Mina; he went to the Jamrah and threw the pebbles at it, after which he went to his lodging in Mina, and sacrificed the animal. He then called for a barber and, turning his right side to him, let him shave it; after which he turned his left side. He then gave (his hair) to the people.

(*Muslim*: 1305)

☾ You may find people with scissors at Marwah, offering (for a small fee) to cut your hair. Many women opt for this, and by doing so, often expose their hair. It is better that they wait until they return to their rooms, and do it in privacy.

☾ For location and cost of barbers for men, see details in chapter 7

UMRAH

If you wish to keep some form of guide (book) with you in order to follow the correct steps for *Umrah*, keep in mind that I have published an *Umrah* pocket guide for this purpose.

⇨ **Performance of *Umrah*:**

Umrah consist of 5 steps:

1. Adopting Ihraam with *Niyah* (at *Meqaat*)
2. Performing *Tawaaf* (7 circuits)
3. Performing 2 *Rak'at Salah* after *Tawaaf*
4. Performing *Sa'ee* (7 laps)
5. Cutting your hair

1. Adopt *Ihraam*:

- Adopt your *Ihraam* clothes and utter your *Niyah* at the *Meqaat* (explained in detail in chapters 5 & 6).

- Recite the *Talbiyah* as often as possible.

- When you enter the *Haram* proceed directly towards the Ka'bah to perform your *Tawaaf*, unless it is time for *Fardh Salah*. Do perform two *Rak'at Tahiyatul-Masjid Salah*, if you plan to sit down prior to performing your *Tawaaf*.

2. Perform *Tawaaf*:

- **Uncover your right shoulder** (men).

- Start at the Hajr-al-Aswad (Black Stone):

  ➤ Kiss it if possible;

  ➤ If not, touch it with your right hand (*Istilam*) and kiss your hand;

  ➤ If this is not possible, then face the Black Stone and with your right hand gesture towards it ONCE only, and DO NOT kiss your hand.

- Say once only:

$$\text{«بِسْمِ اللهِ وَاللهُ أَكْبَرُ»}$$

Bismillahi-wallahu-Akbar

(In the Name of Allah, Allah is the Greatest.)

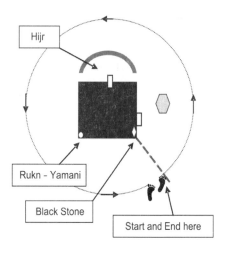

- Proceed in an anti-clockwise (towards the Maqaam Ibraheem) direction.

- Supplicate, make *Dhikr*, recite Qur'an.

- Walk around the Hijr area and not through it.

- Once you reach the **Rukn-al-Yamani** (the southern corner) touch it with your right hand (*Istilam*) and say اللہ أکبر (*Allahu Akbar*). Do not kiss it. If you are unable to touch it, do not gesture towards it, but proceed towards the Hajr-al-Aswad, without saying اللہ أکبر (*Allahu Akbar*). It is *Sunnah* to recite the following between the Rukn-al-Yamani and the Black Stone Corner (note that the *Du'a'* stops at *Adhaaban-Naar*):

﴿رَبَّنَآ ءَاتِنَا فِى ٱلدُّنْيَا حَسَنَةً وَفِى ٱلْأَخِرَةِ حَسَنَةً وَقِنَا عَذَابَ ٱلنَّارِ﴾

Rabbanaa aatina fid-dunya hasanatan wa fil aakhirati hasanatan wa qinaa adhaaban-Naar.

(Oh Allah, give us the good of this world and the good of the Hereafter and protect us from the punishment of Hellfire.)

[*Surah Al-Baqarah* (2), part of *Ayah* 201]

- Once you reach the Hajr-al-Aswad again you have completed 1 circuit.

- Continue by once again either kissing, touching or gesturing towards the Black Stone and say only:

اللهُ أَكْبَرُ

Allahu Akbar

(Allah is the Greatest.)

- Proceed and repeat the aforementioned steps until you have completed 7 circuits.

3. Perform two *Rak'at*:

- Upon completion of the *Tawaaf*, proceed to the Maqaam Ibraheem or any place in the mosque if this area is too crowded.

- It is commendable to say:

$$\text{﴿ وَاتَّخِذُواْ مِن مَّقَامِ إِبْرَهِـعَ مُصَلًّى ﴾}$$

Wattakhithu min Maqaami Ibraheema musalla.

(And take the Station of Ibraheem as a place of prayer.)
[*Surah Al-Baqarah* (2), part of *Ayah* 125]

- Cover your right shoulder and perform 2 *Rak'at* of prayer. I cannot stress enough that it is acceptable to perform the 2 *Rak'at* anywhere in the mosque. As with the kissing of the Black Stone, remember it is best to avoid harming and causing difficulties to fellow Muslims.

- If you are fortunate enough to perform it near the Maqaam, then stand with the Maqaam between you and the Ka'bah (if possible).

- It is *Sunnah* to recite *Suratul-Kafirun* (109) after *Suratul-Fatihah* in the first *Rakah* and *Suratul-Ikhlas* (112), after *Suratul-Fatihah* in the second *Rakah*.

- After finishing the two *Rak'at Salah* it is *Sunnah* to proceed to the well of Zamzam and drink your fill. The well entrance is gone now, so you need to drink from the taps against the wall.

- Then return to the Black Stone and kiss it you are able to do so without crowding other worshippers, saying "*Allahu Akbar*".

- If it is not possible proceed to the *Sa'ee* area without

gesturing or saying "*Allahu Akbar*".

♦ For *Nafl Tawaaf* or *Tawaaf-al-Wadaa*: At this point you are completed.

4. Perform *Sa'ee*:

♦ Proceed to Safaa. When you get close to Safaa it is *Sunnah* to say:

$$﴿ إِنَّ ٱلصَّفَا وَٱلْمَرْوَةَ مِن شَعَآئِرِ ٱللَّهِ ﴾$$

Innassafa walmarwata min sha'aa' irillah.

(Indeed Safaa and Marwah are among the signs of Allah.)

[*Surah Al-Baqarah* (2), part of *Ayah* 158]

♦ Followed by saying:

$$«أَبْدَأُ بِمَا بَدَأَ اللهُ بِهِ»$$

Abda'u bima bada'a Allahu bihi.

(I begin with that which Allah has begun.)

♦ Please note that both the above are only to be said **ONCE,** that is at the beginning of the *Sa'ee* and not at the beginning of every lap.

♦ When ascending Safaa, go up until the Ka'bah is visible (if possible) and facing it, it is Sunnah to repeat the following 3 times while raising your hands as in making *Du'a'* (supplication), and not with your palms facing the Ka'bah. Also do not gesture towards the Ka'bah with your hands as in *Tawaaf*. In between these 3 times you may make your own supplications (i.e. say the following; supplicate; say the following; supplicate; say the following):

» الْحَمْدُ للهِ وَلَا إِلَهَ إِلَّا اللهُ وَاللهُ أَكْبَرُ، لَا إِلَهَ إِلَّا اللهُ وَحْدَهُ لَا

شَرِيكَ لَهُ، لَهُ الْمُلْكُ وَلَهُ الْحَمْدُ يُحْيِي وَيُمِيتُ وَهُوَ عَلَى كُلِّ

شَيْءٍ قَدِيرٌ، لَا إِلَهَ إِلَّا اللهُ وَحْدَهُ، صَدَقَ وَعْدَهُ، وَنَصَرَ عَبْدَهُ،

وَهَزَمَ الأَحْزَابَ وَحْدَهُ».

Alhamdu lillah, wala ilaha illallah, wallahu Akbar. Laa ilaha illallahu wahdahu la shareeka lahu, lahulmulku wa lahulhamdu, yuhyee wa yumeetu wa Huwa ala kulli shay'in Qadeer. La ilaha illallahu wahdahu, sadaqa wa'dahu, wa nasara abdahu, wa hazamal-ahzaaba wahdahu.''

(All praise is due to Allah, none has the right to be worshipped but Allah, and Allah is the Greatest. None has the right to be worshipped but Allah alone, no partners are unto Him, His is the dominion (kingdom) and His is the praise. He gives life and He gives death and He is capable of everything. There is none worthy of worship but Allah alone, who fulfilled His promise, and gave victory to His servant and defeated the Confederates alone.)

(*An-Nasai*: 2977 and *Abu Dawud*: 4547)

♦ Walk towards Marwah. When you arrive at the green fluorescent light, the men should run briskly (if convenient), until the next green light. Women should **NOT** run.

♦ There is no prescribed supplication during the *Sa'ee* or between the two green lights, though you can supplicate and mention Allah as you like. It is also good to recite the Qur'an during the *Sa'ee*. There is nothing from the Prophet (ﷺ) establishing any particular prayer during the *Sa'ee*, but it has been established that Ibn Masood and Ibn Umar (may Allah be pleased with them) used to say:

«رَبِّ اغْفِرْ وَارْحَمْ وَأَنْتَ الأَكْرَمُ»

Rabbighfir warham wa Antal-Akram.

(Oh Allah forgive me and have mercy upon me, for You are the most Mighty and Honourable.)

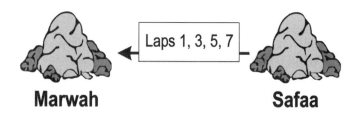

Marwah   **Safaa**

- ☾ But this is without any reference to any particular place where it should be said.

- ◆ Upon reaching Marwah, the 1st lap is complete. Ascend Marwah, face the Ka'bah, and it is commendable to do what was done at Safaa.

- ◆ Proceed back to Safaa (once again men run at the green lights if convenient). The 2nd lap is now complete. Repeat this procedure at Safaa and Marwah until you finish at Marwah, which should be your 7th lap.

- ◆ There is no *Du'a'* at the end of the 7th lap at Marwah.

- ◆ *Sa'ee* is now complete.

    ☾ It is better to perform *Sa'ee* while in the state of *Wudhu'*, but it is permissible to do it without *Wudhu'* (ablution).

5. Proceed to have your hair cut:

- ◆ As mentioned earlier, it is recommended for men to shave their heads and women should cut no more than one

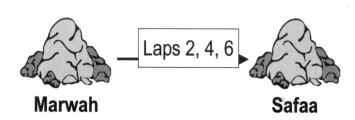

Marwah   **Safaa**

fingertip length (about one inch) from their hair (one place only).

✦ You are now out of the state of *Ihraam*.

✦ **Umrah is complete.**

✦ You may now adopt your normal clothes again.

➔ **Complete:**

• If you feel somewhat concerned or disappointed that you have not performed your *Umrah* 'correctly', don't. Most people feel this way after their first Umrah.

⇨ **What Next?**

➔**What are the best actions?**

• Spend your time attending *Salah* at the *Haram* (remember each *Fardh Salah* in the *Haram* has 100,000 times reward, compared to any other Mosque, except the Prophets mosque in Madinah (1,000) and Al-Quds (500) in Jerusalem).

• Also keep yourself busy with recitation of the Qur'an, *Nafl Salah* and *Nafl Tawaaf*. As mentioned earlier, *Nafl Tawaaf* is one of the best forms of *Ibadah* while in Makkah.

• Many people spend lots of time shopping. Try not to waste your time shopping and in idle discussions. Time is precious, so use it well.

➔ **Performing multiple *Umrahs*:**

✦ If we look at the practice of the Prophet (ﷺ) and of his companions (may Allah be pleased with them), we do not find them doing this at all. They did not try to accumulate many *Umrahs* on the same trip. Had there been any virtue in doing so, they would not have omitted that. **Therefore, doing many Umrahs on the same trip is not recommended.** One may do so only when one wants to do the *Umrah* on behalf of someone else, or in fulfillment of a pledge.

A person, who has already done the *Umrah* and wishes to do another *Umrah*, he is required to leave Makkah and the *Haram* area, enter into *Ihraam* again, and come back to do the same duties again. This is not logical, considering that he is already in the area, which is most blessed on earth, with access to the Ka'bah, the place to which all Muslims turn when they pray.

If you consider the duties that the *Umrah* involves, you will find that they are four: Entering into the state of *Ihraam*; *Tawaaf*; *Sa'ee*; and then releasing oneself from Ihraam by shaving one's head or cutting one's hair. So apart from the *Ihraam* (being in the state of consecration and releasing oneself from it), there are only the *Tawaaf* and *Sa'ee* left. As mentioned previously that the Prophet (ﷺ) described *Tawaaf* as a form of prayer and that it is highly recommended to perform as many voluntary *Tawaafs* as possible while in Makkah.

Sa'ee on the other hand, is a duty of *Umrah* and *Hajj* only. It cannot be done except as part of either duty. It may not be offered voluntarily for any reason. Therefore a person who goes out of Makkah in order to do a second *Umrah* is not able to do anything which he may not do while in Makkah, except for *Sa'ee*, which is not something we are encouraged to volunteer on its own. One can easily do as many *Tawaafs* as one wish while one is inside Makkah, without going through the rituals that a second *Umrah* involves.

- So in summary, we cannot say it is wrong to perform multiple *Umrahs*; also not all scholars agree that you can do *Umrah* on behalf of someone else, so the recommendation here is to stick with the rites that are established with 100% certainty.

Aishah (ﷺ) narrated that the Prophet (ﷺ) said:

«مَنْ أَحْدث في أَمْرِنا هذَا ما لَيْسَ فِيهِ فَهُوَ رَدٌّ» .

"If somebody innovates something which is not in harmony with the principles of our religion, that thing is rejected."

(*Bukhari* : 2697)

- I have seen many people perform *Umrah* almost daily but sleep through the *Fardh Salah* times, due to tiredness.

- Save yourself some energy and do the following instead:

  Anas bin Malik (may Allah be pleased with him) narrated that the Prophet (ﷺ) said:

  «مَنْ صَلَّى الْفَجْرَ فِي جَمَاعَةٍ ثُمَّ قَعَدَ يَذْكُرُ اللهَ حَتَّى تَطْلُعَ الشَّمْسُ ثُمَّ صَلَّى رَكْعَتَيْنِ كَانَتْ لَهُ كَأَجْرِ حَجَّةٍ وعُمْرَةٍ»

  "Whoever performs Salatul-Fajr in congregation and remains in the place (Masjid) busy with Dhikr of Allah, and then performs two Rak'at after sunrise, he will get the reward equal to that of performing Hajj and Umrah."

  (*Tirmidhi* : 586)

- How Great and Merciful is Allah? Do not make things difficult for yourself by exerting your energy in actions that have no basis in the Sunnah. This *Salah* is called *Salatul-Duha*. It is sometimes referred to as *Salatul-Ishraq*.

- Even though you will find many taxis outside the *Haram* shouting "Small *Umrah*" (from Tan'iym) and "Big *Umrah*" (from Ji'ranah), do not be tempted.

- **Question:** How many *Umrahs* did the Prophet (ﷺ) perform in his lifetime?

  ○ **Answer:** 4 (all in the month of *Dhul-Qadah*)

⇨ **Departure from Makkah:**

→ **Going to Madinah:**

- Take this opportunity to visit Madinah if time and finances permit.

- For details about Madinah, see chapter 10, in this book.

- If it is Ramadaan and you do not have pre-arranged accommodation in Madinah, then you may have trouble finding a place to stay as Madinah is extremely crowded during the peak times.

- Ensure that all your luggage is securely packed. Do not place fragile items in your luggage.

- Do not forget to take some Zamzam water with you as it is not readily available in Madinah.

→ **Going Home:**

- Reconfirm your flights at the appropriate time. Do not wait until the last minute.

- Make sure you know which terminal you will be departing from: Hajj Terminal, South Terminal (Saudi Arabian Airlines), or North Terminal (other Airlines). During busy periods such as Ramadaan, *Umrah* flights may also depart from the Hajj Terminal.

- Arrange to ship any cargo you may have well ahead of your departure date.

- Ensure that you have all your luggage and it is securely packed.

- If you happen to have any Saudi Riyals left, do not spend them all, as you may need money at the airport to buy food, in the event of any delays. Also you can always use it when you come again. Alternatively you can keep it and give it as a gift to pilgrims in the future.

- You may also need money for any excess baggage (overweight) charges.

- If you are with a group and your baggage is not overweight, I suggest you do not check in with the group. From experience, you may end up paying, as the group as a whole may have excess baggage, and they will collect money from everybody.

- Some airlines count your Zamzam weight as part of your 20kg allowance, so check with your airline.

- Zamzam is not allowed as carry-on (hand) luggage anymore.

- Do not put the Zamzam water containers inside your suitcase.

- Do not neglect your *Salah* on your way home, even if it means performing it on the aeroplane. Most airlines are obliging, if you request a small space to pray. Normally by the entry door is a good place.

→ **Supplication for the return journey:**

«اللهُ أَكْبَرُ اللهُ أَكْبَرُ اللهُ أَكْبَرُ، سُبْحَانَ الَّذِي سَخَّرَ لَنَا هَذَا وَمَا كُنَّا لَهُ مُقْرِنِينَ، وَإِنَّا إِلَىٰ رَبِّنَا لَمُنْقَلِبُونَ، اللَّهُمَّ! [إِنَّا] نَسْأَلُكَ فِي سَفَرِنَا هَذَا الْبِرَّ وَالتَّقْوَىٰ، وَمِنَ الْعَمَلِ مَا تَرْضَىٰ، اللَّهُمَّ! هَوِّنْ عَلَيْنَا سَفَرَنَا هَذَا، وَاطْوِ عَنَّا بُعْدَهُ، اللَّهُمَّ أَنْتَ الصَّاحِبُ فِي السَّفَرِ، وَالْخَلِيفَةُ فِي الْأَهْلِ، اللَّهُمَّ! إِنِّي أَعُوذُ بِكَ مِنْ وَعْثَاءِ السَّفَرِ، وَكَآبَةِ الْمَنْظَرِ، وَسُوءِ الْمُنْقَلَبِ فِي الْمَالِ وَالْأَهْلِ»، (وَإِذَا رَجَعَ قَالَهُنَّ، وَزَادَ فِيهِنَّ:) «آئِبُونَ، تَائِبُونَ، عَابِدُونَ، لِرَبِّنَا حَامِدُونَ».

Allahu Akbar, Allahu Akbar, Allahu Akbar. Subhanaladhee sakh-khara lana hadhaa wa maa kunnaa lahu muqrineen, wa innaa ilaa Rabbanaa lamunqaliboon. Allahumma (innaa) nasaluka fee safarinaa hadhal-birr wa-taqwaa, wa minal a'mali maa tardaa. Allahumma howwin a'laynaa safaranaa hadhaa, watwi 'annaa bu'dahu. Allahumma Antas-Saahibu fissafari, wal-khalifatu fil-ahli. Allahumma inni a'oodhubika min wa'thaa'is-safari, wa kaabatil-manthari, wa soo'il-

munqalabi filmaali wal-ahli. Ayiboona, taa'iboona, 'aabidoona, lirabbinaa haamidoona.

(Allah is the Greatest, Allah is the Greatest, Allah is the Greatest, How perfect He is, The One Who has placed this (transport) at our service, and we ourselves would not have been capable of that, and to our Lord is our final destiny. O Allah we ask You for *Birr* and *Taqwaa* in this journey of ours, and we ask You for deeds which please You. O Allah, make easy for us this journey of ours and fold up (i.e., shorten) for us its distance. O Allah, You are the companion in travel and the caretaker of the family. O Allah, I seek refuge in You from the hardship of travel and from (finding) a distressing sight or an unhappy return in regard to (my) property and family. We return, repent, worship and praise our Lord.)

(*Muslim* : 3275)

(*Birr* & *Taqwaa* = Two comprehensive terms which individually, refer to all good actions and obedience.)

Chapter 9
Ramadaan

Ramadaan O beautiful Ramadaan...

The details in this chapter about planning, visas, accommodation, *Salah*, etc., is for Ramadaan only. So, please read the other chapters as well to help you with the overall planning of your trip.

Ramadaan is by far the busiest *Umrah* period. Also within Ramadaan, there are busier periods than others. For example, the first ten days are the least busy, followed by the next ten days. The last ten days being almost as busy and crowded as *Hajj*. Having said that, since the new Umrah rules, Ramadaan from day one is extremely busy. My guess is, it is not because the new rules are allowing more people to come; no it is because people are now much more selective as to when they come. If you are going to go through the 'pain' of new booking procedures, paying upfront and new visa regulations, then you may as well make it worth it and come at a time that will yield the highest reward. The term busy is relative to what you are used to, so when I say extremely busy, I mean the Haram is packed from side to side, the walkways outside are full etc. As an example on the 27th night there are about 2 million people in the *Haram* in Makkah. And when I say as busy as *Hajj*, well only those that have been for *Hajj* can relate to that. So be prepared for the crowd!

I have also listed some of the 'negative' things that sometimes happen, so you can be aware and be prepared. Having said this, I would like to mention that Ramadaan in Makkah is 'addictive'. "One Ramadaan in Makkah and you will keep on coming. Ramadaan will never be the same again for you, in any other part of the world." I personally have been blessed to have spent many years in Makkah-al-Mukarramah during Ramadaan, and I will not trade it for anything in the world.

Over the last few years I opted to spend the last ten days in Madinah instead, as Makkah was just getting tooooo full. Well what can I say, Makkah has the reward, but believe me, Madinah is 'something else'. Normally the packages with Madinah instead of Makkah for the last ten days are cheaper, so if finances are tight then Madinah is a good option. Remember, I did not say it is not crowded...

⇨ **Reward of *Umrah* in Ramadaan**

Ibn 'Abbas reported that the Prophet (ﷺ) said:

«عُمْرَةٌ فِي رَمَضَانَ تَعْدِلُ حَجَّةً» .

"An 'Umrah in the month of Ramadaan is equal (in reward) to performing a Hajj."

(*Ahmad* : 2670 and *Ibn Majah* : 2994)

سَمِعْتُ ابْنَ عَبَّاسٍ رَضِيَ اللهُ عَنْهُما يُخْبِرُنا يَقُولُ: قَالَ رَسُولُ اللهِ ﷺ لِامْرَأَةٍ مِنَ الأَنْصَارِ – سَمَّاها ابْنُ عَبَّاسٍ فَنَسِيتُ اسْمَهَا –: «مَا مَنَعَكِ أَنْ تَحُجِّي مَعَنا؟» قَالَتْ: كَانَ لَنا نَاضِحٌ فَرَكِبَهُ أَبُو فُلانٍ وَابْنُهُ، لِزَوْجِها وَابْنِها، وَتَرَكَ نَاضِحًا نَنْضَحُ عَلَيْهِ، قَالَ: «فَإِذَا كَانَ رَمَضَانُ اعْتَمِرِي فِيهِ، فَإِنَّ عُمْرَةً فِي رَمَضَانَ حَجَّةٌ»

I heard Ibn 'Abbas ﷺ saying, "Allāh's Messenger asked an Anṣari woman (Ibn 'Abbas named her but 'Ataa forgot her name), 'What prevented you from performing Hajj with us?' She replied, 'We have a camel and the father of so-and-so and his son (i.e., her husband and her son) rode it and left one camel for us to use for irrigation.' He ﷺ said (to her), 'Perform 'Umrah when Ramadan comes, for 'Umrah in Ramadan is equal to Hajj (in reward),' or said something similar."

(*Bukhari* : 1863)

⇨ **Planning:**

- If you are able to perform *Umrah* in Ramadaan, certainly do so. Once again good planning is important, as the flights are extremely busy.

- Many Muslims prefer to be 'home' for *Eid* and miss one of the most beautifull (not to mention the reward) *Eid* mornings one can imagine. Some people try so hard to be home in time, they not only miss *Eid* in Makkah but they also miss it at home, especially if their home country has *Eid* on the same day as Makkah. My advice is to stay in Makkah. If you have to be home around that time, then ensure your flight is not on *Eid* morning. Remember *Eid* in Makkah is based on the actual sighting of the moon, so it may not be on the same day as the calendar shows. Plan well, and forget about being home for *Eid*. Stay in Makkah!

- Sometimes I am amazed at the lack of planning and priorities some Muslims have when it comes to planning a trip to Makkah, be it for *Umrah* or *Hajj*. One Shabaan I met someone in Madinah who came for *Umrah* for the first time. I asked him about his trip and this is what he told me: "We have just come from Makkah where we spent 3 days and performed a couple of Umrah's; we arrived in Madinah yesterday and we will stay for 8 days, as you know we must complete 40 *Salah's* here; we will then go to Jakarta for 5 days on our way home".

- So what do you think he could have done differently in order to get more reward from his trip? Spend more time in Makkah?; come in Ramadaan as Shabaan is so close?; just two points that come to mind.

- Maybe he had some valid reasons (the 8 days in Madinah is not a valid one, see chapter 10). The point I am trying to make is, look at your trip as a 'business' trip. Where and how will you get the most return (rewards) on your investment?

⇨ **Visas:**

* One of the biggest problems Saudi Arabia faces today is the overstaying of many Muslims on *Umrah* and *Hajj* visas. Overstaying, meaning not by a few days or weeks, no, staying behind to obtain work and remaining indefinitely in the country. Hence its current tough stand on issuing of visas.

* You cannot stay from Ramadaan until *Hajj*. There is no mechanism to convert your *Umrah* visa into a *Hajj* visa. It is not allowed.

* There are no *Umrah* visas issued from the last week of Ramadaan until after *Hajj* (Safar).

• Obtain your *Umrah* visa as early as possible.

• Your travel agent will arrange the visa.

• The maximum visa length has been extended from two weeks to one month.

• If your outbound flights are not confirmed, they will not issue you with a visa.

• If you have no Mahram, they will not issue you with a visa. Some exceptions are made if a woman is over the age of 45.

• If you plan to go for *Hajj* in the same year or plan to perform *Umrah* again within six months, check first with the embassy if you will be able to obtain another visa.

⇨ **Accommodation:**

• Ramadaan accommodation prices are in a league of its own. You may consider it 'supply and demand', but I consider it total exploitation.

• The prices for accommodation during Ramadaan are more than it is during *Hajj* time.

• To give you an idea of the prices:

   ❖ For a double room (average hotel):

Normal price	- SR150.00 per night
1st ten days	- SR350.00 per night
Days 11-20	- SR450.00 per night
Last ten days	- SR700.00 per night

- For the last 10 days it is normally all or nothing. Meaning you cannot take only a few days, you must take all 10 days.

- There are some small rooms in some of the five star hotels that sell for as much as SR35,000.00 for the last ten days only. No it is not a typo, it is thirty five thousand.

- On the other hand, you can rent an entire apartment (2 rooms, kitchen etc.) for about SR14,000 for the entire month of Ramadaan. These apartments are generally further away from the Haram. A similar apartment closer to the Haram will cost you in excess of SR19,000. There is normally a very small price difference for the entire month versus the last ten days only.

- The problem is they sell.

- Madinah accommodation is also expensive, but not as much as Makkah. There are many packages that offer the first twenty days in Makkah and the last ten days in Madinah. As mentioned before this normally cost much less than the reverse option.

- Ridiculous, but true...

⇨ **Processing upon arrival:**

◆ If you are going directly to Makkah, ensure you adopt your *Ihraam* at the *Meqaat*.

* On occasions the authorities use the Hajj Terminal to process the arrivals, due to the sheer number of flights.

* If you arrived at the Hajj Terminal, it is very likely that you will also depart from the Hajj Terminal. Check this with your airline when you reconfirm your flight.

- Once you arrive at Jeddah, be prepared for some delays

due to the number of people and flights arriving at the same time.

- The queues are normally very long and also the processing may take very long at immigration and customs. It has improved considerably over the last few years.

- Keep some dates, water and some biscuits with you in your hand luggage. Many times people are 'stuck' in the queue during *Iftaar* (breaking of fast) time. There are no facilities to buy food inside the immigration area.

- If you are waiting to be processed and you calculate that you will not be done by *Salatul-Maghrib*, arrange to perform *Wudhu'* and prepare yourself to have *Iftaar* and to perform *Salah* inside the immigration area.

- Many people tend to neglect their prayers, while waiting to be processed.

- The immigration and customs officers will stop work at *Iftaar* time, until after *Maghrib*. So, relax and be patient.

- Unlike before when you had to find a taxi yourself to go to Makkah or Madinah, with the new rules, your transport should have been pre-arranged.

- You should be received by a representative from the *Umrah* company who arranged all your accommodation. If the representative is not available, go to the *Hajj* and *Umrah* office at the airport for help.

⇨ **Transport:**

* See in chapter 4 under 'Transport' for details about transport.

- The taxi fares for short trips within and around Makkah are normally much higher than normal during Ramadaan.

⇨ **The starting and completion of the month of Ramadaan:**

The Prophet (ﷺ) said:

«صُومُوا لِرُؤْيَتِهِ وأَفْطِرُوا لِرُؤْيَتِهِ، فإِنْ غُبِّيَ عَلَيْكُمْ فأَكْمِلُوا عِدَّةَ شَعْبَانَ ثَلَاثِينَ».

"Start observing Saum (fasts) on seeing the crescent moon of Ramadaan, and stop observing Saum (fasts) on seeing the crescent moon (of Shawaal), and if the sky is overcast (and you cannot see it), complete thirty days of Shabaan."

(*Bukhari*: 1909)

Narrated 'Abdullâh bin 'Umar (؆) that Allah's Messenger (؀) said:

«الشَّهْرُ تِسْعٌ وَعِشْرُونَ لَيْلَةً فَلَا تَصُومُوا حَتَّى تَرَوْهُ، فإِنْ غُمَّ عَلَيْكُمْ فأَكْمِلُوا الْعِدَّةَ ثَلَاثِينَ».

"The month (can be) 29 nights (i.e. days), and do not observe Saum (fast) till you see the crescent, and if the sky is overcast, then complete (Sha'ban) as 30 days."

(*Bukhari*: 1907)

- Over the last few years there is a great deal of speculation about the moon sighting. I suggest you don't delve into this and just keep in mind that the start and end dates may not match the calendar dates.

- The feeling of everybody starting and finishing at the same time is just so great, after years of having lived in environments where there is constant bickering on the moon issue at Ramadaan time. I call them the moon professors, and they only surface this time of the year. What a great feeling to be away from them! I am sure you will also 'enjoy' this.

⇨ **Working hours/holidays:**

* The working hours for shops, offices and government centres are different from the normal working hours. They open later in the mornings and close after *Salatul-Zuhr*. They normally open again only after *Salatul-Ishaa* and remain open until about 02:00am.

* The food shops are closed all day. They open about 30 minutes before *Salatul-Maghrib* and normally remain open until about thirty minutes before *Salatul-Fajr*.

* It is public holidays in Saudi Arabia starting the last five days of Ramadaan until about a week after *Eid*, which means all government offices, banks etc., are all closed. Most shops remain open.

⇨ **Personal Behaviour:**

• Recognize that you are going on a spiritual trip that necessitates some hardship and sacrifice. It demands from you to be patient. Expect the least relaxation and the maximum rewards from Allah.

• Expect less sleeping, less comfort, less eating, lots of walking, due to the crowds.

• Expect too many people that over-crowd the streets, the hotels, and every other place you can imagine.

• Prepare yourself, so you can transcend all these barriers and remember the Day of Judgement when every human being is to be assembled and to be judged by Allah.

• Avoid sitting in the walkways. If you are 'forced' to perform *Salah* here, move out of the way immediately after the *Fardh Salah*.

• Many people tend to sit and eat in the walkways after *Salatul-Maghrib*, and get upset if people trample over them. Be wise and sit out of the way.

• When you arrive early at the *Haram* for prayer you may find lots of space to sit and perform *Salah* comfortably. Within no time you will find that this 'space of yours' gets eroded bit by bit as the *Haram* starts filling up. Now you can do one of two things. You can 'fight' with every person that tries to sit too close to you, or you can try and accommodate them. From experience, I can guarantee you that you will not be able to hold on to 'your territory' for very long. So avoid stress and adopt an attitude of: "this mosque does not belong to me, we are all guests of Allah, and hence we are all entitled to be in it". This is especially true for the *Jumuah* prayer and during the last ten days of Ramadaan.

- However, when you are late, try not to push in and walk over the top of people. Your rightful place for being late is at the back. You may ask, but why should I adhere to the rules when nobody else does? Simple, Allah knows!

$$\text{﴿وَمَا تَفْعَلُواْ مِنْ خَيْرٍ يَعْلَمْهُ ٱللَّهُ﴾}$$

"...*And whatever good you do, (be sure) Allah knows it...*"

[*Surah Al-Baqarah* (2), part of *Ayah* 197]

- Due to the layout of the roads that lead to the mosque, cars and people are constantly 'mixing' while going to and from the mosque. Be careful while walking or crossing the street as the drivers expect the pedestrians to give way.

- There are always long queues at the public phones and people tend to argue as they are tired, hot and hungry. Keep your composure and try not to get angry. I found the least busy time to do anything, such as phoning or going to the hospital or shop etc., is about fifteen minutes before the *Salah*. After any *Salah* is the 'worst' time to do any of these things.

- If you have a pager or a mobile phone, please turn it off prior to going into the mosque. It is very disturbing when a mobile phones ring during *Salah*. What is even worse is that during *Salatul-Taraaweeh*, people actually have conversations on their mobile phones while the *Salah* is in progress.

- **Spitting:** There is no need to spit all the time while you are fasting. This is a very bad habit and some people do it all the time in Makkah. When you hear that ominous sound that preludes a spit, you better give way, as some people spit in all directions. Well, what more can I say? Don't do it.

⇨ **Performing *Umrah* :**

- How to perform *Umrah* is covered in the previous chapter.

- Be prepared for a large crowd.

- If you are tired and it is during the day, I suggest you delay your *Umrah* until after *Maghrib* or *Taraaweeh* prayer. This way you will be rested and have had something to eat. You will need the energy.

- There is no extra reward or benefit in performing *Umrah* in the hot sun.

- Do not make things difficult for you while you are fasting.

- If you decide to go during the day and you have small children accompanying you, take some water with you. The Zamzam containers are not available during the day, and the children are bound to get thirsty. If you forget, then keep in mind that you can always take them to the Zamzam taps near the *Tawaaf* area.

- The average time it takes to complete an *Umrah* is about two hours.

- **Shoes:** For *Umrah* and *Salah*, I strongly suggest you keep your shoes with you. During Ramadaan the cleaners throw out all plastic bags from inside the mosque. On one occasion we were sitting outside the *Haram* when the cleaners threw out a big bundle of plastic bags and shoes. In no time people converged on this bundle and started trying on shoes for size and took off with it. Some people took many pairs. There were even some baby clothes and milk bottles. I found this very unusual as the shoes all appeared to be good and expensive type shoes. It wasn't shoes or bags that were left behind for a long time. A few hours later, my fears were confirmed when people in *Ihraam* started coming to look for their belongings. I noticed the same cleaner pointing them into the direction where he dumped the shoes. They were all gone! What happened was that these people merely placed their belongings inside the mosque in a place which they deemed to be safe, while they were going to perform *Umrah*. Seems like no place is 'safe' inside the mosque for any parcels or shoe bags, as the cleaners apply different rules, during Ramadaan.

⇨ **Beggars:**

- As with *Hajj*, Ramadaan is a peak time for the beggars. As a matter of fact there are more of them during Ramadaan, as they know people tend to be more generous during this time.

- The authorities are trying to reduce the beggars, but as you can imagine it is a very difficult task.

- Please review the notes on beggars in chapter 7 of this book, where I list the types of beggars you may come across.

- During Ramadaan though, I have experienced two new styles of begging: The first being where they wait for you at the newspaper store to beg or grab your change. The second, being very professional and reaping lots of money in the process. How they do it: Mostly after *Salatul-Asr*, when people are relaxed and reciting Qur'an in the mosque while waiting for *Iftaar*, you will find a man in *Ihraam* standing up and starting to cry real loud. He will then continue by lifting the top of his *Ihraam* to show you how his money belt has been cut, and that all his money and documents have been stolen. He will continue to cry as he takes of the belt to show it to people. In no time people from everywhere will come to give him money as he is still crying. After about fifteen minutes he stops crying, while he puts all the money away and continues to tell his story to anyone who is interested. People are amazed and display outrage that someone can do this to a fellow

Muslim in *Ihraam*. Now before you part with your money. I have seen the same man in the same *Ihraam* with the same belt for more than one week in different parts of the mosques acting out the same scenario. I took the liberty of following him around the mosque area to try to ascertain his credibility. Needless to say that he is a fraud. Worst of all, he is not the only one. If you come across this scene and feel convinced, I suggest you follow him after *Salah* before you part with your money. If you want to give him money anyway, give him, but please still follow him after *Salah* (if you have time) and see how disgusted you feel (as I felt) after you see him repeat his act.

- Last year the authorities arrested groups of beggars and found a great deal of money on them. Thousands that is!

- Many of these beggars even use their babies as a means to gain your sympathy.

- I suggest you give any charity (money) to the men and women that clean the mosque as well as the street cleaners.

- Having said all that, don't despair, as Allah will reward you based on your *Niyah*, even if the receiver is a fraud.

⇨ **The Shameless:**

- If you think the professional beggars are bad, think again!

- At least the beggars give you the option of giving them money or not.

- The following stories are all factual and it shows to what level some Muslims will go to obtain money:

  ➤ "My wallet was stolen from my pocket while I was in the crowd coming out from the mosque."

  ➤ "I was late, so I put my shoes down in front of me, and went into *Sujood*. When I came out of *Sujood*, my shoes were gone."

  ➤ "I had just put my bag down right in front of me, and started performing my *Sunnah Salah*. When I came up from *Sujood*, I noticed my bag and shoes were gone. It had my passport and all my money. I went to report it immediately, but the policeman told me how common this was and that it was not likely that I would get my bag back. Fortunately for me, my passport was found lying in the street and was handed in to my embassy."

➤ "I had just completed my *Umrah* and was very tired. I decided to rest for a while in the mosque as the next *Salah* was only an hour away. I was lying down next to a pillar with my small bag next to me, when a man came to sit next to me with a Qur'an and started reciting. I must have dozed off, because the man was gone and so was my bag, with my money and passport."

➤ "We were both very excited as we left the university in Madinah to go to Makkah for *Umrah*. We got a taxi, placed all our luggage in the trunk, and proceeded to Dhul-Hulaifah (*Meqaat*). Without a second thought, we both jumped out at the *Meqaat* to go into the mosque and to adopt our *Ihraam*. Yes, you've guessed it. When we came out, the taxi was gone with all our luggage. I'm not sure what he was hoping to get, as we are merely students."

• I am trying to highlight that you should be very careful and vigilant with your bag, luggage, money and any valuables that you may have. Not everybody is here for the same reasons you are.

• Don't carry your passport with you to the mosque.

• Don't place any valuable items in your bag and then leave it unattended, even while performing *Salah*.

• Don't carry your wallet in your back or side pocket, during the busy times or in any crowded area. Sad but true!

⇨**Sleep:**

• During Ramadaan, night becomes day and day becomes night!

- If you have children living in the same hotel or apartments as you, then be prepared for noise all night long.

- If you can hear the traffic or car-horns from your room, forget about any sleep.

- If there is any construction near you, forget about sleep.

- If you request any service, such as changing of a bulb, or cleaning of your room, don't be shocked when they turn up at 2:00am to do it.

- Well you say, I will just complain to the hotel management. I have experienced all of the above, at different times, over the last many years, and have tried all avenues, with no success.

- Try to be patient!

⇨ **Shopping:**

- If you plan to do gift shopping, I suggest you do it as early as possible in Ramadaan. Prices generally stay the same, but there are less bargaining (meaning less discount) in the last two weeks. The demand is high. The shops are also very crowded.

- Most shops are closed on *Eid* day. If you plan to go to Jeddah for shopping, keep in mind that many shops are closed for at least three days (*Eid* day and the two days following).

- After *Salah* you may find many street 'vendors' selling all sorts of things, from clothes, toys, electrical items, and watches to pyjamas. You will see them along the street displaying their goods on a bed sheet, while he is holding on to the ends of the sheet and his eyes are ever watchful. The reason for this is that they are illegal traders and plain-clothes police are constantly chasing and arresting them. Many times you will be standing with goods in your hand and the seller will have run away. This is to your advantage, but once I was waiting for my change, when the police came and the vendor ran off breaking the 100 meters world record. Another time I had to run after him to pay him. They do have some good bargains though.

⇨ *Suhur:*

◆ It is recommended to have *Suhur* (morning meal).

Narrated Anas bin Maalik (礪): The Prophet (礪) said:

«تَسَحَّرُوا فإِنَّ فِي السَّحُورِ بَرَكَةً» .

"Take Suhur as there is a blessing in it."

(*Bukhari :* 1923)

◆ It is recommended to have it as close to *Salatul-Fajr* as possible. Some people insist on eating early and also to stop eating long before the *Adhaan*. Many hotels serve *Suhur* around 1:00am. To have *Suhur* that early and to stop long before the *Adhaan* for *Salatul-Fajr*, are contrary to the advise of our beloved Prophet (礪).

عَنْ زَيْدِ بْنِ ثابِتٍ رَضِيَ اللهُ عَنْهُ قالَ : تَسَحَّرْنا مَعَ النَّبِيِّ ﷺ ثُمَّ
قَامَ إِلَى الصَّلَاةِ، قُلْتُ : كَمْ كَانَ بَيْنَ الْأَذَانِ وَالسَّحُورِ؟ قالَ :
قَدْرُ خَمسينَ آيَةً .

Narrated Zaid bin Thaabit (礪): We took the Suhur with the Prophet (礪). Then he stood for As-Salaat (the prayer). I asked, "What was the interval between the Suhur and the Adhaan?" He replied, "The interval was sufficient to recite fifty Verses of the Qur'ân."

(*Bukhari :* 1921)

◆ Many interpret this as the time one should stop eating, before the *Adhaan*. No, it means the *Suhur* was delayed until that amount of time, before the *Adhaan*, which actually means the opposite to what most people understand. Start eating at this time, not stop eating. Another meaning is that it merely indicates the time they took from the start of *Suhur* until the time for *Iqaamah* (at that time, the *Iqaamah* was referred to as *Adhaan*). Either way, it highlights that the *Suhur* was delayed to be very close to *Salatul-Fajr*.

* All the food shops remain open all night until the *Adhaan* for *Salatul-Fajr*.

* There is a big rush just before *Suhur*, so be early to avoid fraying tempers. I have witnessed people fighting for the last available food in restaurants.

⇨ **When to stop Eating:**

﴿وَكُلُوا۟ وَٱشْرَبُوا۟ حَتَّىٰ يَتَبَيَّنَ لَكُمُ ٱلْخَيْطُ ٱلْأَبْيَضُ مِنَ ٱلْخَيْطِ ٱلْأَسْوَدِ مِنَ ٱلْفَجْرِ﴾

"...and eat and drink until the white thread (light) of dawn appears to you distinct from the black thread (darkness of the night)..."

[*Surah Al-Baqarah* (2), part of *Ayah* 187]

It is narrated by 'Adi bin Hâtim (ﷺ) that when the Verses were revealed: "Until the white thread appears to you, distinct from the black thread," I took two (hair) strings one black and the other white, and kept them under my pillow and went on looking at them throughout the night but could not make anything out of it." So, the next morning I went to Allah's Messenger (ﷺ) and told him the whole story. He explained to me,

«إِنَّمَا ذَلِكَ سَوَادُ اللَّيْلِ وَبَيَاضُ النَّهَارِ».

"That Verse means the darkness of night and the whiteness of dawn."

(*Bukhari* : 1916)

It is narrated by Aishah (ﷺ) that Bilal used to pronounce the *Adhaan* at night, so Allah's Messenger (ﷺ) said,

«كُلُوا واشْرَبُوا حَتَّى يُؤَذِّنَ ابْنُ أُمِّ مَكْتُومٍ، فإِنَّهُ لَا يُؤَذِّنُ حَتَّى
يَطْلُعَ الفَجْرُ».

"Carry on taking your meals (eat and drink) till Ibn Umm Maktum pronounces the Adhaan, for he does not pronounce it till it is dawn."

(*Bukhari*: 1918 & 1919)

♦ On numerous occasions I have noticed that people continue to eat or drink and worst of all, smoke, during the *Adhaan* of *Fajr*. The rule is simple. When you hear the *Adhaan* (not when it is completed), you must stop eating immediately. You may finish what you have in your mouth. (i.e., if you are busy chewing on a sandwich, you may finish what you are chewing and not the rest of the sandwich; if you were drinking water or tea and had the cup in your hand, you may complete the last mouthful).

⇨ Buying of food:

- You do not need to take dates or food to the *Haram* as there are many areas in the mosque where people give *Sadaqah* by providing free dates, *Laban*, tea, Arabic coffee etc. Some areas (outside area) even provide soup and other food items. You are not allowed to take food items inside the mosque.

- There are many people that distribute dates and food parcels for free outside the *Haram* area and in the roads leading to the mosque. The behaviour of the Muslims fighting for the free food is even more embarrassing than the mess they make inside the mosque.

- If you plan to buy dates or food for free distribution, be careful when distributing it, as you will be 'mobbed' and you may lose more than you bargained for.

- If you plan to buy food after *Maghrib*, be prepared to stand in long queues and the tempers are worse than those at *Suhur* time. So exercise some patience. Plan ahead of time. Buy food early if possible.

- The courtyard area around the *Haram* is where many people sit to eat, and break their fast. Most men go inside the mosque for *Maghrib*, although many men pray outside, even if it means standing behind women. Avoid it.

⇨ *Iftaar* (breaking of the fast):

It is narrated by Umar bin Al-Khattab that Allah's Messenger (ﷺ) said,

«إِذا أَقْبَلَ اللَّيْلُ مِنْ هَاهُنا وأَدْبَرَ النَّهارُ مِنْ هاهُنا وغَرَبَتِ الشَّمْسُ فَقَدْ أَفْطَرَ الصَّائِمُ».

"When night falls from this side and the day vanishes from this side and the sun sets, then the fasting person should break his fast."

(*Bukhari*: 1954)

It is narrated by Sahl bin Sad: Allah's Messenger (ﷺ) said,

«لا يَزَالُ النَّاسُ بِخَيرٍ ما عَجَّلُوا الفِطْرَ».

"The people will remain on the right path as long as they hasten the breaking of the fast."

(*Bukhari*: 1957)

عَنْ أَنَس بن مَالِكٍ قَالَ: كَانَ رَسُولُ الله ﷺ يُفْطِرُ عَلَى رُطَبَاتٍ قَبْلَ أَنْ يُصَلِّيَ، فإِنْ لَمْ تَكُنْ رُطَبَاتٌ فَعَلَى تَمَرَاتٍ، فإِنْ لَمْ تَكُنْ حَسَا حَسَواتٍ مِنْ مَاءٍ.

It is narrated by Anas (ﷺ) who said: "Allah's Messenger (ﷺ) used to break the fast with fresh dates before praying, and if not fresh dates then with older dates, and if not with dates then with some mouthfuls of water."

(*Abu Dawud*: 2356, *Tirmidhi*: 694 and *Ahmad*: 3/164)

- Ever wondered where the word breakfast (break fast) came from?

- Food items are not allowed inside the mosque. Only dates, tea, fruit etc., are allowed. Many people 'smuggle' all sorts of food inside. The mess people make inside and outside the mosque is a sheer embarrassment for the behaviour of Muslims.

- Avoid breaking your fast, by smoking a cigarette.

- The cleaners will start cleaning up the floors soon after *Maghrib,* and you are expected to move out of the way, otherwise they will clean over the top of you.

⇨ **Cannon announcements:**

* Sometimes you will hear the sound of a cannon shooting at: *Suhur* starting time, *Iftaar* time and also to announce *Eid* (if Ramadaan is only 29 days).

⇨ *Salah* **times:**

* *Salatul-Ishaa* is two hours after *Maghrib,* instead of the normal one and a half-hours.

* *Salatul-Taraaweeh* starts about five minutes after the completion of *Salatul-Ishaa*.

* The time between the *Adhaan* and the *Iqaamah* is fifteen minutes for *Zuhr* and *'Asr* but only ten minutes for *Fajr, Maghrib* and *Ishaa*. On the night before *Eid,* this time for *Ishaa* is fifteen minutes and also for *Fajr* on *Eid* morning, instead of the normal ten minutes.

* The total elapsed time for *Ishaa, Taraaweeh* and *Witr* is only about two hours.

* The total elapsed time for *Qiyam-ul-Layl* and *Witr* is about one and a half to two hours.

* The time between the two *Adhaans* for *Salatul-Jumu'ah* is only 5 minutes.

* Try and be in the mosque at the latest before 11:30am for *Salatul-Jumuah*. After this, you will not be able to find a place inside and you may be forced to sit in the sun outside.

The Ultimate Guide to *Umrah*

* For any of the *Salah*, if you are not inside the mosque at the
  time of *'Iqaamah*, you may be 'caught' in the street as even
  the walkways and entrances will be full.

* There are two *Adhaans* in the morning. One is called one
  hour before the *Adhaan* of *Salatul-Fajr*, and the second is the
  Adhaan for *Salatul-Fajr*.

It is narrated by Abdullah bin Umar that the Prophet
(ﷺ) said,

«إِنَّ بِلَالًا يُنَادِي بِلَيْلٍ، فَكُلُوا وَاشْرَبُوا حَتَّى يُنَادِيَ ابْنُ أُمِّ
مَكْتُومٍ».

*"Bilal pronounces the Adhaan at night so that you may eat
and drink till Ibn Umm Maktum pronounces the Adhaan (for
the Fajr prayer)."*

(*Bukhari* : 620)

◆ **Being Late:** On many occasions, people come late for
  Salatul-Ishaa, and only arrive once *Salatul-Taraaweeh* has
  already started. They then start their own congregation to
  perform *Salatul-Ishaa*. The correct method is to join the
  Taraaweeh congregation and complete your third and
  fourth *Rak'at* once the *Imam* has made *Tasleem* at the end
  of the two *Rak'at Salah* for *Taraaweeh*.

◆ If you arrive and the *Imam* has not started *Taraaweeh Salah*
  then wait, don't start your own *Ishaa* congregation.

⇨ *Salatul-Taraaweeh*:

* If the month of Shaban is only twenty-nine days, and the
  announcement of Ramadaan comes later in the evening
  (after *Salatul-Ishaa*), then the first *Taraaweeh Salah* will be the
  following night.

* If Shaban is thirty days, then the first *Taraaweeh Salah* will
  be performed on the same night (30th day)

* In Makkah and Madinah they perform twenty *Rak'at* for
  Salatul-Taraaweeh.

* The *Salah* starts about five minutes after the completion of *Salatul-Ishaa*.

* There are no extended pauses after every two *Rak'at*, except after the tenth *Rak'at*, when there is a change of *Imam*.

* Generally there are two *Imam*s that lead the *Taraaweeh Salah*, each leading for ten *Rak'at*.

* It normally takes about one and half to two hours to complete.

⇨ 8 or 20?

• The thing I like most about *Salatul-Taraaweeh* in Makkah is that it is always twenty *Rak'at*. No argument. For those who live in countries where there is the constant argument about whether *Salatul-Taraaweeh* should be 8 or 20 *Rak'at*, will know what I mean.

• I do not even plan to delve into the arguments or views here, as most people are quite knowledgeable on this subject, come Ramadaan. I would merely like to make a point to encourage my fellow Muslims to take the opportunity in Makkah and to complete twenty *Rak'at* with the congregation.

• I have witnessed many people leave after eight, only to find them sitting in front of the television or to go shopping.

• Let us draw a hypothetical analogy: Let us say for a moment that your father owns an orchard and he asks you to pick some fruit for him. He promises you that he will give you at least $10.00 for each piece of fruit you pick. However he will not able to pay you directly, but he will place the money in your account for you. As you trust your father, I am sure you will accept the deal, and will try to pick as much fruit as possible, right? Now your Creator, Whom you should trust more than your father, makes you an offer. He tells you that for each *Rak'at* you make He will place a certain amount (no less than 10), in your account with Him. Now why is it that you choose to do less? Is it because you cannot see the reward? Or is it just laziness? Whatever it is, fellow Muslims, do not miss this golden opportunity to 'build-up' your account with Allah. Make 20!

- In Makkah it seems more like 10 or 20, as there is a large exodus after 10 *Rak'at*. Hence, if for some reason you have to leave early, I suggest you leave after 8 or 12 *Rak'at*.

- I cannot understand why we should even discuss about doing less when we have such an incredible 'offer':

Narrated Abu Hurairah: I heard Allah's Messenger (ﷺ) saying regarding Ramadaan:

«مَنْ قَامَ رَمَضَانَ إِيمَانًا وَاحْتِسَابًا غُفِرَ لَهُ مَا تَقَدَّمَ مِنْ ذَنْبِهِ» .

"Whoever prayed at night in it (the month of Ramadaan) out of sincere faith and hoping for a reward from Allah, then all his previous sins will be forgiven."

(*Bukhari* : 37)

⇨ *Salatul-Witr* :

Oh how much disputes we have when it comes to *Salah*, especially during Ramadaan? Why is it so, you may ask? Well my guess is that most of us are merely following what our fathers have been doing. *Salatul-Witr* is no exception and not only in Ramadaan, but during normal days as well. It is very simple, yet we complicate it, mainly due to unsubstantiated views. So fellow Muslims, I have taken the time to find the appropriate *Ahadith* for the views expressed in this book, so I urge you to follow it unless you have authentic proof to the contrary. And saying merely I have heard from so and so, is not enough. Proof!

Jabir reports that the Messenger of Allah (ﷺ) said:

«مَنْ خَافَ مِنْكُمْ أَنْ لاَ يَسْتَيْقِظَ مِنْ آخِرِ اللَّيْلِ ، فَلْيُوتِرْ مِنْ أَوَّلِ اللَّيْلِ ثُمَّ لِيَرْقُدْ . وَمَنْ طَمِعَ مِنْكُمْ أَنْ يَسْتَيْقِظَ مِنْ آخِرِ اللَّيْلِ ،

فَلْيُوتِرْ مِنْ آخِرِ اللَّيْلِ. فَإِنَّ قِرَاءَةَ آخِرِ اللَّيْلِ مَحْضُورَةٌ. وَذٰلِكَ
أَفْضَلُ»۔

"Whoever of you fears that he will not be able to wake during the latter portion (of the night), he should make the Witr prayer during the early part (of the night). And whoever of you believes that he will be able to wake during the latter portion of the night, he should make the Witr prayer during that latter portion as it is the blessed time (the angels are attentive to the prayers in the last portion of the night)."

(*Muslim* : 755, *Tirmidhi* : 455, *Ibn Majah* : 1187 and
Ahmad : 389/3)

عَنْ عَائِشَةَ قَالَتْ: كُلَّ اللَّيْلِ أَوتَرَ رَسُولُ اللهِ ﷺ وانْتَهى وِتْرُهُ
إلى السَّحَرِ۔

It is narrated by 'Aishah (﵂) that Allah's Messsenger (ﷺ) offered Witr prayer at different nights at various hours extending (from the Ishaa prayer) up to the last hour of the night.

(*Bukhari* : 996)

* *Salatul-Witr* is performed in congregation immediately after *Salatul-Taraaweeh*.

* During the last ten days, *Salatul-Witr* is **not** performed after *Salatul-Taraaweeh*, instead it is performed immediately after *Qiyam-ul-Layl* (night prayer). Some people refer to this *Salah* as *Tahajjud*. Though all night prayers (including *Taraaweeh* and *Tahajjud*) are regarded as *Qiyam-ul-Layl*, I will refer to the late prayer as *Qiyam-ul-Layl* for the sake of clarity.

* *Qunoot* (*Du'a'* in the last *Rakah*) is generally performed in *Salatul-Witr*.

* *Salatul-Witr* is generally performed as 2+1 (with two *Tasleems*) or 3 straight (one *Tashahud*). This method also

confuses some people as they may have never experienced *Witr* performed like this.

➤ Three *Rak'at* with one *Tasleem*:

* *Witr* is never performed 2+1 with one *Tasleem* (like *Maghrib*). Why?

Abu Hurrairah reported that the Prophet (ﷺ) said:

«لَا تُوتِرُوا بِثَلَاثٍ، أَوْتِرُوا بِخَمْسٍ أَوْ سَبْعٍ، وَلَا تُشَبِّهُوا بِصَلَاةِ الْمَغْرِبِ»

"Do not pray Witr as three Rak'at, either pray 5 or 7 Rak'at, and do not resemble the Maghrib prayer."

(*Daraqutni* : 1650)

➤ One *Rak'ah*:

* Many Muslims refuse to pray 2+1 as they believe that performing one *Raka'h* of *Salah* is invalid. Below I have listed only two *Ahadith* proving the authenticity of one *Rak'ah*.

أَخْبَرَنِي عَبْدُ اللهِ بْنُ ثَعْلَبَةَ بْنِ صُعَيرٍ - وكانَ رَسُولُ اللهِ ﷺ قَدْ مَسَحَ عَيْنَهُ -: أَنَّهُ رَأَى سَعدَ بْنَ أَبِي وَقَّاصٍ يُوتِرُ بِرَكعَةٍ.

It is narrated by Abdullah bin Thalabah bin Su'air, whose eye Allah's Messenger (ﷺ) had touched, that he had seen Sa'd bin Abi Waqqas offering one Rak'ah only for the Witr prayer.

(*Bukhari* : 6356)

Allah's Messenger (ﷺ) said:

«صَلاةُ اللَّيْلِ مَثْنَى مَثْنَى، فإِذَا خَشِيَ أَحَدُكُمُ الصُّبْحَ صَلَّى رَكْعَةً وَاحِدَةً، تُوتِرُ لَهُ ما قَدْ صَلَّى».

"The night prayer is two by two. If anyone of you fears that the morning fall is approaching, let him conclude the prayer with one Rak'ah, making the number that he prayed odd."

(*Bukhari* : 990)

> ➤ **Do not perform *Salatul-Witr* more than once in the same night:**

Talq bin Ali narrated that he heard the Messenger of Allah (ﷺ) say:

«لَا وِتْرَانِ فِي لَيْلَةٍ»

"There are no two Witr prayers in one night."

(*Abu Dawud*: 1439, *An-Nasa'i*: 1680 and *Tirmidhi*: 470)

عَنْ أَبِي جَمْرَةَ قَالَ: سَأَلْتُ عائِذَ بِنَ عَمْرو - وكانَ مِنْ أَصحابِ النَّبِيِّ ﷺ، مِنْ أَصحابِ الشَّجَرَةِ -: هَلْ يُنْقَضُ الوِتْرُ؟ قَالَ: إِذَا أَوْتَرْتَ مِنْ أَوَّلِهِ فَلَا تُوتِرْ مِنْ آخِرِهِ.

Narrated by Abu Jamrah, I asked Aidh bin Amr, who was one of the Companions of the Prophet (ﷺ), one of those (who gave the allegiance to the Prophet (ﷺ) beneath the Tree: "Can the Witr prayer be repeated (in one night)?" He said, "If you have offered it in the first part of the night, you should not repeat it in the last part of the night."

(*Bukhari*: 4176)

♦ Hence, you should perform *Salatul-Witr* only once in any given night. If you decided after *Salatul-Taraaweeh* to perform *Salatul-Witr* and you later decide to perform *Qiyam-ul-Layl*, then you should not sit during *Salatul-Witr* as many people do. Instead, when the *Imam* completes *Salatul-Witr* after the third *Rak'ah*, you should stand and complete four. These four *Rak'at* will be regarded as *Nafl* for you. More reward!

♦ Whoever has performed the *Salatul-Witr* and then wishes to perform some more *Salah*, he may do so but he is not to repeat the *Witr*.

♦ There is also no evidence from the Qur'an or *Sunnah* that one must sleep before one can perform another *Salah* after having performed *Salatul-Witr*.

عَنْ أُمِّ سَلَمَةَ أَنَّ النَّبِيَّ ﷺ كَانَ يُصَلِّي بَعْدَ الْوِتْرِ رَكْعَتَيْنِ خَفِيفَتَيْنِ، وَهُوَ جَالِسٌ.

"Umm Salamah also narrates that the Prophet (ﷺ) prayed two Rak'at while sitting, after the Witr prayer."

(*Ibn Majah* : 1195, *Tirmidhi* 471 & *Ahmad* : 6/299)

- There are many people who plan to perform *Salatul-Witr* on their own later in the night. Because of this they tend to sit while the congregation is performing *Salatul-Witr* after *Salatul-Taraaweeh*. If you plan to do this I suggest you perform *Salatul-Witr* with the congregation. When they *Tasleem* on the third *Rakah* you stand to complete four *Rak'at*. This way you will obtain reward for four extra *Rak'at Nafl Salah*. Remember, it is Ramadaan and you are in Makkah, so you need to get as much rewards as possible. If you choose not to perform *Salatul-Witr* with the congregation, just because you do not ascribe to the method (2+1), then I suggest you ponder over the following *Hadith*. The emphasis being the reward for praying behind the *Imam* until he has finished:

عَنْ أَبِي ذَرٍّ قَالَ: صُمْنَا مَعَ رَسُولِ اللهِ ﷺ رَمَضَانَ. فَلَمْ يَقُمْ بِنَا شَيْئًا مِنْهُ. حَتَّى بَقِيَ سَبْعُ لَيَالٍ. فَقَامَ بِنَا لَيْلَةَ السَّابِعَةِ حَتَّى مَضَى نَحْوٌ مِنْ ثُلُثِ اللَّيْلِ. ثُمَّ كَانَتِ اللَّيْلَةُ السَّادِسَةُ الَّتِي تَلِيهَا. فَلَمْ يَقُمْهَا. حَتَّى كَانَتِ الْخَامِسَةُ الَّتِي تَلِيهَا، ثُمَّ قَامَ بِنَا حَتَّى مَضَى نَحْوٌ مِنْ شَطْرِ اللَّيْلِ. فَقُلْتُ: يَا رَسُولَ اللهِ لَوْ نَفَّلْتَنَا بَقِيَّةَ لَيْلَتِنَا هٰذِهِ. فَقَالَ: «إِنَّهُ مَنْ قَامَ مَعَ الإِمَامِ حَتَّى يَنْصَرِفَ، فَإِنَّهُ يَعْدِلُ قِيَامَ لَيْلَةٍ» ثُمَّ كَانَتِ الرَّابِعَةُ الَّتِي تَلِيهَا، فَلَمْ يَقُمْهَا. حَتَّى كَانَتِ الثَّالِثَةُ الَّتِي تَلِيهَا. قَالَ، فَجَمَعَ نِسَاءَهُ وَأَهْلَهُ وَاجْتَمَعَ النَّاسُ. قَالَ، فَقَامَ بِنَا حَتَّى خَشِينَا أَنْ يَفُوتَنَا الْفَلَاحُ. قِيلَ: وَمَا الْفَلَاحُ؟ قَالَ: السُّحُورُ. قَالَ، ثُمَّ لَمْ يَقُمْ

بِنَا شَيْئاً مِنْ بَقِيَّةِ الشَّهْرِ.

It is narrated by Abu Dharr: "We fasted with the Messenger of Allah (ﷺ) during Ramadaan, but he did not make us get up at night for prayer at any time during the month till seven nights remained; then he made us get up for prayer till a third of the night had passed. When the sixth remaining night came, he did not make us get up for prayer. When the fifth remaining night came, he made us stand in prayer till a half of the night had gone." So I said: "Oh, Messenger of Allah, I wish you had led us in supererogatory prayers during the whole of tonight." He said: When a man prays with an Imam till he finishes (the Imam) he is reckoned as having spent a whole night in prayer. On the fourth remaining night he did not make us get up. "When the third remaining night came, he gathered his family, his wives, and the people and prayed with us till we were afraid we should miss the Falah (success)." I said: "What is Falah?" He said: "The meal before daybreak. Then he did not make us get up for prayer during the remainder of the month."

(*Ibn Majah* : 1327 and *Abu-Dawud* : 1370)

➢ **Other methods of *Witr*:**

* As many Muslims are not aware of the various methods of how *Qiyam-ul-Layl* and *Witr* can be performed, I decided to include a brief of some of the methods. I will merely explain the manner. This should wet your appetite to learn more on this subject.

Abu Ayyub Al-Ansari reported that Allah's Messenger (ﷺ) said:

«الْوِتَرُ حَقٌّ فَمَنْ شَاءَ فَلْيُوتِرْ بِخَمْسٍ، وَمَنْ شَاءَ فَلْيُوتِرْ بِثَلَاثٍ وَمَنْ شَاءَ فَلْيُوتِرْ بِوَاحِدَةٍ»

"Witr is true (as a recommended act of worship). Anyone who wishes may pray five (Rak'at); and anyone who wishes may

pray three; and anyone who wishes may pray one."

(*Al-Hakim* 1/302)

1. Pray thirteen *Rak'at* in pairs, starting with a short pair, followed by a very long pair, then a shorter pair, then a shorter pair, then a shorter pair, then a shorter pair, then one *Rak'ah* for *Witr*.

2. Pray thirteen *Rak'at*, making *Tasleem* at the end of each pair of the first eight, and then praying *Witr* as five *Rak'at*, with no sitting or *Tasleem* except in the last one.

3. Pray eleven *Rak'at*, making *Tasleem* at the end of each pair, and concluding with one *Rakah* for *Witr*.

4. Pray eleven *Raka't*, four with only one *Tasleem*, then four more in the same way, then three.

5. Pray eleven *Rak'at*, performing the first eight without sitting (for *Tashahhud*) except in the eighth, and then, without *Tasleem*, pray *Witr* as one *Rak'ah* concluded with *Tasleem*. Then pray two *Rak'at* while sitting.

⇨ Qur'an Recitation:

♦ There is no other time of the year like Ramadaan, when so many Muslims busy themselves with reciting the Qur'an. Be one of them!

♦ Take the time to understand the meaning, instead of just trying to complete the entire Qur'an as quick as possible.

♦ You will notice some people keeping the Qur'an in their hands while 'following' the *Imam* during *Salatul-Taraaweeh*. This is not recommended.

♦ Don't read aloud while you are in the mosque to avoid disturbing you fellow Muslims.

♦ Do not place the Qur'an on the floor.

* The entire Qur'an is recited over the course of 29 nights during *Salatul-Taraaweeh*.

• Familiarise yourself with the places of *Sajdah-Tilaawah*

(place of prostration while reciting or listening to the Qur'an).

- Many people embarrass themselves when they go into *Ruku'* instead of *Sujud* for *Sajdah-Tilaawah*.

- *Sajdah-Tilaawah* is done on the following nights in *Salatul-Taraaweeh*: 8th, 12th, 13th, 14th, 15th, 16th (x2), 18th (x2), 20th, 23rd, 26th, 29th (x2).

- Also for *Salatul-Fajr* it is *Sunnah* to recite *Surah Sajdah* on a Friday. Once again, be aware that a *Sajdah-Tilaawah* will be performed in the first *Rak'ah*.

⇨ *Du'a'* :

Narrated by Abdullah bin 'Amr bin Al-'Aas who said that Allah's Messenger (ﷺ) said:

«إِنَّ لِلصَّائِمِ عِنْدَ فِطْرِهِ لَدَعْوَةً مَا تُرَدُّ» .

"Indeed there is for the fasting person, when he breaks his fast, a supplication which is not rejected."

(*Ibn Majah* : 1753)

* So use this opportunity and supplicate as much as you can while fasting and when breaking your fast.

* *Du'a'* (*Qunoot*) in congregation is performed almost every night in the last *Rak'at* of *Salatul-Witr*. Occasionally (one or two nights) it is not done (to indicate that it is not *Wajib*).

* *Du'a'* is also performed in the last *Rak'at* after the completion of the Qur'an recitation (normally on the 29th night).

* These *Du'a's* are normally quite long. The average time is about fifteen minutes. A few years ago the *Du'a'* on the 27th night was about fifty minutes. So rest those feet, and don't delay going to the toilet, thinking that the *Salah* is almost done.

* **Recording:** If you are interested in buying an audio cassette of the *Du'a'*, they are normally available the very

next day (sometimes within hours) from the cassette shops.

⇨ *Tawaaf*:

♦ As with any other time, performing *Tawaaf* is one of the best forms of *Ibadah* while in Makkah.

* Women are stopped from entering the *Tawaaf* area about half an hour before *Salah*.

• As with *Hajj*, during Ramadaan the *Tawaaf* area is very full at most times.

• Some of the busiest times are: After *Salatul-Asr* until *Salatul-Maghrib*; in the morning about one hour before *Salatul-Fajr*. During the last ten days, even after *Salatul-Maghrib* it is very busy.

• In the past the least busiest time was between 7:00am and about 10:00am. The last few years there seems to be no quiet time anymore, not even in the middle of the day.

⇨ *Sadaqah* (Charity):

عَنِ ابْنِ عَبَّاسٍ رَضِيَ اللهُ عَنْهُما قَالَ: كَانَ النَّبِيُّ ﷺ أَجْوَدَ النَّاسِ بِالخَيْرِ، وكَانَ أَجْوَدَ ما يَكُونُ فِي رَمَضَانَ، حِينَ يَلْقَاهُ جِبْرِيلُ، وكَانَ جِبْرِيلُ عَلَيْهِ السَّلامُ يَلْقَاهُ كُلَّ لَيْلَةٍ فِي رَمَضَانَ حَتَّى يَنْسَلِخَ، يَعْرِضُ عَلَيْهِ النَّبِيُّ ﷺ القُرْآنَ، فَإِذَا لَقِيَه جِبْرِيلُ عَلَيْهِ السَّلامُ، كَانَ أَجْوَدَ بِالخَيْرِ مِنَ الرِّيحِ المُرْسَلَةِ.

"It is narrated by Ibn Abbas ؓ that the Prophet (ﷺ) was the most generous amongst the people, and he used to be more so in the month of Ramadaan when Gabriel visited him, and Gabriel used to meet him on every night of Ramadaan till the end of the month. The Prophet (ﷺ) used to recite the Noble Qur'an to Gabriel, and when Gabriel met him, he used to be more generous than a fast wind (which causes rain and welfare)."

(*Bukhari* : 1902)

Allah's Messenger (ﷺ) said:

«مَنْ فَطَّرَ صَائِمًا كَانَ لَهُ مِثْلُ أَجْرِهِ غَيْرَ أَنَّهُ لَا يَنْقُصُ مِنْ أَجْرِ الصَّائِمِ شَيْئًا».

"He who gives food for a fasting person to break his fast, he will receive the same reward as him, except that nothing will be reduced from the fasting person's reward."

(*Ahmad* : 4/115, *Tirmidhi* : 807 and *Ibn Majah* : 1746)

◆ So what are you waiting for?

◆ Give as much charity as you can. Be it money, dates, food, kindness, etc.

⇨ *Fidyah* (Expiation):

◆ For those that are unable to fast, due to sickness or otherwise, and need to pay expiation (see *Surah* 2, *Ayah* 184), can buy or make food/date parcels to give out at the mosque area.

• Once again, be careful while distributing any food as it can be very hazardous due to the unruly behaviour of certain Muslims.

⇨ Last ten days:

عَنْ عَائِشَةَ رَضِيَ اللهُ عَنْها قَالَتْ: كَانَ النَّبِيُّ ﷺ إِذا دَخَلَ الْعَشْرُ شَدَّ مِئْزَرَهُ وَأَحْيَا لَيْلَهُ وَأَيْقَظَ أَهْلَهُ.

"Narrated by Aishah ﷺ that with the start of the last ten days of Ramadaan, the Prophet (ﷺ) used to tighten his waist belt (i.e. work hard) and used to pray all the night, and used to keep his family awake for the prayers."

(*Bukhari* : 2024)

كَانَ رَسُولُ اللهِ ﷺ يَجْتَهِدُ فِي الْعَشْرِ الْأَوَاخِرِ، مَا لَا يَجْتَهِدُ فِي غَيْرِهِ.

"Allah's Messenger (ﷺ) used to exert himself in devotion

during the last ten nights to a greater extent than at any other time."

(*Muslim* : 1175)

- This is by far the busiest time in Makkah.

- Adopt a different schedule for going to the *Haram* as it gets very full much earlier than in the previous days.

- There is not much, if any, sleep during the last 10 days.

⇨ *Qiyamul-Layl* (Night Prayer):

♦ There are numerous *Ayat* and *Ahadith* that tells us about the great benefits for the night prayers:

$$﴿ وَالَّذِينَ يَبِيتُونَ لِرَبِّهِمْ سُجَّدًا وَقِيَامًا ﴾$$

"And those who spend the night in worship of their Lord, prostrate and standing."

[*Surah Al-Furqan* (25), *Ayah* 64]

'Amr bin Abasah reports that he heard the Prophet (ﷺ) say:

«أَقْرَبُ مَا يَكُونُ الرَّبُّ مِنَ الْعَبْدِ فِي جَوْفِ اللَّيْلِ الْآخِرِ فَإِنِ اسْتَطَعْتَ أَنْ تَكُونَ مِمَّنْ يَذْكُرُ اللهَ فِي تِلْكَ السَّاعَةِ فَكُنْ».

"The closest that a slave comes to his Lord is during the middle of the latter portion of the night. If you can be among those who remember Allah, the Exalted One, at that time then do so."

[*Tirmidhi* : 3579, *Ahmad* : 4/111-112 and *Ibn Khuzaimah* : 1147]

حَدَّثَنِي أَبُو مُسْلِمٍ قَالَ: قُلْتُ لِأَبِي ذَرٍّ: أَيُّ قِيَامِ اللَّيْلِ أَفْضَلُ؟ قَالَ أَبُو ذَرٍّ: سَأَلْتُ رَسُولَ اللهِ ﷺ كَمَا سَأَلْتَنِي فَقَالَ: جَوْفُ اللَّيْلِ الْغَابِرِ أَوْ نِصْفُ اللَّيْلِ وَقَلِيلٌ فَاعِلُهُ.

Abu Muslim asked Abu Dharr: "Which late-night prayer is the best?" He said: "I asked the Messenger of Allah (ﷺ) the same that you asked me and he said, 'The (one done during) middle of the latter half of the night, and very few do it.' "

(Ahmad 5/179)

* *Qiyamul-Layl Salah* in the mosque starts on the 21st night (20th day) of Ramadaan.

* This *Salah* normally starts at 1:00am. This time may change, so check it with someone on the day.

* It consists of ten *Rak'at*.

* Normally they start the recitation from *Surah Al-Baqarah* again. (There were some years when they continued the recitation from where *Salatul-Taraaweeh* finished on the night).

* Every two *Rak'at* takes approximately fifteen minutes to complete. There is a longer pause in all the actions of the *Salah* with an even extended pause in the *Ruku'* (to make more *Dhikr*) and in the *Sujud* (for you to make *Du'a'*).

* This *Salah*, including *Salatul-Witr*, normally takes about one and half to two hours to complete.

* Take a prayer mat with you, just in case you do not get a space on the carpet. The *Sujood* is very long and your forehead will hurt after a while on the marble.

* As this *Salah* is not a normal practice in many parts of the world during Ramadaan, many people that are in Makkah are not aware of it, until after a few nights have already passed.

* Many people are aware of it, but claim that they are too tired. They watch television instead. What a tragedy! Fellow Muslims, do not miss this great opportunity to gain so much reward.

* As a friend once told me, when I was getting agitated with the people watching television and missing the *Taraaweeh Salah*: "What do you expect? Do you think that people that never attend *Taraaweeh Salah* when they are at home, will suddenly now attend because they are in Makkah?" I was

more optimistic and believed that because they had made the effort to come all the way to Makkah that they will behave differently. Well, sad as it is, old habits die hard. The point I am trying to make is that, don't believe that being in Makkah will 'make' you go to mosque, when it is not part of your habit already.

* One year, we spent hours trying to convince people of the benefits of *Qiyam-ul-Layl*. Fellow Muslims, do not waste your money and precious time. Prayer is better than sleep!

⇨ *I'tikaf*:

عَنْ عَائِشَةَ رَضِيَ اللهُ عَنْهَا قَالَتْ: كَانَ النَّبِيُّ ﷺ يَعْتَكِفُ فِي الْعَشْرِ الأَوَاخِرِ مِنْ رَمَضَانَ، فَكُنْتُ أَضْرِبُ لَهُ خِبَاءً فَيُصَلِّي الصُّبْحَ ثُمَّ يَدْخُلُهُ.

"Aishah ؓ said that the Prophet (ﷺ) used to practice I'tikaf in the last ten days of Ramadaan and I used to pitch a tent for him, and after offering the morning prayer, he used to enter the tent."

(*Bukhari* : 2033)

أَنَّ النَّبِيَّ ﷺ كَانَ يَعْتَكِفُ الْعَشْرَ الأَوَاخِرَ مِنْ رَمَضَانَ حَتَّى تَوَفَّاهُ اللهُ تَعَالَى، ثُمَّ اعْتَكَفَ أَزْوَاجُهُ مِنْ بَعْدِهِ.

"The Prophet (ﷺ) used to practice I'tikaf in the last ten days of Ramadaan till he died and then his wives used to practice I'tikaf after him."

(*Bukhari* : 2026)

♦ *I'tikaf* is when one spends a length of time (normally in the last ten days of Ramadaan) in a mosque without indulging in any marital relations or worldly affairs. Where possible, the person does not leave the mosque premises at all.

➢ **How it is done in Makkah:**

   * On the 20th day after *Salatul-Asr*, the *Haram* fills

up with many people who will perform *I'tikaf*.

* You will notice clothes and *Ihraams* on almost every pillar in the mosque as each one claims his territory for the next ten days.

* There are also women in *I'tikaf*, in separate areas of the mosque. There are no designated areas, but people just claim space on a first come first serve basis.

* As there are no *Wudhu'* or toilet facilities on the mosque premises and also no food is allowed inside the *Haram*, those in *I'tikaf* are 'forced' to leave the mosque premises. As long as it is only for the essential needs (toilet, shower, eating etc.) then the *I'tikaf* rules are not violated.

• If you plan to perform *I'tikaf*: If you performed *Umrah* before going into *I'tikaf* (not a requirement) and you had a shower and changed into your normal clothes, be aware that the guards will not allow you to enter the mosque with your *Ihraam* in a bag or in your hands. As many people use their *Ihraam* as a blanket, I suggest you change into your clothes inside the mosque. Alternatively you can wear (hide)·the *Ihraam* underneath your clothes.

• The guards are normally very strict as to what you can or cannot take inside the mosque. With this in mind, I am sure you will be as amazed as I am, when you see some of the things people managed to 'smuggle' in.

• **Madinah:** The rules are similar in Madinah. However they are a bit more organized. There are designated areas where you are allowed to stay and they have a registration process. Ask one of the guards at the doors for directions to the processing area. I suggest you check this out a few days before the 20th Ramadaan.

⇨ *Laylat-ul-Qadr* **(Night of Decree):**

• Note the title. It is not night of power, it is night of decree.

- On which night is it?

It is narrated by 'Aishah 🌸 that Allah's Messenger (ﷺ) said:

«تَحَرَّوْا لَيْلَةَ القَدْرِ في الوِتْرِ مِنَ العَشْرِ الأَوَاخِرِ مِنْ رَمَضَانَ».

"Search for the Night of Qadr in the odd nights of the last ten days of Ramadaan."

(Bukhari : 2017)

It is narrated by Ubadah bin As-Samit that the Prophet (ﷺ) came out to inform us about the Night of *Qadr* but two Muslims were quarreling with each other. So, the Prophet (ﷺ) said:

«خَرَجْتُ لأُخْبِرَكُمْ بِلَيْلَةِ القَدْرِ فَتَلاحَى فُلانٌ وفُلانٌ فَرُفِعَتْ وعَسىٰ أَنْ يَكُونَ خَيْرًا لَكُمْ، فالتَمِسُوها في التَّاسِعَةِ والسَّابعةِ والخَامِسَةِ».

"I came out to inform you about the Night of Qadr but such-and-such persons were quarreling, so the news about it had been taken away; yet that might be for your own good, so search for it on the 29th, 27th and 25th (of Ramadaan)."

(Bukhari : 2023)

Narrated by Ibn Abbas that Allah's Messenger (ﷺ) said:

«هِيَ فِي الْعَشْرِ الأَوَاخِر، هِيَ فِي تِسْعٍ يَمْضِينَ، أَوْ فِي سَبْعٍ يَبْقَيْنَ»

"The Night of Qadr is in the last ten nights of the month (Ramadaan), either on the first nine or in the last (remaining) seven nights (of Ramadaan)."

Ibn 'Abbas added:

«التمسُوا في أَرْبَعٍ وعشرِينَ».

"Search for it on the twenty-fourth (of Ramadaan)."

(Bukhari : 2022)

- What is the reward of this night?

Surah Al-Qadr (97)

﴿إِنَّا أَنزَلْنَٰهُ فِى لَيْلَةِ ٱلْقَدْرِ ۞ وَمَآ أَدْرَىٰكَ مَا لَيْلَةُ ٱلْقَدْرِ ۞ لَيْلَةُ ٱلْقَدْرِ خَيْرٌ مِّنْ أَلْفِ شَهْرٍ ۞ تَنَزَّلُ ٱلْمَلَٰٓئِكَةُ وَٱلرُّوحُ فِيهَا بِإِذْنِ رَبِّهِم مِّن كُلِّ أَمْرٍ ۞ سَلَٰمٌ هِىَ حَتَّىٰ مَطْلَعِ ٱلْفَجْرِ﴾

1. *Verily We have sent it (this Qur'an) down in the Night of Al-Qadr (Decree)*

2. *And what will make you know what the night of Al-Qadr (Decree) is?*

3. *The Night of Al-Qadr (Decree) is better than a thousand months (i.e. worshipping Allah in that night is better than worshipping Him a thousand months, i.e. 83 years and 4 months).*

4. *Therein descend the angels and the Ruh (Jibreel (Gabriel)) by Allah's Permission with all Decrees.*

5. *Peace! (All that night, there is Peace and Goodness from Allah to His believing slaves) until the appearance of dawn.*

- I have mentioned only three out of many *Ahadith* about the instruction to look for the Night of Decree in the last ten nights of Ramadaan. Yet, you find so many Muslims claiming that it is on the 27th night. Do they know better than the Prophet (ﷺ)?

- So, contrary to popular belief, the Night of *Al-Qadr* (Decree) is not necessarily on the 27th night of Ramadaan. It is clear from the *Ahadith* that it can be any night in the last ten nights. Hence coming only on the 27th night and believing that it is *Laylat-ul-Qadr* is a great loss for many Muslims around the world, not to mention those in Makkah. I am not saying it cannot be on the 27th night. What if it was on the 25th night? Then you have certainly missed out, big time! So, if you are able, seek for the Night of *Al-Qadr* (Decree) in the last ten nights, and if you are not able to do that, then at least seek for it in the odd nights (21, 23, 25, 27 & 29).

⇨ **27th Night:**

• It seems that no matter how much you teach or explain to certain Muslims the above, they still come for *Umrah* specifically on the 27th night. If you think the mess they make with the food, or the fighting for the free food is a shame, then you have not seen the behaviour of some of the Muslims on this night in the *Tawaaf* area. Fellow Muslims, I urge you. If you have to perform *Umrah* on this night, then please check your personal behaviour, as you are in the House of Allah in the most auspicious month, on one of the most auspicious nights.

• This is the busiest night in Ramadaan. There are times when there are over two million people in and around the *Haram* on this night.

• If you wish to secure a place inside the mosque, you must do so after *Salatul-Asr*. Do not leave until after *Salatul-Taraaweeh*. If you plan to return for *Qiyam-ul-Layl*, then you should be back at least an hour before the *Salah* starts.

• There is normally a very long *Du'aa'* in the last *Rak'at* of *Salatul-Witr*, so rest your feet. Go to the toilet early if you need to, as the *Du'a'* extended to almost 50 minutes during one year.

• I suggest you bring your own food instead of buying on this night, as the shops are extremely crowded. Our practice over the last few years has been, to take plenty of dates, tea and some small sandwiches. We secure a place on the roof after *Salatul-Asr* and only leave an hour after *Salatul-Taraaweeh* to go and eat something more substantial and to use the toilets. We immediately return to our space, which we secured with our prayer mats. It also helps to leave at least one person to 'guard' your space. Obviously you have to be creative as to how you get the sandwiches into the mosque. If you do take food of any kind inside, treat it as you would your own house do not mess on the floor or carpets.

- If you are late, not even your 'protected' space will be available. On many occasions the actual doors of the *Haram* gets closed to avoid any more people from entering, as it is already like a can of sardines inside. Corner to corner, there is no space, not even for a fly.

- After *Qiyam-ul-Layl*, you may leave to eat something for *Suhur*. Once again the food shops are extremely crowded.

- Ensure that you return early enough for *Salatul-Fajr*. Not as crowded as in the night, but still full.

- Do not even consider to perform *Nafl Tawaaf* on this night, as you will be 'crushed' in the crowds. If you wish to do so, then try to do it around midnight when there is a lull in the crowd.

- Almost the entire area around the Ka'bah is cleared (no place for *Salah*) to allow room for those performing *Tawaaf*. For those who have performed *Hajj* and can remember the crowds during *Tawaaf-al-Ifadah*, will know what I am talking about. For those who haven't performed *Hajj*, and wish to observe, I suggest you go to the roof area to watch.

⇨ **29th Night — Completion of the Qur'an recitation:**

- This is normally on the 29th night (28th day). This is a 'very special event' for me personally.

- It is just as busy and crowded as on the 27th night. Except there are not that many people performing *Umrah*.

- The issues of crowds, food, and securing a place in the *Haram* for *Ishaa* and *Taraaweeh*, are the same as that of the 27th night.

- The completion of the Qur'an recitation is normally at the end of *Salatul-Taraaweeh*, followed by a very long *Du'a'* (rest your feet during the day), in the last *Rak'at*, before *Ruku'* (note, before and not after *Ruku'*).

- *Salatul-Witr* is performed after *Qiyam-ul-Layl* and not after *Salatul-Taraaweeh*.

⇨ *Zakaat-ul-Fitr*

◆ Below are some *Ahadith* from Bukhari in relation to *Zakaat-ul-Fitr*. You will notice that all of them indicate that this *Zakaat* should be given in kind and not in the form of money, as many Muslims do today.

◆ It must be given before the *Eid Salah*.

عَنِ ابْنِ عُمَرَ رَضِيَ اللهُ عَنْهُمَا قَالَ: فَرَضَ رَسُولُ اللهِ ﷺ زَكَاةَ الفِطْرِ صَاعًا مِنْ تَمْرٍ أَوْ صَاعًا مِنْ شَعِيرٍ عَلَى العَبْدِ وَالحُرِّ، وَالذَّكَرِ وَالأُنْثَى وَالصَّغِيرِ وَالكَبِيرِ مِنَ المُسْلِمِينَ، وَأَمَرَ بِهَا أَنْ تُؤَدَّى قَبْلَ خُرُوجِ النَّاسِ إِلَى الصَّلاةِ.

"It is narrated by Ibn Umar ﷺ that Allah's Messenger (ﷺ) enjoined the payment of one Sa' of dates or one Sa' of barley as Zakaat-ul-Fitr on every Muslim slave or free, male or female, young or old, and he ordered that it be paid before the people went out to offer the Eid prayer. (One Sa' = 3 kilograms approx.)"

(Bukhari : 1503)

عَنِ ابْنِ عُمَرَ رَضِيَ اللهُ عَنْهُمَا: أَنَّ رَسُولَ اللهِ ﷺ فَرَضَ زَكَاةَ الفِطْرِ صَاعًا مِنْ تَمْرٍ، أَوْ صَاعًا مِنْ شَعِيرٍ عَلَى كُلِّ حُرٍّ أَوْ عَبْدٍ، ذَكَرٍ أَوْ أُنْثَى مِنَ المُسْلِمِينَ.

"It is narrated by Ibn Umar ﷺ that Allah's Messenger (ﷺ) made it incumbent on all the slaves or free Muslims, male or female, to pay one Sa' of dates or barley as Zakaatul-Fitr."

(Bukhari : 1504)

عَنْ أَبِي سَعِيدٍ الخُدْرِيِّ رَضِيَ اللهُ عَنْهُ قَالَ: كُنَّا نُخْرِجُ زَكَاةَ

الفِطْرِ صَاعًا مِنْ طَعَامٍ، أَوْ صَاعًا مِنْ شَعِيرٍ، أَوْ صَاعًا مِنْ
تَمْرٍ، أَوْ صَاعًا مِنْ أَقِطٍ، أَوْ صَاعًا مِنْ زَبِيبٍ.

"Narrated by Abu Sa'id Al-Khudri ﷺ : We used to give one
Sa' of meal or one Sa' of barley or one Sa' of dates, or one Sa'
of cottage cheese or one Sa' of raisins (dried grapes) as Zakaat-
ul-Fitr."

(Bukhari : 1506)

عَنِ ابْنِ عُمَرَ رَضِيَ اللهُ عَنْهُما قَالَ: فَرَضَ النَّبِيُّ ﷺ صَدَقَةَ
الفِطْرِ - أَوْ قَالَ: رَمَضَانَ - عَلَى الذَّكَرِ وَالأُنْثَى، وَالحُرِّ
وَالمَمْلُوكِ، صَاعًا مِنْ تَمْرٍ أَوْ صَاعًا مِنْ شَعِيرٍ، فَعَدَلَ النَّاسُ
بِهِ نِصْفَ صَاعٍ مِنْ بُرٍّ.

"It is narrated by Abdullah bin Umar ﷺ that the Prophet
(ﷺ) ordered (Muslims) to give one Sa' of dates or one Sa' of
barley as Zakaatul-Fitr. The people rewarded two Mudds of
wheat as equal to that."

(Bukhari : 1511)

عَنِ ابْنِ عُمَرَ رَضِيَ اللهُ عَنْهُما: أَنَّ النَّبِيَّ ﷺ أَمَرَ بِزَكَاةِ الفِطْرِ
قَبْلَ خُرُوجِ النَّاسِ إِلَى الصَّلَاةِ.

"It is narrated by Ibn Umar ﷺ that the Prophet (ﷺ) ordered
the people to pay Zakaatul-Fitr before going to the Eid prayer."

(Bukhari : 1509)

* About three days before *Eid* most of the shops and many
  street vendors will prepare special bags of rice which you
  can buy to distribute as *Zakaat-ul-Fitr*.

* There are many poor people waiting next to the sellers that
  at times grab the rice from you. Unfortunately, not all the
  people waiting there 'qualify' for *Zakaat-ul-Fitr*. Some of
  them have collected more rice than what the vendor has to

sell. What do you do? Try to find some other means, if possible, to distribute your *Zakaat-ul-Fitr*. It is best to give it in the place where you will have *Eid*.

*   It is the duty of the father (husband) to give the *Zakaat-ul-Fitr* on behalf of everybody he is responsible for.

⇨ *Zakaat-ul-Maal :*

*   This is the compulsory *Zakaat* that you have to pay 2.5% on the money (gold, silver, goods etc.) that you have had in your possession over the last year. This is just a reminder. Ramadaan is a good time to pay this money, even though it can be paid at anytime during the year. If you do it every year in Ramadaan, then you don't have to worry about remembering when the year has passed. Many people become mathematicians when calculating their *Zakaat*, meaning they count to the last penny (cents) and seconds just to make sure they don't pay too much *Zakaat* too early. How much is too much *Zakaat*? My fellow Muslims, we spend hundreds of dollars on worldly things without giving it a second thought, yet when it comes to *Zakaat* we find all sorts of excuses. Err on the side of caution, so you will not be answerable on the Day of Judgement for unpaid *Zakaat*!

*   There is no need to guess or seek people's opinions as to who is eligible for *Zakaat*, when it is already clearly defined in *Surah Taubah* (9), *Ayah* 60.

⇨ *Eid-ul-Fitr :*

➢ **Announcement:**

*   The debate as to whether the end of Ramadaan is determined by the actual sighting of the moon continues and I don't think it will end soon. So, my suggestion is, seeing that the authorities claim that this is their basis, let's leave it at that and enjoy for once everyone in the same country having *Eid* on the same day.

- Is it *Eid* or not, how will you know? This is something else I find quite strange. The only way to find out is from the television, radio or from someone who happened to watch the television. Why they don't announce it in the mosque or simply make *Takbir* is what we have been wondering for years. No, they simply don't make *Taraaweeh*, and that is the 'announcement'.

- On the 29th day, the digital clocks in the *Haram* will show the time for *Salatul-Ishaa* to be one and half-hours after *Salatul-Maghrib*, instead of two hours. Many people interpret this as the *Eid* announcement. No it is not. I am not sure why it is done, but I guess it is done, just in case it is *Eid*, so nobody will be late for *Salatul-Ishaa*. If Ramadaan is thirty days, *Salatul-Ishaa* will be two hours after *Salatul-Maghrib*, even though the clocks show otherwise.

- If it is thirty days, *Taraaweeh Salah* will still be performed on the night of the 30th (29th day), even though they have completed the recitation of the entire Qur'an the night before. They normally continue reciting from where they stopped during *Qiyam-ul-Layl* on the previous night.

- If Ramadaan is only 29 days, then obviously there will be no *Taraaweeh Salah* on the 30th night.

- *Salatul-Ishaa* will now start again at its original time, which is one and half-hours after *Salatul-Maghrib*, instead of two hours. Remember this, as many people miss *Ishaa Salah* on the last day, as they come too late.

- There is a max-exodus of people from Makkah at this stage. All those in *I'tikaf* leave the mosque and many people prepare to go home.

➢ *Salatul-Eid* :

- *Salatul-Eid* starts about one and half-hours after *Salatul-Fajr*, followed by the *Eid Khutbah*. If you look at the digital clock, it will show the time of sunrise (*Al-Shurook*). *Salatul-Eid* is about twenty minutes after this time.

عَنْ عَبْدِ اللهِ بِن عُمَرَ: أَنَّ رَسُولَ اللهِ ﷺ كَانَ يُصَلِّي فِي الْأَضْحَى وَالْفِطْرِ ثُمَّ يَخْطُبُ بَعْدَ الصَّلَاةِ.

"It is narrated by Abdullah bin Umar ؓ that Allah's Messenger (ﷺ) used to offer the prayer of Eid-ul-Adha and Eid-ul-Fitr and then deliver the Khutbah after the prayer."

(*Bukhari* : 957)

عَنْ جَابِرٍ قَالَ: كَانَ النَّبِيُّ ﷺ إِذَا كَانَ يَوْمُ عِيدٍ خَالَفَ الطَّرِيقَ.

"It is narrated by Jabir (bin Abdullah ؓ) that on the Day of Eid the Prophet (ﷺ) used to return (after offering the Eid prayer) through a way different from that by which he went."

(*Bukhari* : 986)

- Even though many people leave on the night before *Eid*, *Salatul-Eid* is still extremely crowded. You must be early to get a place inside the mosque. Plan to stay in the mosque after *Salatul-Fajr*.

- *Dhikr* is normally performed in groups and over the loud speakers inside the *Haram*, about fifteen minutes after *Salatul-Fajr*.

- Some people distribute dates, chocolates, tea and coffee.

عَنْ أَنَسِ بْنِ مَالِكٍ قَالَ: كَانَ رَسُولُ اللهِ ﷺ لَا يَغْدُو يَوْمَ الْفِطْرِ حَتَّى يَأْكُلَ تَمَرَاتٍ.

"It is narrated by Anas bin Malik (ؓ) that Allah's Messenger (ﷺ) never proceeded (for the prayer) on the Day of Eidul-Fitr unless he had eaten some dates. (Anas also narrated that the Prophet (ﷺ) used to eat odd number of dates.)"

(*Bukhari* : 953)

➢ *Eid* Day:

- After *Eid Salah* there is a complete exodus of people and the streets are packed for about two hours.

- The rest of the day is extremely quiet, a sort of an anticlimax after the hectic last ten days.

- Most of the shops are closed.

- This is maybe when you will regret not having gone home for *Eid*. Don't! Enjoy the peace and quiet in Makkah.

⇨ Fasting Missed Days:

- ◆ The maximum number of days one can fast in Ramadaan is 30 days and the minimum is 29 days.

- Why mention it? Well, an issue arises under the following conditions:

  - ▪ You left home (your country) and they did not start fasting yet, but Makkah has.

  - ▪ You already had *Eid* in Makkah, and arrive home while the people are still fasting.

- If any of above situations apply to you, just keep the first point in mind. Let us look at some **examples:**

  1. You arrive in Makkah during the first day of Ramadaan and you haven't started fasting yet. If Ramadaan is 29 days in Makkah, then you need to 'pay-back' one day; If Ramadaan is 30 days in Makkah, then you don't need to 'pay-back' any days.

  2. You arrive in Makkah during the second day of Ramadaan and you haven't started fasting yet. If Ramadaan is 29 days in Makkah, then you need to 'pay-back' two fasting days. If Ramadaan is 29 days in Makkah, then you need to 'pay-back' only one day.

  3. You fasted 29 days in Makkah and arrive home while they are still fasting. You need not fast with them, but you can if you wish.

4. You fasted 30 days in Makkah and arrive home while they are still fasting. You should not fast with them.

☪ For points 3 and 4, there may be some other aspects to consider before making your decision to fast or not. Such as: did Ramadaan start with the actual sighting of the moon; was Shaban 30 days due to cloud; you cannot fast more than 30 days due to cloud; you cannot fast more than 30 days, etc. If you decide not to fast, then you must refrain from eating in public. So as I said before, it is best to stay in Makkah until *Eid*. What about arriving when they have Eid and you already celebrated *Eid* in Makkah? Enjoy *Eid* again!

⇨ Madinah:

- I also had the privilege of spending time in Madinah during Ramadaan. As stated before, it is something worth experiencing. Apart from the obvious things, such as *Umrah, Tawaaf* etc. that does not apply to Madinah, all of the things mentioned (food, suhur, *Salah* times, etc.) in this chapter, also applies to Madinah. However it is not as busy and rushed and the people are much better behaved. See next chapter for complete details.

⇨ 6 Days of Shawaal:

- Although most people leave Makkah before or immediately after *Eid-ul-Fitr*, there are a few who stay on longer. If you do, do not forget the reward of fasting six days in Shawaal. There is no better place to start your six days. They do not have to be consecutive days and you should 'make up' missed Ramadaan days first.

  Abu Ayyub Al-Ansari (ﷺ) reported that the Prophet (ﷺ) said:

«مَنْ صَامَ رَمَضَانَ ثُمَّ أَتْبَعَهُ سِتًّا مِنْ شَوَّالٍ، كَانَ كَصِيَامِ الدَّهْرِ».

"Whoever fasts during the month of Ramadaan and then follows it with six days of Shawaal will be (rewarded) as if he had fasted the entire year."

(Muslim : 1164)

[(30 x 10 = 300 for Ramadaan) + (6 x 10 = 60 for Shawaal) = 360 - One *Hijrah* year]

Abu Sa'id Al-Khudri (ﷺ) reported Allah's Messenger (ﷺ) as saying:

«مَنْ صَامَ يَوْمًا فِي سَبِيلِ اللهِ، بَاعَدَ اللهُ وَجْهَهُ عَنِ النَّارِ سَبْعِينَ خَرِيفًا».

"He who observes fast for a day in the way of Allah He would remove his face from the Hell to the extent of seventy years distance."

(Muslim : 1153)

♦ Wouldn't you like to be removed that far from Hell, by simply fasting the 6 days of Shawaal? But guess what, that is not all. If the reward for fasting 6 days equals to that of fasting for one year, then the distance you may be removed from Hell is not 6 x the distance of seventy years, but rather, 360 x the distance of seventy years. How far that is, only Allah knows, but I am sure no one can claim that they do not need this reward...

Chapter 10
Al-Madinah Al-Munawwarah

Narrated Anas (ﷺ) that the Prophet (ﷺ) said:

«المَدِينَةُ حَرَمٌ مِنْ كَذَا إِلى كَذَا ، لا يُقْطَعُ شَجَرُها ، ولا يُحْدَثُ فِيها حَدَثٌ ، مَنْ أَحْدَثَ فِيهَا حَدَثًا فَعَلَيْهِ لَعْنَةُ اللهِ والمَلائِكَةِ والنَّاسِ أَجْمَعِينَ» .

"Al-Madinah is a sanctuary from that place to that. Its trees should not be cut and no heresy should be innovated nor any sin should be committed in it, and whoever innovates in it heresy or commits sins (bad deeds), then he will incur the curse of Allah, the angels, and all the people."

(*Bukhari* : 1867 & *Muslim* : 1366)

⇨ The importance of Madinah:

Abdullah bin Zaid bin Asim (رضي الله عنه) reported Allah's Messenger (ﷺ) as saying:

«إِنَّ إِبْرَاهِيمَ حَرَّمَ مَكَّةَ وَدَعَا لِأَهْلِهَا، وَإِنِّي حَرَّمْتُ الْمَدِينَةَ كَمَا حَرَّمَ إِبْرَاهِيمُ مَكَّةَ، وَإِنِّي دَعَوْتُ فِي صَاعِهَا وَمُدِّهَا بِمِثْلَي مَا دَعَا بِهِ إِبْرَاهِيمُ لِأَهْلِ مَكَّةَ».

"Verily Ibraheem declared Makkah sacred and supplicated (for blessings to be showered) upon its inhabitants, and I declare Madinah to be sacred as Ibraheem declared Makkah to be sacred. I have supplicated (Allah for His blessings to be showered) in its sa' and its Mudd (two standards of weight and measurement) twice as did Ibraheem for the inhabitants of Makkah."

(*Muslim*: 1360)

⇨ The rewards of praying in the *Haram* in Madinah:

Abu Hurairah (رضي الله عنه) reported that Allah's Messenger (ﷺ) said:

«صَلَاةٌ فِي مَسْجِدِ رَسُولِ اللهِ ﷺ أَفْضَلُ مِنْ أَلْفِ صَلَاةٍ فِيمَا سِوَاهُ مِنَ الْمَسَاجِدِ، إِلَّا الْمَسْجِدَ الْحَرَامَ».

"A prayer in my mosque is a thousand times more excellent than a prayer in any other mosque, except Masjid-al-Haram (Makkah)."

(*Muslim* : 1394)

⇨ About the people of Madinah:

Narrated Sa'd (رضي الله عنه) that he heard the Prophet (ﷺ) saying:

«لَا يَكِيدُ أَهْلَ الْمَدِينَةِ أَحَدٌ إِلَّا انْمَاعَ، كَمَا يَنْمَاعُ الْمِلْحُ فِي الْمَاءِ».

"None plots against the people of Al-Madinah but that he will

be dissolved (destroyed) like the salt is dissolved in water."

(*Bukhari* : 1877 and *Muslim* : 3361)

Other names of Madinah:

♦ As narrated in various *Ahadith* in Bukhari, Madinah was also referred to as **Yathrib** and **Taybah** by the Prophet (ﷺ).

⇨ Visiting the Prophet's mosque before or after *Umrah*:

♦ Visiting the city of Madinah is not a devotional rite of *Umrah* and has nothing to do with *Umrah*. However it is highly commendable to visit the Prophet's (ﷺ) mosque.

→ Etiquette of the Prophet's mosque:

➢ As with any other mosque, enter with your right foot and recite the supplication (see chapter 7, entering the *Haram*) for entering the *Masjid*.

➢ Perform two *Rak'at* (*Tahiyatul-Masjid*).

➢ Do not push and walk over fellow Muslims in the *Masjid*.

➢ Proceed to the front of the *Masjid* to visit the graves of Allah's Messenger (ﷺ) and his two Companions, Abu Bakr and Umar (may Allah be pleased with them), if possible. How to do this is covered next. Also this does not have to be done each time you enter the mosque. On many occasions it is extremely crowded at the front of the mosque.

➢ Walking backwards away from the tomb to leave the *Masjid* is an innovation.

➢ Send salutations on the Messenger (ﷺ) as often possible:

The Prophet (ﷺ) said:

«مَنْ صَلَّىٰ عَلَيَّ وَاحِدَةً، صَلَّى اللهُ عَلَيْهِ عَشْرًا».

"Whoever asks Allah to bless me once, Allah will bless him for that ten times."

(*Muslim* : 408)

→ Etiquette of visiting the graves:

Abu Hurairah (؄) relates that the Prophet (ﷺ) said:

«لَا تَجْعَلُوا بُيُوتَكُمْ قُبُوراً، وَلَا تَجْعَلُوا قَبْرِي عِيداً، وَصَلُّوا عَلَيَّ فَإِنَّ صَلَاتَكُمْ تَبْلُغُنِي حَيْثُ كُنْتُمْ».

"Do not make your houses graves and do not make my grave a place of festivity and merry-making (but) invoke blessings upon me for your blessings will reach me, wherever you may be."

(*Abu Dawud* : 2042)

- ◆ It is improper (even sinful) for a visitor to the Prophet's ﷺ mosque to stand before the graves and indulge in the following:

  - ✗ Crying, beseeching from the Prophet ﷺ, and supplicating to the Prophet ﷺ;

  - ✗ Supplicating long *Du'a's* and seeking the Prophet's ﷺ intercession;

  - ✗ Touching and kissing the lattice and walls.

The Prophet (ﷺ) said:

«لا تُطْرُونِي كما أطْرَتِ النَّصَارَى ابنَ مَرْيَمَ».

"Do not praise me as the Christians did Eesa bin Maryam (Jesus)."

(*Bukhari* : 3445)

- * Following is a picture of the front (gates) of the graves inside the mosque.

- ◆ Once you are at the middle gates do the following:

- ◆ Facing the graves (if possible) say:

السَّلَامُ عَلَيْكَ يَا رَسُولَ اللهِ وَرَحْمَةُ اللهِ وَبَرَكَاتُهُ

Assalaamu 'alayka yaa Rasullulah wa rahmatullahi wa barakaatuhu.

(Peace be upon you, O Messenger of Allah, and Allah's mercy and blessings.)

* Move about two steps to the right and extend your greetings to Abu-Bakr (﷽):

السَّلَامُ عَلَيْكَ يَاأَبَابَكْرٍ

Assalaamu 'alayka yaa Abu-Bakr.

(Peace be upon you, O Abu Bakr.)

* Move another step or two to the right and extend greetings to Umar (﷽):

السَّلَامُ عَلَيْكَ يَا عُمَر

Assalaamu 'alayka yaa Umar.

(Peace be upon you, O 'Umar.)

♦ If it is crowded, it is quite acceptable just to walk past the graves (or from anywhere in the mosque) and pronounce the greetings as above.

♦ There is no need to pass the graves after every *Salah*. Also the long *Du'a's* and greetings as many books teach have no authentic evidence in the *Sunnah*.

♦ Sending greetings on behalf of someone also has no evidence in the *Sunnah*. The *Hadith* related earlier in the chapter, indicates that one can send greetings upon the Prophet (ﷺ) from wherever one is in the world.

→ *Raudah-tul-Jannah :*

♦ Try to perform *Salah* in the area called '*Raudah-tul-Jannah*'. This area is marked by white pillars and different coloured carpet, close to the front of the mosque. See the diagram later in this chapter for the location. (There are also other white pillars which are outside this area.)

Abdullah bin Zaid Al-Ansari (ﷺ) narrated that the Prophet (ﷺ) said:

$$ «مَا بَيْنَ مِنْبَرِي وَبَيْتِي رَوْضَةٌ مِنْ رِيَاضِ الْجَنَّةِ» . $$

"Between my house and my pulpit is a garden from the gardens of Paradise."

(*Muslim* : 1390)

* There are special times for ladies to enter the *Raudah-tul-Jannah* area. Normally from about 7.00am to 11am and also after *Zuhr Salah*. These times vary from year to year, so ask one of the guards at the door for the appropriate times.

• This area is always busy. You have to go very early, as it is sometimes impossible to get a chance to perform *Salah* in this area.

• On Fridays people sit in this area from after *Salatul-Fajr* until after *Jumu'ah*.

- Avoid performing *Salah* in the forbidden times. Do not contravene a law with an action that is not part of the *Sunnah*.

- If you are fortunate to get a chance and you wish to make *Du'a'*, do it in the *Sajdah* of your *Salah*, as the guards will move you as soon as you sit down to make *Du'a'*.

→ *Salah* **in General:**

♦ The *Haram* is locked everyday about one hour after *Ishaa* until *Tahajjud* (about 3.00am, depending on the season).

- All the aspects of *Salah* (*Sutrah, Sunnah, Nafl, Janazah*, where to sit) mentioned for Makkah are applicable to Madinah as well.

- As there is no *Tawaaf*, try to spend your time with all the other aspects of *Ibadah* as mentioned for Makkah.

- There are no special rewards to make *Salah* in the 'old *Mihrab'*. You will notice many people queuing and pushing to make *Salah* in the small pulpit located next to the *Raudah*. Some people even go to the extent of performing *Salah* in the forbidden times in this area. Once again do not contravene a law with an action that is not part of the *Sunnah*.

- The *Haram* gets very full even by 4.00am. So be early for your prayers, in order to get a place inside the mosque. The mosque has been extended and is now quite large and has two levels (ground and roof level).

- The new section is air-conditioned.

→ **Personal Behaviour:**

- You are in Madinah. The city of our beloved Prophet (ﷺ). All the aspects regarding personal behaviour in the previous chapters apply to Madinah also.

- Let the two opening *Ahadith* in this chapter guide your behaviour.

⇨ **Staying 8 days in Madinah?**

◆ There is no authentic evidence from the Qur'an or the *Sunnah* about any additional benefit in staying 8 days (performing 40 prayers) in Madinah. The reason many people insist on this is based on a *Da'eef* (weak) *Hadith* about performing 40 prayers in the Prophet's ﷺ mosque. This *Hadith* is *Da'eef* (weak) or a distortion of the *Sahih Hadith* which says, 40 days in **any** *Masjid* with *Takbira-tul-Ihram* (first *Takbir*), and not 40 prayers in Madinah.

◆ Let me relate the answer given by a renowned scholar when asked the following question:

➢ Question: - "Is the offering of 40 consecutive prayers in the Prophet's mosque a must?"

➢ Answer: - "Many people tend to think that offering 40 prayers with the congregation in the Prophet's mosque has a special significance. Well, if it did, then there should be something associated with this number which should make it preferable to an even larger number. The fact is that there is none. If you offer 41 prayers in the Prophet's mosque, whether consecutive or not, you are better off than offering 40 prayers. The reason is that Allah gives us for every prayer we offer there the reward of 1000 prayers anywhere else (except Makkah). Hence the more prayers we offer the greater the reward."

◆ Let us look at the mathematical calculation:

➢ One *Salah* in Madinah = 1000 rewards, hence 40 prayers in Madinah = 40,000 (40 x 1000). One *Salah* in Makkah = 100,000 rewards. Meaning that 8 days in Madinah equates to less than half of the reward for one *Salah* in Makkah. Shouldn't this encourage any person to get to Makkah as soon as possible or stay longer in Makkah?

• Don't get me wrong. If time and finances permit, it is good to stay as long as possible. I personally love Madinah very much. However, do not let your stay in Madinah 'affect' the time you should spend in Makkah, as there is much more reward being in Makkah.

- Let me relate two stories to highlight how we sometimes lose sight of our priorities:

  o "During the *Hajj* year of 1409 (1989) we ascribed to the same view about the 40 prayers in Madinah. There were four of us (two couples) that were 'counting' together. One of the ladies started menstruating (even after taking pills to ensure this wouldn't happen, in order to make the 40) after the count was at 30. She was devastated and needed special counseling. At *Salah* number 36, my wife developed a severe bout of the flu. In order for her not to miss the 40 prayers in the *Masjid* we virtually forced her to the *Masjid*. We made our life very difficult due to ignorance! (My wife still reminds me of it)."

  o In 1419/1998 I met a friend of mine in Madinah. He came for *Umrah* with his family. I enquired about his trip and his itinerary. This was his response: "We have just come from Makkah where we spent 3 days and performed a couple of *Umrahs*; We arrived in Madinah yesterday and we will stay for 8 days, as you know we must complete 40 *Salahs* here; We will then go to Jakarta for 5 days on our way home, *In Sha Allah*." Ok at least he came you might say. My point is, try to get the most reward out of your trip.

⇨ **Visiting other sites around Madinah:**

→ **Al-Baqee Cemetery:**

◆ It is *Sunnah* to visit the graveyards:

The Prophet (ﷺ) said:

«زُورُوا الْقُبُورَ . فَإِنَّهَا تُذَكِّرُكُمُ الآخِرَةَ» .

"Visit graves in that these remind you of the Hereafter."
(*Ibn Majah* : 1569 and *Abu Dawud* : 3235)

- Many of the Companions and family members of the Prophet (ﷺ) are buried in Al-Baqee Cemetery. There are no marked gravestones to indicate specific graves. It is not necessary to know or to dwell over any particular gravesite.

- The *Sunnah Du'a'* one should recite at any graveyard:

«السَّلَامُ عَلَيْكُمْ دَارَ قَوْمٍ مُؤْمِنِينَ، وَأَتَاكُمْ مَاتُوعَدُونَ غَدًا، مُؤَجَّلُون، وَإِنَّا - إِنْ شَاءَ اللهُ - بِكُمْ لَاحِقُونَ»

Assalaamu alaykum daara qawmin mu'minin, wa atakum ma Tū'adun ghadan, mu'ajjalūn, wa innaa in sha-allahu bikum laahiqoon.

(*Muslim* : 974)

(Peace be upon the Muslim people of these dwellings. That which was promised to you for the tomorrow has reached you. You were given respite. And we will be joining you soon, if Allah wills.)

* Women are not allowed to enter the gravesite.

* You will notice at the entrance of Al-Baqee Cemetery a big sign, warning women against the visiting of the graves.

- With regards to women visiting the gravesites, including that of the Prophet (ﷺ); the issue is addressed in chapter 3 ('About Women').

- The cemetery gates are locked and are open only at certain times. Normally it is open after *Salatul-Fajr* and *Asr*.

- If you wish to enter the cemetery and see how a burial is performed in Madinah, I suggest you follow (help carry) the bier (*Janazah*) from the mosque. Be prepared to carry all the way.

→ Quba Mosque:

- There is no specific supplication for the Quba Mosque, but it is one of the places recommended to visit, while you are in Madinah:

Sahl bin Hunaif (ﷺ) reported that the Prophet (ﷺ) said:

«مَنْ تَطَهَّرَ فِي بَيْتِهِ، ثُمَّ أَتَىٰ مَسْجِدَ قُبَاءٍ، فَصَلَّى فِيهِ صَلاَةً، كَانَ لَهُ كَأَجْرِ عُمْرَةٍ» .

"One who does Wudhu' at home, then offers prayers in Quba Mosque is entitled to the reward of an Umrah."

(Ahmad : 3 / 487, Nasa'i : 700, Ibn Majah : 1412 and Hakim : 3 / 12)

❖ Quba Mosque is closed almost immediately after *Salatul-Ishaa*. It reopens around 4:00am.

→ Other:

• There are many other mosques and sites of interest to visit in Madinah, however keep in mind that there is no religious merit in it, except for visiting the graves at Uhud.

• As in Makkah, if the visit to any place may mean missing *Salah* in the *Haram*, avoid it or ensure that you are back in time for *Salah*.

• Many groups visit the 'Seven Mosques' and people push and fight to perform *Salah* inside these small mosques. There is no need. There is even doubt about the authenticity of these mosques as it is difficult to comprehend why the Companions would build mosques so close to each other.

• A place worth visiting is the Mountain of Uhud where the battle of Uhud took place. There you will also find the gravesite of Hamzah and the other Companions (ﷺ), who were martyred during the battle. Many people make various supplications here, even to Hamzah. This is *Shirk!* The only supplication you should make here is the one mentioned earlier when visiting a grave.

• Another place of interest to visit is the King Fahd Qur'an Printing Press where they print the Qur'ans you find in the mosques. You need to make an appointment to visit this facility. Most travel agents know the procedures to follow in order to obtain permission for a visit.

⇨ **Some erroneous statements about visiting Madinah:**

♦ Visiting the Prophet's grave is neither obligatory nor a condition for *Hajj* or *Umrah*. Many books quote various *Ahadith* about visiting the grave after or before *Hajj* or *Umrah*. This causes undue stress on those who are unable to do so. These references have no authentic source. Below are some of these statements:

  ✗ One who performs *Hajj* and does not visit me, wrongs me.

  ✗ One who visits me after my death is as if he visited me during my life.

  ✗ One who visits me and my ancestor Ibraheem within a year, I guarantee for him *Jannah* with Allah.

  ✗ One who visits my grave, my intercession for him is certainly due.

♦ Extending greetings on behalf of other people (this is a very common practice) also has no basis in the *Sunnah*.

⇨ **General information about your visit to Madinah:**

→ **Doors of the *Haram*:**

* As in Makkah the doors of the *Haram* have names and can be used as a means of identifying your location.

* Some of the door names are: Baab-us-Salaam; Baab-ur-Rahmah; Baab-ul-Jibreel; Baab-un-Nisaa; Baab-us-Siddiq; Baab-ul-Abdul Aziz.

→ **General layout of the Mosque (*Raudah* and the graves):**

• Follow the 'procedure' below and you can achieve, praying in *Raudah*, *Fardh* in the front row and passing the graves:-

  ➢ In relation to the diagram: ❶ Be early and enter from the appropriate door nearest to your location; Proceed to the *Raudah* area ❷ and perform your *Tahiyatul-Masjid* and *Sunnah Salah* here; Move towards the first row ❸ and perform your *Fardh Salah* here; After *Salah* wait for the crowd to be less while you perform *Dhikr*, *Tasbih*, reciting Qur'an, etc.; Proceed towards the door ❺ while passing by the graves ❹ and extending your greetings.

- If you exit from this door ❺ you will be in the general area of Al-Baqee Cemetery.

→ **Access to the *Haram*:**

- The doors are all numbered and unlike Makkah, there are specific doors for men and women to enter. There is no need to memorise the door numbers, as the entrances are rather obvious.

- Some door numbers that may be of use are:

  ○ The graves are near door number 41

  ○ Door no 29 is where the ladies enter from to go to *Raudah-tul-Jannah*.

  ○ Access to roof area (men only) is via doors 6, 10, 15, 27, 31.

- All the larger doors have wheelchair ramps for easy access.

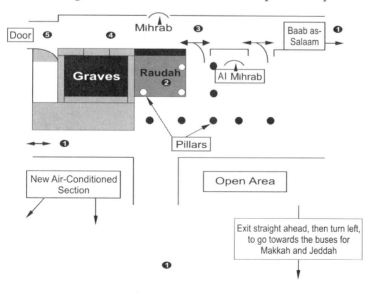

⇨ **Medical Facilities:**

* There are specialist hospitals in and around Madinah.

- There used to be a medical facility right outside the mosque, but this has been broken down. If you need medical help, I suggest you ask one of the pharmacies for the closest facility, as they may have built a new one.

- On many occasions you can get a 'consultation' and medication for minor issues (common cold, sore limbs etc.) from the pharmacist himself.

→ **Toilets:**

- There are lots and lots of toilets and *Wudhu'* facilities around the *Haram* area, both for men and women.

- The women's toilet locations are:

  ○ Near doors 12, 13, 21, 23, 24, 25, 26, 29.

  ○ These doors are also the entrances to the *Masjid* for the women.

- The men's toilet locations are near doors 1, 5, 6, 7, 8, 14, 16, 17, 18, 19, 20, 21, 32, 38.

→ **Friday (*Jumu'ah Salah*):**

- As in Makkah, one should endeavour to go early for *Jumu'ah Salah*, as it gets extremely crowded.

- Many people sit in the *Raudah-tul-Jannah* area from after *Salatul-Fajr until* after *Jumu'ah Salah*.

- There are also two *Adhaans* performed and they are only about 5 minutes apart.

→ **Zamzam:**

- The water contained in the grey containers inside the *Haram* is Zamzam water.

- As in Makkah, some of the containers contain room temperature Zamzam. It has writing on it (in Arabic):

"Zamzam water, not cold".

- If you did not get a chance to get Zamzam to take home in Makkah, there is a Zamzam filling 'station' outside the mosque near door number eight (8).

→ Children:

- At the *Haram* in Madinah they do not allow any boys, regardless of age (infants excluded) to enter the female section of the mosque. Even if they are with their mothers. So, if you have younger boys, send them with their father, otherwise they will be forced to sit outside. I am not sure of the logic of this, but it happens.

→ Shopping:

- As with Makkah there are plenty of shopping opportunities. Once again, do not spend too much time shopping as it can be better spent in *Ibadah*.

- Many people wonder whether it is better (or cheaper) to buy in Makkah or Madinah. A simple rule: If you like the item and the price, buy it! You may not find it again, let alone the shop.

- Madinah has one of the best fresh date markets.

→ 2 *Adhaans*:

- As with Makkah Madinah has two *Adhaans* in the morning, one about an hour before *Fajr* and the *Fajr Adhaan* itself.

→ Leaving Madinah:

- Do not walk backwards out of the *Haram*.

- There are no specified supplications, but one should read the supplication when departing from any mosque.

➢ To Makkah:

- You need to prepare yourself for *Ihraam* conditions (i.e., *Ghusl*, trim nails if required).

- You will stop at the *Meqaat* Dhul-Hulaifah where you will adopt *Ihraam* (you may put on your *Ihraam* clothes at your hotel prior to leaving) and make your *Niyah* at the *Meqaat*.

- The bus will also stop at certain checkpoints.

➤ **For Home:**

- Ensure that all your luggage is secure and marked (labeled) correctly.

- Do not spend all your Riyals, as you may need these for food or excess baggage charges.

Chapter 11
About *Hajj*

I have included this short chapter on *Hajj*, merely as a reminder for those that have not performed *Hajj* yet.

⇨ *Hajj*, the Call

﴿وَأَذِّن فِى ٱلنَّاسِ بِٱلْحَجِّ يَأْتُوكَ رِجَالًا وَعَلَىٰ كُلِّ ضَامِرٍ يَأْتِينَ مِن كُلِّ فَجٍّ عَمِيقٍ﴾

"And proclaim to mankind Al-Hajj (pilgrimage). They will come to you on foot and on every lean camel, they will come from every deep and distant (wide) mountain highway (to perform Hajj)."

[*Surah Al-Hajj (22), Ayah 27*]

⇨ *Hajj*, an Obligation

﴿إِنَّ أَوَّلَ بَيْتٍ وُضِعَ لِلنَّاسِ لَلَّذِى بِبَكَّةَ مُبَارَكًا وَهُدًى لِّلْعَٰلَمِينَ ۝ فِيهِ ءَايَٰتٌ بَيِّنَٰتٌ مَّقَامُ إِبْرَٰهِيمَ وَمَن دَخَلَهُ كَانَ ءَامِنًا وَلِلَّهِ عَلَى ٱلنَّاسِ حِجُّ ٱلْبَيْتِ مَنِ ٱسْتَطَاعَ إِلَيْهِ سَبِيلًا وَمَن كَفَرَ فَإِنَّ ٱللَّهَ غَنِىٌّ عَنِ ٱلْعَٰلَمِينَ﴾

"Verily, the first House (of worship) appointed for Mankind was that at Bakkah (Makkah), full of blessing, and a guidance for Al-Alamin (mankind and jinns). In it are manifest signs (for example) the Maqaam (place) of Ibraheem; whosoever enters it, he attains security. And Hajj (pilgrimage to Makkah) to the House (Ka'bah) is a duty that mankind owes to Allah, those who can afford the expenses (for one's conveyance, provision and residence); and whoever disbelieves (i.e. denies Hajj, then he is a disbeliever of Allah), then Allah stands not in need of any of the Alamin (mankind and jinn)."

[*Surah Al-Imran (3), Ayat 96-97*]

As we can see from the preceding *Ayat*, *Hajj* is not only the fifth pillar of Islam, but it is an actual duty we owe unto Allah! So when do you plan to fulfill this duty?

⇨ **Reward of *Hajj*:**

The Prophet (ﷺ) said:

«مَنْ حَجَّ لِلَّهِ فَلَمْ يَرْفُثْ وَلَمْ يَفْسُقْ رَجَعَ كَيَوْمِ وَلَدَتْهُ أُمُّهُ» .

"He who performs Hajj for Allah's pleasure and avoids all lewdness and sins will return after Hajj free from all sins as he was the day his mother gave birth to him."

(*Bukhari*: 1521 and *Muslim*: 1350)

⇨ **Who should go?**

Allah does not wish to make things difficult for the Muslims. Apart from the duty being *Fardh* (compulsory) only once in a lifetime, there are certain other conditions that have to be met to be 'eligible':

1. To be a Muslim
2. To have reached puberty
3. To be of sound mind
4. To be free (not a slave)
5. To have the financial means[*]
6. To possess the physical means[**]
7. To have a *Mahram* (for women)

[*] It is important to note that one does not have to be debt free in order to be eligible to perform *Hajj*.

[**] If your physical disablement is of a permanent nature, and you have the money, then it is advisable to send (deputise) somebody to perform the *Hajj* on your behalf. *Umrah* is different and less strenuous.

⇨ When should one go?

- One should expedite the performance of *Hajj*. It is reported on the authority of 'Abdullah bin 'Abbas (☺) that the Prophet (ﷺ) said:

«مَنْ أَرَادَ الْحَجَّ فَلْيَتَعَجَّلْ . فَإِنَّهُ قَدْ يَمْرَضُ الْمَرِيضُ، وَتَضِلُّ الضَّالَّةُ، وَتَعْرِضُ الْحَاجَةُ».

"Expedite the performance of the duty of Hajj. For nobody knows what may obstruct one."

(*Ibn Majah* : 2883 & *Ahmad* 1/214)

- Once you have met all the conditions, it is important to perform your *Fardh Hajj* as soon as possible. Many people tend to leave this obligation until much later in their life. It is so much easier and better if one undertakes this journey while one is young and has the health and strength.

- Instead of going into great detail about *Hajj*, I have listed a short quiz. See how you go. Needless to say you will find all the answers in the book: "Getting the Best out of *Hajj*". The quiz is followed by the pillars, obligatory rites and a summary flow of the *Hajj* days.

⇨ *Hajj* Quiz:

1. How many methods of *Hajj* are there?
2. Which method did the Prophet (ﷺ) perform?
3. Which method did the Prophet (ﷺ) recommend?
4. Which method does the residence of Makkah perform?
5. In which Islamic month is the actual *Hajj* performed?
6. How many days is *Hajj*?
7. What are the calendar days of the actual *Hajj*?
8. Which *Surah* (and *Ay'at*) in the Qur'an indicates that *Hajj* is an obligation?
9. What are the different places that one will be in during the

Hajj days?

10. How many sacrifices are obligatory for the *Tamattu* and *Qiran* pilgrim?

11. What is this sacfrifice called?

12. In which *Surah* and *Ayah* in the Qur'an can one find the ruling for Q10?

13. Which is the most important day of *Hajj*?

⇨ Pillars (*Arkan*) of *Hajj*:

The pillars of *Hajj* are the rites that are compulsory for the validity and completion of the *Hajj*.

1. *Ihraam* (with *Niyah*).
2. Standing at Arafat.
3. *Tawaaf-Al-Ifadah*.
4. *Sa'ee* for *Hajj*.

⇨ Obligatory rites of *Hajj*:

The obligatory rites of *Hajj* are the rites that if omitted requires the pilgrim to offer an expiation.

1. *Ihraam* at the *Meqaat*.
2. Being at Arafat until sunset.
3. To spend the night (or part of) in Muzdalifah.
4. To *Ramy* (cast pebbles) at the *Jamr'at*.
5. To shave the head or cut the hair.
6. To spend the nights of *Tashreek* in Mina.
7. To perform *Tawaaf-ul-Wadaa* (menstruating women may omit this without expiation).

⇨ *Hajj* Days at a Glance:

8th Dhul-Hijja (*Yaum-at-Tarweya*)

This day the pilgrims adopt *Ihraam* and proceed from Makkah to Mina where they pray 5 prayers (*Zuhr* - *Fajr*)

9th Dhul-Hijja (*Yaum-ul-Arafat*)

This day the pilgrims go to Arafat where they spend the day in supplication after combining *Zuhr* and *Asr* prayers until sunset.

Mabeet-fi-Muzdalifah:

After sunset the pilgrims leave for Muzdalifah where they pray *Maghrib* and *Ishaa* joined. They spend the night or part of it here, and depart for Mina just before sunrise.

10th Dhul-Hijja (*Yaum-ul-Hajj-il-Akbar*)

This day the pilgrims return to Mina and *Ramy* (throw 7 pebbles) at the big *Jamrah*; perform their sacrifice; cut their hair; go to Makkah to perform *Tawaaf-al-Ifadah* and *Sa'ee* for *Hajj;* and then return to Mina.

11th-13th Dhul-Hijja (*Ayaam-at-Tashreeq*):

The pilgrims spend the next 2 or 3 days in Mina, *Ramy* all three *Jamrat* on all three days. They may leave for Makkah before sunset on the 12th or stay until the 13th.

Makkah:

The pilgrims return to Makkah and perform *Tawaaf-al-Widaa* (farewell *Tawaaf*) as the last rite before departing for home.

Hajj is complete

⇨ *Fidyah* (Expiation):

- The *Fidyah* is a means of compensation (mercy from Allah) for a missed action or for transgressing a *Hajj* related law.

- It is important to keep in mind that the expiation is for the purpose mentioned above and should not be used (as many pilgrims do) to intentionally omit an action and opt to sacrifice instead. The sacrifice is commonly referred to as *Dumm*.

- The sacrifices must be done in the Makkah, Mina or Muzdalifah area. It cannot be done in the pilgrim's home country or any other place for that matter. The pilgrim may also share with 6 others (7 in total) in the sacrifice of a camel or cow.

- A pillar of *Hajj* cannot be omitted, as there is no expiation for it. *Hajj* is not completed (valid). Also indulging in sexual relations prior to all the pillars being completed invalidates the *Hajj*.

Some specific rulings:

- The expiation for passing the *Meqaat* without *Ihraam*:

  ☾ Sacrifice of one sheep or goat.

- The expiation (*Fidyah*) for violating the *Ihraam* restrictions (e.g., cutting your hair due to an ailment in your scalp; need to remove a nail due to injury, men: applying perfume, wearing fitted clothes, covering their heads):

  ☾ Fast for 3 days or feed 6 poor persons or sacrifice one sheep or goat.

Remember to go
ma

Checklists:

➤ Vacation/Tickets/Visas etc.

Action	Details	Done?
Arrange vacation		
Plan trip		
Make Bookings		
Vaccinations		
Traveller's Cheques		
Passports	Valid for more than six months	
Suitcases	~~All ways take less~~	
Doctor	Letter for special medicines; Vaccinations Certificates	Remeber to have them early 2 each
Visas photos	Obtain photos for visas	
Visa	Obtain all required visas	
Extra photos	Obtain some extra photos for the trip	they give you six
Letter from local Muslim society	Required for Visa application	

➤ **What to Study:**

Topic	Done?	Remarks
Salah		
Travelling *Salah*		
Janazah Salah		
Talbiyah		
Ihraam requirements/ restrictions		
Umrah rites		
Sunnah Du'a'		
Remember to do W at airport, you can't do W on the plane dont miss salah		

➢ Questions related to the *Umrah* Package

Question	Answer
How far is the hotel from the mosque (by time)?	
Are there any hills or hilly streets on the way?	
Are there any stairs to climb to get to the building?	
How many persons will share a room?	
Do the rooms have telephones, fridges, air-conditioning etc.?	
Do the people who manage the hotel speak English (receptionist)?	
Do they provide room cleaning service?	
Do they provide laundry facilities?	
Is food included? If yes, what type of food is provided?	
Are there kitchen/cooking facilities in the rooms?	
Who will represent the agent during the trip?	

Package Evaluation Table: *(see example in chapter 2)*

		Packages:				
Overall Scores						
Total for High	H					
Total for Medium	M					
Total for Low	L					
Criteria:		Scores:				
Agent Reputation						
Cost:						
Airfare						
Accommodation						
Other						
Accommodation:						
Location						
Type						
Couple-room						
En-suite						
Facilities						
Other:						
Food						
Madinah						
Flight schedules						
Transport						
# days in Makkah						

➢ Things to Buy and Pack

Item	Details	Bought	Packed
Ihraam	If you plan to go to Madinah first, then you may purchase it there		
Medicine:	Tablets for Pain & Fever		
	Antibiotics		
	Cough Medicine		
	Diarrhea Tablets		
	Throat Lozenges		
Toiletries:	Shampoo		
	Toothpaste		
	Scent free soap		
	Moisturising Cream		
	Miswak		
	Sunscreen		
Moneybelt			

Umbrella			
Towels (dark coloured)	Not all places provide towels *Write how you feel*		
5,2,2016 Alisha			
		Hungry tired	
5,2,2016 Zara	- Sick, hungry	bored	

➤ Travellers cheques:

Number	Amount	Date and Place Cashed

➢ Important points to Remember:

Item	When
Change Money to Riyals	Bank/Airport

➢ **Parcels to deliver; things to buy; messages; for others:**

Action	For Whom?	From Whom?	√

➢ **Memorable Moments:**

Moment	Date	Place
Feel like Crying the ground all the pro	5/2/2016	All meddinah Walked on

➢ People I met:

Name	Tel. No	Address/E-Mail

➢Important Contact Numbers:

Name	Tel. No	Fax. No	E-mail address

➤Things (Gifts) to buy:

Person	Item	Budget	√
TOTAL COST:			

> *Umrah:*

No	Action	√
01	Trim nails, if required	
02	Shave under arms, if required	
03	Shave pubic hair, if required	
04	*Ghusl*	
05	Apply Perfume (men only)	
06	*Meqaat* reached (or before)	
07	Adopt *Ihraam*	
08	Niyah for Umrah	
09	Recite *Talbiyah*	
10	Read *Du'aa'* when entering *Haram* (mosque)	
11	Expose right shoulder (men)	
12	Start at the Hajr-al-Aswad and say *"Bismillahi Allahu Akbar"*	
13	Kiss/Touch/Gesture to Black Stone	
14	Men *Raml* (slow running) in first 3 rounds	
15	Touch the Rukn-al-Yamani Corner if possible	
16	Read *"Rabanaa Aatina..."*	
17	Kiss/touch or gesture and say *"Allahu Akbar"* as you pass the Black Stone	
18	Complete 7 rounds (circuits)	
19	Cover the right shoulder (men)	
20	Perform 2 *Rak'at* near Maqaam Ibraheem or any convenient place in the mosque	
21	Read *Surah Al-Kafirun* (109) in 1st *Rakah* after *Suratul-Fatihah*	
22	Read *Surah Al-Ikhlaas* (112) in 2nd *Rakah* after *Suratul-Fatihah*	
23	Drink Zamzam	

24	Kiss/Touch Black Stone if possible	
25	Proceed to Safaa	
26	Read "*Inaas-Safaa......*"	
27	Read "*Allahu Akbar....*" x 3, with *Du'a'* in between	
28	Start *Sa'ee* from Safaa	
29	Men *Raml* (slow running) between the green lights	
30	Stop at Marwah and do the same as at Safaa (step 27)	
31	Complete 7 laps (Safaa to Marwah = 1)	
32	Cut Hair or shave head (men)	
33	Remove *Ihraam*, adopt normal clothes	
34	*Ihraam* restrictions lifted	
35	*Tawaaf-ul-Wadaa'* (before leaving for home)	

➢ Rites missed that require payment of *Fidyah* (expiation/*Dumm*):

Rite:	Expiation?
Violating the *Ihraam* restrictions (i.e., cutting your hair or nails, applying perfume, men wearing fitted clothes or covering their head)	Fast for 3 days or feed 6 poor persons or sacrifice 1 sheep or goat
Sexual relations while in *Ihraam* and *Umrah* not complete	*Ghusl,* Complete *Umrah* rites; Sacrifice one sheep or goat*; Go outside *Haram* boundary and redo *Ihraam* (*Niyah*), redo *Umrah*
Passing the *Meqaat* without *Ihraam*	Sacrifice one sheep or goat*
Not shaving or cutting your hair	Sacrifice one sheep or goat*

* Option = Share with 6 others (7 in total) in a camel or a cow. All sacrifices must be performed in the Makkah (*Haram*) area.

➢ Notes:

Remarks	Related to

➢ **Passport & Emergency Details:**
(keep a photocopy of this page)

Passport Details
Name:
Passport Number:
Nationality:
Place of Issue:
Date of Issue:
Expiry Date:

Emergency Details

Blood Type:	Allergies
Name:	
Relationship:	
Address:	
Country code:	City Code:
Home:	Office:
Mobile:	Fax:
Internet Address:	

Agent and Hotel Details:
(make a photocopy of this page and leave it with a relative at home)

Local Agent Details
Company Name:
Contact Name:
Contact Number:
Internet Address:

Saudi Agent Details
Company Name:
Contact Name:
Contact Number: 966 + city code
Internet Address:

Makkah Hotel Details
Hotel Name:
Contact Number: 9662
Internet Address:

Madinah Hotel Details
Hotel Name:
Contact Number: 9664
Internet Address:

In Closing

I sincerely hope that the information in this book is of use to those intending to perform *Umrah*. If it is all correct then it is from Allah and if there are any mistakes then it is from me. As the *Niyah* of this book is to provide accurate, realistic and useful information, I would appreciate any comments, suggestions and constructive criticism, in order to improve the book.

The Prophet (ﷺ) said:

«مَثَلُ ما بَعَثَنِي اللهُ مِنَ الهُدَى وَالعِلْمِ كَمَثَلِ الغَيْثِ الكَثِيرِ أَصَابَ أَرْضًا، فَكانَ مِنْها نَقِيَّةٌ، قَبِلَتِ المَاءَ، فَأَنْبَتَتِ الكَلأَ وَالعُشْبَ الكَثِيرَ، وكانَتْ مِنْها أَجادِبُ، أَمْسَكَتِ الماءَ، فَنَفَعَ اللهُ بِها النَّاسَ فَشَرِبُوا وسَقَوْا وَزَرَعُوا، وَأَصَابَ مِنْها طائِفَةً أُخْرَى، إِنَّما هِيَ قِيعانٌ لا تُمْسِكُ ماءً وَلا تُنْبِتُ كَلأً، فَذلِكَ مَثَلُ مَنْ فَقُهَ فِي دِينِ اللهِ وَنَفَعَهُ ما بَعَثَنِي اللهُ بِهِ فَعَلِمَ وَعَلَّمَ، وَمَثَلُ مَنْ لَمْ يَرْفَعْ بِذلِكَ رَأْسًا وَلَمْ يَقْبَلْ هُدَى اللهِ الَّذِي أُرْسِلْتُ بِهِ».

"The example of guidance and knowledge with which Allah has sent me is like abundant rain falling on the earth. Some of which was fertile soil that absorbed rain-water and brought forth vegetation and grass in abundance. (And) another portion of it was hard and held the rain water and Allah benefited the people with it and they utilized it for drinking, (making their animals drink from it) and to irrigate the land for cultivation. (And) a portion of it was barren which could neither hold water nor bring forth vegetation (then that land gave no benefits). The first is the example of the person who comprehends Allah's religion (Islam) and gets benefit (from the knowledge) which Allah has revealed through me (the Prophet) and learns and then teaches it to others. The (last

example is that of a) person who does not care for it and does not take Allah's guidance revealed through me (he is like the barren land)."

(*Bukhari* : 79)

We all know that the shortest distance between two points is a straight line. So, the surest way of ensuring that we obtain the highest reward for our *Umrah* is to follow a straight line. The straight line being, to perform it the way our Prophet (ﷺ) performed it.

"I bear witness that there is none worthy of worship except Allah and I bear witness that Muhammad is His Messenger."

And Allah knows best!

Abu Muneer Ismail Davids

Umrah - Glossary

Ahadith	-	Plural for *Hadith*.
Arafat	-	Name of the area located 11 km from Mina, where the pilgrims spend the 9th of Dhul-Hijjah. Sometimes spelt Arafah.
Aswad	-	Black.
Aurah	-	Parts of the body that must be covered.
Ayat	-	Plural for *Ayah* (Verse from the Qur'an).
Ayaam	-	Days.
Barakah	-	Blessings of Allah.
Dhikr	-	Mentioning Allah's Name and attributes (in *Ibadah*).
Du'a'	-	Supplication; Invocation.
Dumm	-	Blood; The sacrifice of a goat, sheep etc., in order to compensate for failing to perform a *Wajib* act of *Hajj* or for violating a *Ihraam* regulation.
Dhul-Hijja	-	The 12th month of the Muslim (*Hijrah*) calendar.
Dhul-Qadah	-	The 11th month.
Eid	-	A celebration for Muslims.
Eid-ul-Adha	-	The 10th of Dhu-Hijjah. The day of celebration after the day of Arafat.
Eid-ul-Fitr	-	The 1st of Shawaal. The day of celebration after the month of fasting in Ramadaan.
Fidyah	-	Expiation for a missed rite (normally by sacrificing a sheep or a goat).
Ghusl	-	Taking a bath in a special ceremonial way. After menstruation, after sexual relations, before adopting *Ihraam*, etc.
Hady	-	The obligatory sacrifice (sheep, goat, etc.) for the *Tamattu* & Qiran pilgrims.
Hajr-al-Aswad	-	The Black Stone implanted in the corner of the Ka'bah.
Hajj-Tamattu	-	*Hajj* performed with *Umrah* preceding it (two *Niy'at*).
Halq	-	Shaving one's hair.
Haraam	-	Forbidden, prohibited.

Haram	-	The mosques in Makkah and in Madinah are commonly referred to as the *Haram*, also the areas around them.
Idtiba'	-	Uncovering the right shoulder (men) while in *Ihraam*.
Ifrad	-	*Hajj-Ifrad* is *Hajj* only, without *Umrah*.
Iftaar	-	Breaking of the fast at sunset.
Ihraam	-	The state of ritual consecration. The ceremonial state of making *Umrah* or *Hajj* or the garments themselves.
Istilam	-	Touching the Black Stone or Rukn-al-Yamani Corner.
I'tikaf	-	Spending a length of time (normally the last 10 days of Ramadaan) in a mosque without going out (except for bare necessities) or indulging in any marital relations or worldly affairs.
Jamrah	-	The pillars in Mina for stoning, signifying the place where the *Shaytaan* tempted Prophet Ibraheem.
Jamr'at (Jimaar)	-	Plural for *Jamrah*
Janazah	-	The dead
Kiswat	-	The cloth that covers the Ka'bah.
Maqaam-Ibraheem	-	The station where Prophet Ibraheem stood while building the Ka'bah. (It was moved from its original place, which was next to the Ka'bah).
Meqaat	-	Boundary of the area around Makkah, which a pilgrim or *Mutamir* should not pass without being in *Ihraam*.
Mina (Muna)	-	One of the *Hajj* ceremonial sites, 8 km from Makkah.
Muhrim	-	A person in *Ihraam*
Mutamatti	-	A pilgrim performing *Hajj-Tamattu*.
Muzdalifah	-	One of the *Hajj* ceremonial sites, between Mina & Arafat.
Qiran	-	*Hajj* with *Umrah* without coming out of *Ihraam* after *Umrah*.
Quba	-	The name of a mosque in Madinah.

Qudoom	-	Welcome *Tawaaf*, done by Ifrad and Qiran pilgrims.
Raml	-	A brisk walking in the first 3 rounds of *Tawaaf* while in *Ihraam*.
Rida	-	The upper cloth of the *Ihraam*.
Ramy	-	Stoning of the Jamr'at.
Rukn-al-Yamani	-	The Corner of the Ka'bah which faces Yemen.
Sa'ee	-	The walk made between Safaa and Marwah.
Safaa	-	The hill where you start your *Sa'ee*.
Shawaal	-	The 10th month of the Hijrah calendar.
Shubriah	-	A stretcher like chair, used to carry pilgrims for *Tawaaf*.
Suhur	-	The meal taken before dawn with the intention of fasting for that day.
Takbir	-	Saying "Allahu Akbar".
Talbiyah	-	The supplication one recites once in *Ihraam* and having made the intention.
Tamattu	-	'Enjoyable' form of *Hajj*. *Hajj* and *Umrah* together. After *Umrah* one comes out of the state of *Ihraam* until the 8th of Dhul-Hijjah with *Niyah* for *Hajj*.
Tawaaf	-	Circumambulation of the Ka'bah.
Tawaaf-ul-Ifadah	-	*Tawaaf* for *Hajj* (pillar of *Hajj*).
Tawaaf-ul-Wadaa'	-	Farewell *Tawaaf*.
Umrah	-	Minor *Hajj*, the combination of *Tawaaf* & *Sa'ee*.
Zakaat-ul-Fitr	-	A charity to be paid in kind to poor Muslims in Ramadaan, before the *Eid* prayer.
Zakaat-ul-Maal	-	Compulsory 'tax' of 2.5% that all Muslims pay on money, gold and silver (if it exceeds a certain value), and 12 months have passed 'over it'.
Zamzam	-	The sacred well inside the *Haram* in Makkah. The water from it is commonly known as Zamzam.
Zawaal	-	When the sun is at its zenith. Midday.

Bibliography
(Referring to the English Translations)

1. **Airlines,** Saudi Arabian. *How to perform Umrah,* published by Islamic Awareness Group in Saudi Arabian Airlines (Jeddah)

2. **Al-Albaanee,** Shaikh Muhammad Naasir-ud-Deen. *The Prophet's Prayer,* published by Al-Haneef Publications (Suffolk) - 1993

3. **Al-Albaanee,** Shaikh Muhammad Naasir-ud-Deen. *The Rites of Hajj & Umrah from the book of Sunnah and narrations from the pious predecessors,* produced by Jami'at Ihyaa' Minhaj Al-Sunnah (U.K.) - 1994

4. **Al-Fouzan,** Dr. Saleh ibn Fouzan. *Explanation of What a Pilgrim and a Muslim Performing Umrah should do,* published by Al-*Imam* Mohammad ibn Saud Islamic University - 1991

5. **Al-Jehani,** *Imam* Ahmad (Lecturer). *Student Notes from Hajj Classes,* notes taken: Author (Jeddah) - 1990-2004

6. **Al-Qahtaani,** Sa'eed ibn Ali ibn Wahf. *Fortification of the Muslim through remembrance and supplication from the Qur'an & Sunnah,* published by Dar-al-Khair (Jeddah) - 1996

7. **Al-Shoura,** Ibraheem. *Opinions of the selected sects about the Pilgrimage, the lesser Pilgrimage and the visit,* published by Dar Al-Arabia (Lebanon)

8. **Al-Uthaimeen,** Shaikh Muhammad As-Salih. *How to perform the rituals of Hajj and Umrah,* published by the Dawah Centre (Jeddah) - 1992

9. **Author** and Fellow Pilgrims. *Notes and Interview Material,* Notes taken: Author (Jeddah) - 1989-2004

10. **Bin Baz,** Shaikh Abdul Aziz Bin Abdullah. *Hajj, Umrah and Ziyarah (in light of the Qur'an and Sunnah),* published by

Maktaba Darussalam (Riyadh) - 1995

11. **Bin Baz,** Shaikh Abdul Aziz Bin Abdullah. *Important Fatwas regarding the rites of Hajj and Umrah*, published by the Islamic Ministry (Riyadh) - 1993

12. **Khan,** Dr. Muhammad Muhsin. *Summarized Sahih Al-Bukhari*, published by Dar-us-Salam Publications (Riyadh) - 1994

13. **Khan,** Dr. Muhammad Muhsin. *The Noble Qur'an (in the English Language)*, published by Dar-us-Salam Publications (Riyadh) - 1996

14. **KSA,** Presidency of Islamic Research. *A Guide to Hajj, Umrah and visiting the Prophet's Mosque* published by Presidency of Islamic Research (Riyadh) - 1991

15. **Philips,** Dr. Abu Ameenah Bilal. *Hajj and Umrah*, published by Abul Qasim Publishing House (Jeddah) - 1993

16. **Philips,** Dr. Abu Ameenah Bilal. *Islamic Rules on Menstruation and post-natal bleeding*, published by Dar-al-Fatah Publications (Sharjah) - 1995

17. **Sabiq,** As-Sayyid. *Fiqh us-Sunnah Volumes 1, 2 & 5*, published by International Islamic Publishing House (Jeddah) - 1992

18. **Saqib,** M.A.K. *A Guide to Prayer in Islam*, published by Ta-Ha Publishers & Muslim Book Centre (UK) - 1986

19. **Siddiqi,** Abdul Hamid. *Sahih Muslim Volumes 1-4*, published by Dar-al-Arabia (Lebanon)

20. **Zeno,** Muhammad bin Jamil. *The Pillars of Islam & Iman*, published by Dar-us-Salam Publications (Riyadh) - 1996

INDEX